THE ETHICAL DIMENSIONS OF GLOBAL CHANGE

UNIVERSITY OF READING EUROPEAN AND
INTERNATIONAL STUDIES

General Editor: Christoph Bluth

This series includes books which discuss some of the major
contemporary European and international issues from a comparative
perspective. National experiences with a relevance for broader European
and international issues are also covered by this series.

The collection is interdisciplinary in nature with the aim of bringing
together studies that emphasise the role of political, economic, historical
and cultural factors in shaping the course of international co-operation
and international conflicts, particularly from the point of view of Europe
and its relations with the rest of the world.

The influence of the processes of European integration (economic,
political, cultural) on both Europe and the rest of the world, as well as
the impact on Europe of global integration processes and non-European
integration schemes are some of the themes that run through the volumes
included in the series.

The Ethical Dimensions of Global Change

Edited by

Barry Holden

Senior Lecturer in Politics
University of Reading

First published in Great Britain 1996 by
MACMILLAN PRESS LTD
Houndmills, Basingstoke, Hampshire RG21 6XS
and London
Companies and representatives
throughout the world

A catalogue record for this book is available
from the British Library.

ISBN 0–333–65071–9

First published in the United States of America 1996 by
ST. MARTIN'S PRESS, INC.,
Scholarly and Reference Division,
175 Fifth Avenue,
New York, N.Y. 10010

ISBN 0–312–15954–4

Library of Congress Cataloging-in-Publication Data applied for

10   9   8   7   6   5   4   3   2   1
05   04   03   02   01   00   99   98   97   96

Printed and bound in Great Britain by
Antony Rowe Ltd, Chippenham, Wiltshire

Contents

Preface

This book is the outcome of a workshop hosted by the Department of Politics at the University of Reading in October 1994. The contributors to the book were participants at that workshop. The chapters that follow are for the most part versions of the papers they presented, modified in the light of the discussion at the time and subsequent correspondence amongst the authors.

I would like to thank Mrs Ann Cade for all her work on the word processor and without whom this book would not have been possible. Under considerable pressure, and in addition to her normal work, she coped efficiently and uncomplainingly with technical details and the processing of repeated drafts of chapters; I am profoundly grateful. I should also like to thank Aspasia Lioliou for providing encouragement and ideas for the workshop, the contributors for efficient delivery of drafts and completed chapters and Peter M. Jones also for his technical assistance, Martin Griffin for the figure design and the Typography Department at the University of Reading for final preparation of the manuscript. Finally my thanks are due to members of my family: to my daughter, Karen, for invaluable help in getting the project off the ground and subsequent expert assistance, and to my wife, Barbara, for yet again putting up with the total disruption of normal family life during the preparation of a book.

Reading University   *Barry Holden*

Notes on Contributors

Anthony Coates is a Lecturer in Politics at the University of Reading. His teaching responsibilities and research interests are in the field of political theory. His current research centres on the ethics of war and he is completing a book on the theory of the just war.

Ken Dark has taught at Oxford and Cambridge and is currently both a lecturer at the University of Reading and a Fellow of the University of Cambridge. He is a member of Chatham House and the International Institute of Strategic Studies. His research centres on long term change and crisis in the international system.

Barry Holden (editor) teaches in the field of political theory and international ethics. His research interests have moved on from democracy within the state to democracy within the international system. He is the author of *The Nature of Democracy* and *Understanding Liberal Democracy*.

Kimberly Hutchings is a Lecturer in Political Theory at the University of Edinburgh and is the author of *Kant, Critique and Politics*. She has written on the political theory of Kant and Hegel, international relations theory and contemporary continental political philosophy.

Peter M. Jones is a Lecturer in the Department of Politics at the University of Reading. His teaching and research interests are in the field of international relations in which he has published articles and edited *The Yearbook of Foreign Policy Analysis*. He is also co-author of *British Foreign Secretaries since 1945* and *British Public Attitudes to Nuclear Defence*.

R. J. Barry Jones is a Senior Lecturer and Head of the Department of Politics at the University of Reading. He is the author of *Conflict and Control in the World Economy: Contemporary Economic Realism and Neo-mercantilism* and *Globalisation and Interdependence in the International Political Economy*. He has also co-edited four books in the field of international political economy.

Sheldon G. Levy is Professor of Social Psychology at Wayne State University in Detroit. He is a past president of the Peace Science Society. His major current research interest is into attitudes toward the conduct of war.

Andrew Mason is a Lecturer in Philosophy at the University of Reading. He was previously a Lecturer in Politics at the University of Hull. He is the author of *Explaining Political Disagreement* and is currently working on a book on the notion of community, which explores the nature and value of community and the different levels at which it might be realised (subnational, national and global).

Matthew Paterson is a Lecturer in the Department of International Relations at the University of Keele. His research interests include international environmental politics (particularly global warming, on which he has published articles and contributions to books), international political economy and international relations theory.

Nick Wheeler is a Lecturer in International Politics at the University of Wales at Aberystwyth. He was previously a Lecturer in Politics at the University of Hull. His research interests are in international relations theory and security studies. He is the co-author of *The British Origins of Nuclear Strategy, 1944–55* and he is co-author (with Ken Booth) of *The Security Dilemma* (Macmillan, forthcoming 1996).

John Williams teaches at the University of Warwick. He worked for a year as a research intern at the Saferworld Foundation, producing two papers on post-Soviet nuclear proliferation and Middle East arms purchases after the Gulf War.

PART 1

Analysing Global Change

Introduction

Barry Holden

We are currently in a period of global change. But, more than this, it is a period of change which is of especial importance: 'As the twentieth century draws to its close, we are becoming aware of historic transformations of human society.'[1] Not only are the transformations 'historic' but they have been happening with great rapidity: 'over a period of less than three years – from major shifts in Soviet foreign policy by 1988 to the collapse of a conservative coup in Moscow in 1991 – the world underwent a cataclysm that was something like the functional equivalent of World War III.'[2] The extent and the speed of the change has, indeed, been astonishing: the 'cataclysm impressively demonstrates that radical change can sometimes happen with astonishing speed' and the 'transformation is as astounding in retrospect as it was at the time.'[3] Fred Halliday sums it up in these words:

> In the late 1980s and early 1990s the world underwent a strategic and intellectual earthquake, comparable in [its] effects – though not, at least initially, in the human suffering – [to those] caused by the First and Second World Wars. A hegemonic system, and its attendant distribution of power, collapsed. The map of states was redrawn, and around twenty new sovereign states were created. A degree of uncertainty unparalleled since the 1930s prevailed in the international arena.[4]

The emphasis of such portrayals of this dramatic period of change is on the nature and importance of its contemporary dimension: ushered in by the fall of communism, it began very recently and has happened very quickly. It should, nonetheless, also be understood in a more extended historical context. The 'cataclysm' can only be properly appreciated as such when seen as bringing to an end a longer period of history. As Halliday puts it, 'a cataclysm of great proportions had occurred, and one that brought to an end not only the Cold War and the challenge of the Bolshevik Revolution but also a longer period of international history in which a movement of contestation of the hegemonic capitalist form was identifiable.' Indeed he goes on to suggest 'that 1989 brought to the end a period of history that began in 1789 with the French Revolution.'[5] This extension of perspective alerts us to the longer historical record and the point that history is replete with 'periods of change'; Dark in fact considers the longer view in Chapter 1. And of course this is not 'the first generation to live on the cusp of a great transformation.'[6] This is indeed all true; yet there *is* something special about the current period of change: 'there is a distinction between the contemporary experience of change and that of earlier generations: never before has change come so rapidly – in some ways all at once – on such a global scale, and with such global visibility.'[7]

The current period of global change, then, is clearly of very great significance. As such the need for analysis and reflection is manifest and this is what informs the present book. The aim is not to give a general survey of the turmoil in the world nor to consider the accompanying theoretical confusion in the discipline of international relations; both are well covered elsewhere.[8] Rather the intention is to consider in a little detail certain aspects of the current period of change, whether they be specific to it or part of a wider process of change.

The focus will be in particular on some ethical dimensions. Ideas form a crucial part of the substance of global structures and processes,[9] and global change both reflects and provokes changes in those ideas. This applies to ethical ideas no less than others and is seen at a very general level and in the development of more particular issues. The chapters that follow will be concerned with both. There is also a duality of purpose; one which reflects the difference between 'is' and 'ought' whilst rejecting the old positivist notion of a logical gulf between them. Because ethical ideas are constituents of global structures and processes, appraisal of the ideas and their changing nature is a part of explaining and understanding changing events and processes. Equally, though, such appraisal also involves moral evaluation and sometimes it is this that is central.

The first chapter of the book sets the current period in the context of a consideration of global change as such. In this chapter Dark discusses the concept of 'global change' and considers how such change should be studied. In doing so he shows the range and diversity of matters that need to be encompassed within such a study, many of which raise important ethical issues. He argues that whilst drawing on various other disciplines the study of global change should properly be located within the field of international relations.

Part Two is concerned with analysis of ethical ideas primarily from the perspective of explaining and understanding changing global structures and processes. The chapter by Barry Jones takes up some very general questions about the nature and possibilities of change in international relations. These relate to the character and role of ethical principles in the functioning of the international realm and involve an examination of the tension between constructionist and structuralist approaches to the study of international relations, through a discussion of the processes and prospects of changing principles of international conduct. The subject of Williams's chapter is the notion of legitimacy. This is a concept that is not only central in international relations but one that is shown to have a key ethical component, thus highlighting the ethical or normative dimension of the structure of the international system. Changes in this dimension are portrayed through an analysis of the evolutionary and historically dynamic development of the concept.

Part Three is concerned with what has been called 'The New World Order': the ethical dimension of the newly emerging international system was often seen, at least initially, as having a key aspect referred to in terms of a new world order. P. M. Jones considers the question of whether 'The New World Order' proclaimed by President Bush does – or did – in fact have any moral element, or whether it was a return to a less stable balance of power structured by the interests of the main powers rather than norms of international morality. One of the key issues involved in this controversy is the emphasis given to humanitarian intervention and this is taken up in the chapter by Mason and Wheeler. It has been held, indeed, that an important feature of 'The New World Order' is a new emphasis on the justification of humanitarian intervention and Mason and Wheeler consider and assess contrasting 'realist' objections to possible justifications. They conclude that such objections do not refute justifications in at least one class of cases, mass murder.

In Part Four potential cosmopolitan aspects of the new ethical dimensions of international relations are considered. In her chapter Hutchings discusses the norms of citizenship and examines the possibility of constructing a viable notion of global citizenship despite the resurgence of nationalism and the recent dominance of the nation state construction of individual political allegiance. She argues that the processes of globalization mean that individuals' personal lives are increasingly internationally mediated, politically, economically, environmentally and ethically, and that a concept of citizenship should be formulated which reflects this – although this is unlikely to be a single, 'global' concept. In my chapter I consider some similar implications of globalization, in this case focussing on potential changes widening the traditional state-bound concept of 'the people' handed down by democratic theory. This is part of my examination of 'cosmopolitan democracy' and the contribution this might make to combating global warming by bringing in popular pressure and an international or global perspective.

Environmental issues – of which the global warming problem is arguably the most important – are in fact increasingly salient in international affairs and have become an important source of change. These issues raise significant moral questions and they give such change another key ethical dimension. This is the subject matter of Part Five. In his chapter on 'Ecological Change and Political Crisis' Dark surveys the wider background. In examining the contention that ecological crises have caused political crises he considers a wide range of ecological processes and environmental issues over a broad sweep of history, covering such matters as the incidence of plagues, population growth and astronomical impacts as well as global warming. Paterson's chapter, on the other hand, is specifically concerned with the global warming problem and some of the moral issues it raises. It focusses on the argument that international justice is central to resolving the problem. It reviews the conceptions of justice invoked in the literature on climate change and seeks to relate them to the recent philosophical discussions of international justice.

Part Six turns to a crucial ethical dimension of international affairs – moral assessments of war. The two chapters here consider ethical issues raised by perceptions of war in a changing world. Coates's chapter examines moral evaluations of war raised by judgements about its role in 'The New World Order'. He assesses the current relevance of the just war tradition and considers moral objections to applying just war ideas today brought by both 'idealists' and 'realists'. He concludes that a war can be waged for a moral purpose but that without the restraining influence of national interest such a war is neither likely to happen nor to be kept within acceptable moral bounds. In his chapter Levy uses empirical evidence to examine popular perceptions of war in today's world. In particular he inquires into notions of moral culpability by investigating the circumstances under which individuals would support or oppose excessive loss of life in armed combat.

In sum *The Ethical Dimensions of Global Change* contains an analysis of some critical developments in a changing world. Attention is particularly focussed on ethical ideas and moral issues, but as these are embedded in and posed by the changing structure of international affairs the following chapters provide a consideration of some key features of the international realm.

Notes and References

1   M. Shaw, *Global Society and International Relations* (Cambridge: Polity Press, 1994), p. 3.

2   J. Mueller, *Quiet Cataclysm: Reflections on the Recent Transformation of World Politics* (New York: Harper Collins, 1995), p. 1.

3   Mueller, *Quiet Cataclysm*, p. 3.

4   F. Halliday, *Rethinking International Relations* (London: Macmillan, 1994), p. 216.

5   Halliday, *Rethinking International Relations*, p. 217.

6   The Report of the Commission on Global Governance, *Our Global Neighbourhood* (Oxford: Oxford University Press, 1995), p. 11.

7   *Our Global Neighbourhood*, p. 12.

8   For example, Halliday, *Rethinking International Relations*, especially Chapters 10 and 11.

9   See Barry Jones's chapter in this volume.

1

Defining Global Change

Ken Dark

1. Introduction

Since the collapse of the Soviet Union, international relations scholars have increasingly turned their attention towards the question of change.[1] Some studies have concentrated on explaining the reasons for the sudden collapse of the USSR while others have focussed on the end of the Cold War but, to an extent, both of these aspects have been incorporated within, and superseded by, a growth in broader studies of the explanation and processes of change.[2]

Building upon the theoretical foundations laid by a small group of scholars such as Jones, Gilpin, Holsti, Modelski and Wallerstein, during the 1970s and 1980s, such studies have been the centre of attention for many younger scholars working within international relations and related fields.[3] They have also included an increasing number of contributions from scholars working outside of conventional political science, such as the work of Hall in sociology and Kennedy in history.[4] Due to the potential for these studies to produce scenarios for the future development of international affairs, they have attracted a large amount of media, public, business and military attention. This latter facet has been exemplified by the very great amount of attention afforded to Paul Kennedy's view that the United States is on the brink of dramatic decline.[5]

The growth in this field and the level of sustained activity which this has produced, has led to there being a sizeable body of researchers both inside and outside of the usual bounds of international relations, concentrating their activity on questions relating to the study of change in world affairs. For example in the last year there have been a considerable number of books and research seminars addressing this question and two internet discussion lists (the World Systems Network and the Global Change Network) are committed to this perspective on international relations.

Such is the level of this activity that it seems timely to recognise 'global change' as a sub-discipline within international relations, analogous to 'international political economy' or 'security studies'. In terms of research output and the number of scholars actively participating in such research (especially when those working outside the academic study of international relations are also counted) the scale of work on this area certainly exceeds that of some recognised sub-disciplines within international relations.

The purpose of this chapter is not only to define this sub-discipline formally, but to show how it relates to other aspects of research in international relations. The intention is also to demonstrate the common theme which lies behind the other chapters in this volume, although most of the scholars involved are not primarily researchers on global change, nor does the range of topics here cover more than a few of the far wider range of themes which this sub-discipline addresses. The intention is not to attempt a definition of the meaning of 'change' as such, as this has been widely discussed by other scholars, nor to propose new interpretations or explanations of the changes involved in world history; but a definition of 'global change' is needed.

The easiest way to define 'global change', and to show that it must be considered that the term refers to a distinct sub-discipline within international relations, is to set out this sub-discipline's scope. That is, by showing the range of interrelated topics which may be included under this heading, it is possible to recognise that these both clarify the meaning of the term 'global change' itself and demonstrate that it can be used to refer to a specific type of scholarly investigation within the discipline of international relations.

At its simplest, of course, 'global change' can be taken to mean change affecting, or within, the world. This is, however, far too broad a definition to be of much use here. What is needed is a clarification of exactly what aspects of change can be grouped into this category. Accordingly the present approach seems a straightforward way of both defining and delimiting this subject.

There will be an attempt, then, to give a brief outline of the scope of global change and thereby to demonstrate why it is a distinct field of study and why it may be situated within the discipline of international relations. Plainly, in a short account, it is only possible to sketch the general contours of the field rather than explore any of its aspects in depth. Nor is there a claim that the following list of topics is completely exhaustive and they are all, to

some extent, interrelated. However all of the main themes of current research
have been included.

2. The Scope of Global Change

States

The rise and fall of individual states and of interstate systems has been a
major focus for existing studies of global change.[6] This has included work
on the collapse of the USSR, the end of the Roman Empire and the process
of decolonisation in the twentieth century.[7] Comparative studies have included
work on state formation and state collapse, in addition to patterns of hegemony.[8] In considering the state studies of global change have, therefore,
examined both intrastate and interstate factors and have looked at changes
in the form of relations (for example forms of diplomacy) between states.
This has included a major focus on interstate warfare, revolution and
specifics of change within and between governments, change in ruling
groups and the existence and role of interest groups. This has been a centre
of interest for the majority of studies of global change such as those undertaken by Modelski and Kennedy.[9]

International Systems

This has been another major focus of research, encompassing work by all of
those scholars mentioned in the previous section. Interest has concentrated
on the rise and decline of international systems, especially the possibilities
of cross-cultural generalisations concerning the pattern of relationships
within international systems and the role of empire and hegemony in defining them.[10] There has been a wide range of approaches to this topic ranging
from realist, state-centric views through world systems approaches to
Wilkinson's urban-based perspective, concentrating on relations between
cities.[11] A key characteristic of most of these studies has been an interest in
the possibility of cyclical patterning in change within and between international systems through time.[12]

Institutions

Similar issues have been approached in relation to the study of international
institutions and their domestic counterparts. Although this has not yet been
the subject of much published work, studies in progress are taking a similar
view of this area to that which has been employed in discussing international
systems and states.[13]

Other Non-State Actors

Although similar approaches might be adopted in relation to the study of other non-state actors, this has not been an issue so far addressed by scholars of global change. Changes that might be examined include those of the emergence and decline of specific actors, changes in the number and role of such actors and in their relationships with states, international institutions and international systems.

Social Organisation

All states and non-state actors must have some form of social organisation and the character of these actors relates to the wider forms of social organisation existing within the societies which produced them and within which they existed. Consequently, social organisation is closely linked to the topics already mentioned and is an obvious area where studies of change might be undertaken. Pioneering work on this topic has already been started in a number of disciplines related to international relations – for example, Friedman's work in anthropology – and a few such studies have been attempted by scholars working within international relations.[14] Notable among these is the recent book by Scholte, addressing these issues in relation to questions of globalisation in the modern world.[15]

Cultural Aspects

Culture, as defined by anthropologists, encompasses not merely art, music and the like, but broader aspects of human societies including social customs and attitudes. This is, again, obviously linked to core concerns in the study of global change and must be seen as another potential topic for research within this sub-discipline. Again, much work conducted outside of the conventional boundaries of international relations has already been undertaken on the question of change in human cultures world-wide. In addition to questions of the emergence and decline of specific cultures, there are issues of culture-contact and the relationship of one culture to others over time.

Religion

All known human societies include a religious aspect. Much work has been completed by scholars in other fields on the relationship between religion and change and on change in religious beliefs and practices. This work is of immediate relevance to international relations for many reasons and the globalisation of the major world religions is a striking characteristic of the modern period.[16] Consequently the study of global change must include the study of religious issues.

Ethical and Normative Questions

Related to religious issues and to studies of international systems and actors, the philosophical dimensions of change constitute another topic which clearly lies within this sub-discipline. There are the questions of change in ethical or normative systems and those of the ethical and normative questions raised by the changes studied in other aspects of this field. Much of the focus of this present book is on these questions and this makes a clear link between global change and political philosophy, as in the study of the implications for the theory of democracy of change in other aspects of international affairs.

Geopolitics and Other Geographical Dimensions of Change

Global change must include an appreciation of the spatial dimension of change, including – but not exclusively – geopolitical change. Here a connection may be made with the study of international geopolitics undertaken by Taylor and, through that, we may see a further link between contemporary studies of geopolitics and the world systems analysis school within global change studies.[17] The relevant range of geographical questions encompasses changes in the boundaries of states and international systems, questions of geographical permeability, economic and social geography and the mapping of cultural and religious aspects. A series of recent atlases, such as *The Times Atlas of World History* and *The New State of the World Atlas*, have begun to show the potential of this approach and, again, there is much relevant work already in existence which has been undertaken by scholars outside of international relations.[18]

Ecological Change

Closely related to geographical dimensions of change are changes in ecological relationships – those relationships between animals, plants and the physical environment which form the biological context in which human societies conduct world politics. Given the closeness of this intrinsic relationship and the ubiquity of change in biological systems, the study of ecological change must be encompassed within the sub-discipline of global change. Much work undertaken on contemporary climate change and other ecological factors, such as pollution, has led to the establishment of a large body of work within international relations on this subject.

Demographic Change

Demography (human population studies) is, of course, closely connected to both geography and ecology. Because it is the change involving human populations that is the concern of the study of global change, this must be a central aspect of that study. Demographic studies encompass change in the age-structure, nutrition, life expectancy and health of global populations and the movement of population between one area and another. Human migration of this sort is already on the agenda of many international relations programmes and so requires no drastic revision in our understanding of the scope and nature of the study of international relations in order to be encompassed within this sub-discipline.[19]

Change in Security Issues
Changes in this area include the development and abandonment of weapons systems, tactics and strategies and the emergence and decline of specific threats.[20] Perceptual changes are also a key factor here, for example in the changing perceptions of the nature and even existence of threats and challenges to individual, institutional or national security.

Technological Change
Economic and security issues relate closely to changes in technology and these may also be included in the range of topics considered by global change studies. The invention and spread of technologies, the relationship between one technology and another and the role of technology in promoting or retarding change in other aspects of international affairs are all key areas of concern. The importance of technological change has been emphasised, for example, in recent studies linking the development of electronic communications with changes in international economics and in studies of the 'rise of the West' in world history.[21]

Economic Change
The study of economic change has been one of the main features of most recent work on global change.[22] While it is not necessary to accord economic factors a primary role in the explanation of global change, most studies of the rise and fall of states and international systems have attempted to employ international economics as a means of understanding aspects of these changes.[23] The range of issues covered by the study of economic change is very wide-ranging, including at least the following: the emergence and decline of specific economic actors, such as commercial companies; the emergence and decline of economic regimes and behavioural norms; changes in the mode of exchange or in the mode of production; changes in the means of exchange; changes in the relationship between economic activity and other aspects of international affairs; and changes in economic geography.

Communication and Information Exchange

A related, but not identical topic is the ease of communication and flow of information between geographical areas, individuals and other actors. Changes in this area include change in the means of transport, of exchanging information and the rate of information exchange, linguistic change, changes in literacy rates and in the extent to which non-linguistic forms of information exchange are employed, and the effects of information exchange on other aspects of world affairs. As the present writer has argued elsewhere we may see economic exchanges as a form of information exchange: as units of exchange, prices and records of commodities can be seen as pieces of information flowing through the international system by means of modes of communication.[24] Although applicable to any monetary economy this interpretation of the relationship between information exchange and economic activity is most clearly seen in the global financial markets of the modern world.[25] In a situation where commodities and shares are bought and sold entirely through linguistic and numerical exchanges, without materials being exchanged directly, economics can be clearly seen as a form of information flow. This does not, in itself, mean that we can say that all economic activity is a form of information-exchange, but information-exchange is an aspect of all economics.

3. Global Change and World History

If such a wide range of topics may be encompassed within the sub-discipline of global change in international relations, and it can be shown (as is attempted in setting out the above list) that each of the component topics is either already part of conventional studies of international relations or has a close relationship to topics which are within the conventional scope of the subject, then this raises the question of the relationship between the study of global change and other disciplines. If global change includes so many topics then what differentiates it, as a sub-discipline within international relations, from the study of 'world history' within the discipline of history?[26]

There are several characteristics shared by international relations approaches to global change which differentiate these from 'world history' and which are likely to be developed in future work within the discipline of international relations. The first of these is the importance assigned to comparative and generalising approaches: these are not currently in fashion among historians.[27] Second there is the theoretical component of work on global change within international relations: this is in contrast to the relatively atheoretical (or, to be more exact, 'historical particularist') approach taken by historians. Another aspect which most studies by international relations scholars have shared, is the opinion that cyclical patterns, at least in some aspects of the world's affairs and at some times, might be discerned in history. Few, if any, historians would agree with this view. Finally there is the far greater importance assigned to long-term approaches in international relations studies of global change than is usual in historical work.[28] This is perhaps ironical, as one might expect that historians would be interested in long-term approaches, but the historical particularist paradigm of contemporary historical studies views the idea of long-term change as a misconception and reduces history to a sequence of incomparable unique events. The explanation of each event is seen in terms of the preceding events in the sequence, rather than in terms of shared processes of change identifiable in several analogous situations. Consequently, historians have tended to attempt to explain change using the study of short-term factors alone, in contrast to the long-term perspective employed to analyse change by international relations scholars.

This final difference is becoming more strongly accentuated as international relations scholars have been increasingly adopting longer time-spans in their analyses.[29] Currently a substantial number of scholars working within the world systems school, in addition to both Wilkinson and Modelski, have employed time-spans in international relations stretching beyond not only the modern period but into the pre-medieval period.[30] The chronological scope of the study of global change has, perhaps, been usefully defined by Adam Watson's work.[31] In Watson's view, all interstate systems must be considered open to analysis by scholars of international relations in their study of change, while Ferguson has adopted a still broader view, that one should include 'chiefdoms' (to use the anthropological term), highly complex non-state societies, in addition to states.[32] Whichever of these two options is adopted, this renders the chronological range of the sub-discipline of global change wide enough to encompass, for example, Classical and Hellenistic Greece, the Roman and Byzantine Empires, ancient China, the Mayan civilisation and medieval Europe as well as the modern world.

It is, therefore, possible to define the field of global change as distinct and separable from the historian's study of world history. Plainly, there is a great overlap in the data employed, as is also inevitably the case with several other disciplines. Some of these, notably anthropology, palaeoecology and archaeology, have strongly-developed theoretical traditions of their own and it is imperative that the next stage in the study of global change in international relations draws heavily upon these theoretical perspectives.

Nor can global change be easily encompassed within economic, geographical or sociological approaches to the study of change. In part, the range

Analysing Global Change

of issues involved necessitates this view, but so too does the distinctiveness of the chronological range, theoretical character and shared interests of the work so far undertaken within the sub-discipline. For example few sociologists would want to include studies of entirely natural biological change within their subject, nor would economists usually see their field as encompassing cultural factors such as art or sport or, for instance, linguistic change. As such studies need include no spatial dimension, geography can also be ruled out. Once again the field seems quite distinct from those addressed in other subjects.

The positive case for encompassing this area of study within international relations is straightforward. On the one hand we have seen that many links exist between aspects of the study of global change and conventional topics of interest within international relations. This alone may suggest that not only does global change belong within the scope of international relations but that it can be seen as lying at the centre of the field's disciplinary concerns. On the other hand it is notable that many precedents for the inclusion of global change as a sub-discipline within international relations can be recognised in the discipline's history.[33] Whether one considers the contribution of Toynbee or of Wight, it is clear that major scholars in the development of international relations as an independent field of study were, themselves, directly involved in the analysis of global change.

4. Conclusion

It can be seen that there are strong grounds for defining a sub-discipline of global change as lying at the core of international relations. This subject is already the focus of much research activity and is attracting many younger scholars, so it is likely to increase in scale and importance within the discipline during the next phase of its development. This may have important implications for the character of international relations as an academic field after the end of the Cold War. It might be argued that in returning to the concerns of earlier scholars in this way, the 'return to history' in international relations can be taken to have an ambiguous meaning.

Notes and References

1   For example, C. W. Kegley Jnr, 'How Did the Cold War Die? Principles for an Autopsy', *Mershon International Studies Review*, 38, Supplement 1 (March, 1994), 11–14.

2   Reviewed in K. R. Dark, *The Waves of Time?* (forthcoming).

3   R. Gilpin, *War and Change in World Politics* (Cambridge and New York: Cambridge University Press, 1981); O. R. Holsti, R. M. Siverson and A. L. George (eds), *Change in the International System* (Boulder, Colo.: Westview Press and Bowker Publishing, 1980); B. Buzan and R. J. B. Jones (eds), *Change and the Study of International Relations: The Evaded Dimension* (London and New York: Pinter and St Martin's Press, 1981); G. Modelski, 'The Long Cycle of Global Politics and the Nation-State', *Comparative Studies in Society and History*, 20 (1978), 214–35; I. Wallerstein, *The Modern World System: Capitalist Agriculture and the Origins of the European World-Economy in the Sixteenth Century* (New York: Academic Press, 1974).

4   P. Kennedy, *The Rise and Fall of the Great Powers* (London: Fontana, 1989); J. A. Hall, *Powers and Liberties* (London: Penguin, 1985).

5   Kennedy, *The Rise and Fall of the Great Powers*; Hall, *Powers and Liberties*.

6   For example G. Modelski (ed.), *Exploring Long Cycles* (Boulder, Colo.: Lynne Rienner, 1987).

7   B. Buzan, C. A. Jones and R. Little, *The Logic of Anarchy: Neorealism to Structural Realism* (New York: Columbia University Press, 1993); M. Bowker and R. Brown (eds), *From Cold War to Collapse: Theory and World Politics in the 1980s* (Cambridge: Cambridge University Press, 1992). See also the works cited in M. Cox, 'Rethinking the End of the Cold War', *Review of International Studies*, 20 (1994) 187–99; S. Corbridge, 'Colonialism, Post-Colonialism and the Political Geography of the Third World', in J. Taylor (ed.), *Political Geography of the Twentieth Century. A Global Analysis* (London: Belhaven Press, 1993).

8   J. A. Tainter, *The Collapse of Complex Societies* (Cambridge: Cambridge University Press, 1988); R. J. Johnston, 'The Rise and Decline of the Corporate-Welfare State: A Comparative Analysis in a Global Context', in Taylor (ed.), *Political Geography*.

9   Modelski (ed.), *Exploring Long Cycles*; Kennedy, *The Rise and Fall of the Great Powers*.

10 B. Buzan and R. Little, 'The Idea of International System: Theory Meets History', *International Journal of Political Science*, forthcoming; and *An Introduction to the International System: Theory Meets History* (Oxford: Oxford University Press, forthcoming); A. G. Frank, 'A Theoretical Introduction to 5000 Years of World Systems History', *Review* 13 (1990) 155–248; B. K. Gills and A. G. Frank, 'World Sys-

tems Cycles, Crises and Hegemonial Shifts, 1700 B.C. to 1700 A.D.',
Review 15 (1992) 621–87.

11   D. Wilkinson, 'Civilizations, Cores, World Economies and Oikumnes',
in A. G. Frank and B. K. Gills (eds), *The World System. Five Hundred
Years or Five Thousand?* (London: Routledge, 1993).

12   For example J. Levy, 'Long Cycles, Hegemonic Transitions, and the
Long Peace', in C. W. Kegley (ed.), *The Long Postwar Peace* (New
York: Harper Collins, 1991).

13   This is the topic of current doctoral research by A. L. Harris at the
University of Reading.

14   J. Friedman, *Cultural Identity and Global Process* (London: Sage,
1994).

15   R. J. B. Jones, *Globalisation and Interdependence in the International
Political Economy* (London: Pinter, 1995); J. A. Scholte, *International
Relations of Social Change* (Buckingham: Open University Press,
1993).

16   Eloquently illustrated in J. O'Brien and M. Palmer, *The State of Religion Atlas* (London: Simon and Schuster, 1993).

17   P. J. Taylor, *Political Geography: World-economy, Nation-state and
Locality* (London: Longman, 1989).

18   M. Kidron and R. Segal, *The New State of the World Atlas* (London:
Simon and Schuster, 1991); G. Barraclough (ed.), *The Times Atlas of
World History* (London: Times Books, 1994).

19   S. Castles and M. J. Miller, *The Age of Migration: International
Population Movements in the Modern World* (New York: Guilford,
1993).

20   B. Buzan, *People States and Fear*, 2nd ed. (Hemel Hempstead: Harvester Wheatsheaf, 1991); J. A. Tickner, 'Re-visioning Security' in K.
Booth and S. Smith (eds), *International Relations Theory Today* (Cambridge: Polity Press, 1995).

21   R. O'Brien, *Global Financial Integration: The End of Geography*
(London: Royal Institute of International Affairs, 1992).

22   For examples see: H. McRae, *The World in 2020* (London: Harper-
Collins, 1994); J. A. Frieden and D. A. Lake, *International Political
Economy* 2nd ed. (London: Unwin Hyman, 1991); J. Goldstein, *Long
Cycles: Prosperity and War in the Modern Age* (New Haven, Conn.
and London: Yale University Press, 1988); J. Gilpin, *War and Change
in World Politics* (New York: Cambridge University Press, 1983); and
The Political Economy of International Relations (Princeton, N.J.:
Princeton University Press, 1987); R. A. Isaak, *International Political*

Economy: Managing World Change (Englewood Cliffs, N.J.: Prentice-Hall, 1990).

23 The most famous example is, of course, Kennedy, *The Rise and Fall of the Great Powers.*

24 Dark, *The Waves of Time?*

25 O'Brien, *Global Financial Integration.*

26 R. Little, 'International Relations and Large-Scale Historical Change', in A. J. R. Groom and M. Light (eds), *Contemporary International Relations: A Guide to Theory* (London: Pinter, 1994), esp. pp. 16–17.

27 R. G. Collingwood, *The Idea of History* (London: Oxford University Press, 1946); K. Popper, *The Poverty of Historicism*, 2nd ed. (London: Routledge, 1961).

28 For example, compare Kennedy, *The Rise and Fall of the Great Powers* and Goldstein, *Long Cycles.*

29 A. G. Frank and B. K. Gills (eds), *The World System. Five Hundred Years or Five Thousand?* (London: Routledge, 1993).

30 Frank and Gills (eds), *The World System.*

31 A. Watson, *The Evolution of International Society: A Comparative Historical Analysis* (London: Routledge, 1992).

32 See the contributions by Y. Ferguson and others in T. Earle (ed.), *Chiefdoms: Power, Economy and Ideology* (Cambridge: Cambridge University Press, 1991).

33 Note the importance attached to the study of change by the 'English School' and historical materialist studies of international relations, both of which have been recently discussed in F. Halliday, *Rethinking International Relations* (London: Macmillan, 1994).

PART 2

The Normative Structure of the International System

2

Construction and Constraint in the Promotion of Change in the Principles of International Conduct

R. J. Barry Jones

1. Introduction

This chapter focusses upon change as a major source of insight into the dynamics of the human condition. The immediate concern is with the sources and patterns of change in the sub-set of the general wider domain of human ethical principles and practices associated with a system of nominally sovereign states. The difficulty of analysing change will be identified through a discussion of the conflicting claims of structural and voluntaristic perspectives and the problems affecting their possible resolution through structuration theory.

The positivistic 'social science' that has attained dominance during the twentieth century would attribute the norms, principles and 'laws' that influence international conduct to the problems and imperatives generated within the conduct of international affairs. The structures of common situations are thus endowed with explanatory power.

The reassertion of 'critical' dispositions within the 'social sciences' has, however, evoked a secular echo of the more humanistic views of principle and practice that prevailed in earlier eras. Indeed human volition has regained a clear primacy in the more extreme forms of intellectual voluntarism of recent popularity, particularly discourse analysis.

The debate between structural and more voluntaristic perspectives upon international affairs can throw considerable light upon the nature of international conduct and developments. It is also an issue that demands serious consideration if the study of international affairs is not to be condemned to indefinite intellectual and methodological schism.

2. Kenneth Waltz's Realist Structuralism

Contextual determinism is implicit in the work of Kenneth Waltz, particularly in his highly influential *Theory of International Politics*.[1] Condemning the majority of alternative approaches to international relations as inherently *reductionist*, Waltz advocated an analytical approach that emphasised the centrality of distribution of capability and potential 'power' amongst the member states of an international system. The particular patterns of interconnectedness in the political and military domain were thus identified as both definitive of any international system and a major influence upon its internal developments.

Only a 'structuralist' approach of the form favoured by Waltz could, in his view, constitute a truly systemic approach to the study of international relations and avoid the fragmented empiricism of more reductionist perspectives. Such an approach was, moreover, quintessentially holistic, with the opportunities and constraints of individual actors being determined largely by their location within the system-wide distribution of capabilities and potential 'power'.

The theories that are required for the description and analysis of complex holistic phenomena in human affairs actually operate at two levels. The validity of any holistic notion has to rest upon appropriate philosophical and methodological foundations. Such foundations sometimes sail close to metaphysics, but they always involve basic propositions about the 'realities' that underlie the complexities of life that present themselves to the senses. Such fundamentals of any holistic approach remain essentially 'meta-theoretical' in that they furnish a broad interpretative framework rather than propositions about reality that are, in any precise manner, testable against that reality.[2] All holistic theories of international relations and the international political economy ultimately rest upon some such 'meta-theoretical' foundations, with the 'Platonic form' of 'scientific realism' frequently filling this role.

Holistic approaches to international relations also involve substantive levels of theory, however. Such theories conventionally embrace primary propositions about the fundamental factors or forces that drive international relations and/or the international political economy and secondary propositions that identify a number of empirical phenomena that are deemed to be shaped by those fundamental factors or forces. The structure of such theories is akin to that of Noam Chomsky's theory of the deep structural foundations of all human languages. The theory rests upon basic propositions about the implications of the human nervous system for the basic structures of all languages and the argument that all human languages despite their superficial diversity could be reduced to, or derived logically from, the deep structure if only the 'transformational rules', whereby deep structures are actually translated into surface languages, could be identified.

The example of Chomsky's structural theory of language illustrates the difficulties that commonly attend holistic theories of human activity. Day-to-day 'realities' are highly diverse. Without an ability to specify appropriate transformational rules, attributions of causal force to deep structural factors and forces remain merely a matter of interpretative plausibility. Evidence will be readily found to support the propositions of the favoured theory, but the same empirical 'reality' will invariably provide evidence for alternative approaches.

Extreme holism thus drifts dangerously close to a form of metaphysical determinism. All human volition, let alone the influence of any particular individuals, is now denied a significant role in human developments. Some feature, force, compulsive process or extra-terrestrial influence is identified as decisive. Human consciousness can only be a derivative, and an imperfect reflection, of the determining force that is intrinsic to the aggregate reality of the human condition. The most to which the individual can aspire is an appreciation of the imperatives inherent in the human system: any ambition for their modification or reversal would clearly be futile. Ethics, from such a perspective, must therefore ultimately reflect the requirements of the system within which they arise. Functionalist imperatives thus exert their influence, with little room for human volition. Such an approach is both morally repugnant and intellectually suspect to many students of human affairs.

3. Ultra-Voluntarism and Extreme Individualism

The ultra-voluntarist alternative to the more extreme and deterministic forms of holism encounters equally serious intellectual and analytical difficulties. Such ultra-voluntarism ultimately drifts into the propositions that have been popularised in recent years by deconstructionists and discourse analysts.[3] Ethics would be attributed to spontaneous intellectual impulses with no more than random acceptance and transitory (at best) institutionalisation within such a perspective.

The notion that reality can be constructed and reconstructed at will, however, is credible only for novelists and the inmates of some medical institutions. The remainder of humanity has to accommodate to the 'realities' of one kind or another that are encountered in the 'external' world of people and things. The sources of the ethical considerations and constraints confronted by most people are thus rather more substantial and enduring than mere ephemeral intellectual caprice.

Extreme individualistic voluntarism also leaves the question of the origin of human ideas and understandings in an unsatisfactory backwater. The acquisition of such intellectual equipment might be attributed to spontaneous and unaided development by each individual, but this bears no correspondence to the patterns of language acquisition and intellectual development of most human infants. The alternative is to acknowledge the social character of intellectual development and cultural acquisition, but simply evade its wider implications for the analysis of human affairs.

4. The Agent-Structure Issue

A parallel expression of the complex and problematical relationship between the behaviour of individual actors and the holistic phenomena that they may collectively create is to be found in the 'agent-structure' issue that has recently attracted considerable attention within the study of international relations.[4] This is more than merely a matter of 'levels of analysis' for it confronts the issue of the ontological status of both individuals and aggregate entities in human affairs.[5] The problems here can be illustrated by two extreme arguments. The first possible argument is that it is only individuals that really exist and that all other conceptions of the human condition involve unwarranted invocation of imagined collectivities: 'there is no society!' The opposing argument contends that holistic phenomena exist and are capable of exerting a causal influence upon human developments that transcends the volition and expectations of any of the human beings involved. Both positions offer considerable attractions to those who are psychologically disposed towards their respective appeals but both leave substantial problems unresolved.

The problematical relationship between individual action and the nature and development of aggregate human phenomena has thus been a matter of more than academic interest. The issue confronted revolutionary Marxists with acute difficulties and dilemmas during the later years of the nineteenth century and the early years of the twentieth. Marxist revolutionaries wondered whether they could merely sit back and await the arrival of the inevitable socialist revolution passively, or whether the inevitable socialist revolution would be 'inevitable' only if they initiated appropriate actions.[6] The debate over this issue was one of theoretical ferocity and practical anxiety. It has, moreover, remained a problematical issue for those who continue to identify themselves as Marxists.

Such issues thus relate to that of the causal connection between the institutional structure of the international system and central developments in world affairs. The perspective provided by 'structuration theory' offers, as will be shown later, a methodology that partially bridges the rationalist/ reflective divide by identifying the intersubjective basis of the behavioural patterns that characterise the international political economy and its institutional features. The realm of international relations is thus one of constant structuration and restructuration by sentient human beings, all seeking to realise their expectations in a world of collectively constructed 'realities' and constraints.

5. Structuration and the Construction of Complex Systems of Human Activity

A systematic resolution of the agent-structure issue would thus be most helpful for students of human affairs. An approach to the study of human affairs that avoids both the positivism of much traditional 'social science' and the extreme voluntarism of 'critical' perspectives is possible through a *constructionist* approach to human action and institutions. Such an approach emphasises the foundation of human actions and institutions in shared values, beliefs, understandings and expectations of the participants in any economic, social or political order, while acknowledging that the complex of interacting and mutually reinforcing behaviour thus generated constitutes a 'reality' of considerable force, pattern and durability.[7] This approach encourages attention to the practical processes and the uneven historical record through which the patterns of contemporary international relations and their institutional foundations have been established.

The *constructionist* perspective thus starts from the proposition that human behaviour is, in the first instance, determined by the beliefs, understandings and expectations of the individual human actor. Such beliefs, understandings and expectations are in turn derived primarily from the society within which the individual is educated and further influenced by his, or her, life-time set of experiences. Most significantly, however, the individual actor interacts with other actors who by virtue of a common culture share many of the same beliefs, understandings and expectations. Each individual's set of beliefs, understandings and expectations is thus likely to be reinforced by the behaviour of all those other members of the same society whose own behaviour is directed by a comparable set of beliefs, understandings and expectations. The actions of each individual thus contribute to a pattern of broadly similar actions by other individuals. Moreover dissonant behaviour by any individual is challenged, and ultimately constrained, by the adverse or uncomprehending reactions of others. A collective 'reality' is thus created and recreated constantly by the complementarity amongst the actions of individuals and the sets of shared beliefs, understandings and expectations upon which they rest. Cohesive societies thus rest upon sets of mutually supporting intersubjectivities amongst their members and constitute a 'reality' that is more, and has greater durability and force, than the behaviour of its individual members, but which remains a product of the sum of complementary behaviours.

Methodologically such an approach has a clear starting point on the *reflective* side of Robert Keohane's distinction between *reflective* (or *cognitive*) and *rationalistic* approaches to the study of international relations and the international political economy.[8] However the central role that is also ascribed to the 'realities' that are generated through the complex sets of self-reinforcing intersubjectivities of the members of societies, economies and polities, re-admits those empirical complexities that may generate important unintended outcomes and unexpected consequences. These are of a kind that require a form of analysis that comes close to that of the rationalistic approach while not necessarily accepting the ontological presumptions of its more extreme forms. The simple distinction between reflective and rationalistic approaches to international relations may thus be not that easy to sustain in practice if analysis is not to be unduly restricted by a priori methodological constraints, or confined to the 'understanding' side of the understanding/ explanation divide in 'social science'.[9]

The constructionist approach to human conduct and institutions corresponds closely to Anthony Giddens' concept of 'structuration'.[10] This perspective, while sharing the methodological difficulties of constructionism discussed earlier, finds ready application at the level of well-established and widely recognised societies. The fit between the actions of individuals and the explicit beliefs, understandings and expectations of other members of a society is readily observable where it exists, and dramatic by its absence where it does not. The fate of individuals who find themselves trying to function in unfamiliar societies illustrates the point with considerable force.

The appropriateness of concepts of structuration to international relations is, however, rather more problematical. The actors in international relations are not sentient human beings like the members of normal societies. This difference lies at the heart of many of the difficulties encountered by the concept of 'international society'.[11] Structuration remains a valid concept at the international level, however, if it is recognised that the processes involved will be more complex than those of domestic societies, will operate at a number of 'levels' and will be mediated by a range of complex institutions including state bureaucracies, political structures and information systems. The complexity, and distance from most sentient human beings, of much that takes place at the international level of activity thus reinforces Margaret Archer's wider contention that it is necessary to maintain, and operate, an analytical distinction between the levels of agent and structure in the analysis of social developments.[12] The explanation of fundamental change reduces, in Archer's view, to one of spontaneous changes of collective outlook unless the mechanisms operative at the structural level can be accessed; and such 'spontaneous changes' of collective outlook become increasingly problematical with the increasing scale and complexity of the collectivities involved.

6. The Constructed 'Reality' of a System of States

Far from being automatic and self-generating conditions, most developments in international relations have thus arisen as a result of the patterning of the modern world into sovereign states and the uneven manner in which these states have then acted and interacted. International relations are, it will be argued, always inherently changeable, as well as manipulable; and it is in the realms of the 'political' that the immediate sources of such change or manipulation are to be found.

The contemporary 'reality' of international relations certainly exhibits the evidence of past construction. The institutionalisation of the sovereignty of states, and the use of power balancing mechanisms, have come to form the basis of what some analysts have dubbed an *international society*:[13] a 'society', albeit of states (or their ruling groups), devoted to the interests and maintenance of those states (or ruling groups).[14] The *system* brought into being was thus, as is also demonstrated by Williams's contribution to this volume, a product of the character, needs and interests of its constituent parts – the member *states* – or, rather, of the dominant interests within those states: the European system of states did not simply spring into life immaculately.

The international system that was created during the emergence of modern Europe, far from shaping the character of its member states unidirectionally, as has often been implied in realist writings on international relations,[15] was far more a political construction of its constituent states. As Williams also points out these states had, initially, been constructed to serve the interests of dynastic ruling groups. The threats posed to their continued suzerainty by ideologically motivated forces, or by hegemonically minded fellow rulers, had prompted the self-interested identification of appropriate 'rules of conduct' within a fundamentally statist political order. The gradual secularisation of the basis of legitimacy for the leaders of states reinforced the need to elaborate a philosophy of the state as a natural and necessary form of human political organization. With the subsequent, albeit gradual, democ- ratisation of political life in the European states the legitimisation of the state increasingly required its 'nationalisation', as a means of incorporating the interests and support of each state's citizenry. The 'nation state' was the potent product of this process of consolidation of territorial control, and progressive legitimisation, within the territories of Europe's consolidating states.

Politics is as much about fundamental political orders as it is a matter of day-to-day control of office or the making of rules and decisions. The polit- ical order prevailing encompasses three basic levels of political life. At the foundational level of a political order are the basic principles that identify the 'legitimate' members of that political order and their proper patterns of interaction. At the institutional or constitutional level are treaties, constitu- tions, organisational structures and any other well-established arrangements which give expression to the fundamentals of the political order. At the day- to-day level of politics negotiations are undertaken, elections are held, poli- cies are formulated by office-holders and the proposals and performances of governmental executives are deliberated upon by legislative bodies. In the political order that crystallised within Europe states, rather than individuals or other groupings and associations, were enshrined as the legitimate mem- bers of the order. A succession of peace treaties, 'concerts', leagues, diplo- matic practices and increasingly formalised institutions gave institutional expression to that statist order. A plethora of diplomatic exchanges, threats, bribes and periodic armed conflicts constituted the day-to-day stuff of an interstate political order.[16] Such behaviour at the level of day-to-day inter- state politics provided the regular nourishment for the underlying principles of that basic order.

The 'reality' of contemporary international relations is thus an essentially constructed political phenomenon with the 'legitimate' members and their basic rules and institutions of international relations all defined by the fun- damental order of nominally sovereign states. While such a 'reality' is neither 'natural' nor unchangeable it is, however, as suggested by Margaret Archer's critique of pure structuration theory, a 'reality' with profound and enduring implications for the probabilities of, and constraints upon, behaviours and developments.

The 'realities' constructed by human activity are, moreover, highly complex and characteristically beset by contradictions. It is in the implications and inherent tensions of such constructed international realities that many of the impulses for change in the ethical principles of international conduct, and the legal constraints upon international behaviour, can be found.

7. Contradictions and Constraints in a System of States

The analytical challenge confronting those who wish to avoid the extremes of holistic determinism or individualistic voluntarism is to identify the general sources of ethical concern and commitment in a system of nominally sovereign states. For the student of *inter*-national relations a primary task is to differentiate those ethical issues that derive from a system of states itself, and those that derive from other sources but which confront a system of states with particular problems.

Much of the traditional debate about the principles of international conduct turns upon the problems generated by a system of states: the justice of war; the conditions under which internal sovereignty might be compromised; the status of treaties and other forms of international agreement and so on. Here it is the complications, and often contradictions, of the states-system itself that form the major source of difficulty, debate and development at the ethical level.

Contradictions embraced by the principles and practices of the United Nations demonstrate many of the difficulties arising at this level of international conduct. The tension between pre-emptive action to deter or diminish the dangers of armed aggression and the sanctification of domestic jurisdiction and state inviolability in Article 2.7 of the Charter of the United Nations exemplifies such a problem.

A growing area of difficulty for contemporary international ethics, however, stems from practical problems or ethical sensitivities deriving, partly or wholly, from sources other than the states-system itself. The challenge to slavery, and its implications for the international trade in slaves and the domestic jurisdiction of the southern states of the United States, provides an earlier example of such an 'external' ethical impulse impacting upon the states-system. The inherent tension between the declaratory universalism of the Universal Declaration of Human Rights, and the embedded statism of Article 2.7 of the Charter of the United Nations, furnishes a contemporary example; and the kinds of complexities involved are illustrated in Hutchings's contribution to this volume.

Recent concerns with, and complications relating to, the issues of global equity, resource management and ecological protection crystallise many of the ethical and practical dilemmas posed by the collision of a states-system with other concerns; and key questions here are discussed in the chapters by Holden and Paterson in this volume. Jamborees, such as the Rio Earth Summit, convey the impression that consultation and negotiation at the level of interstate relations may offer part of the solution to a range of the problems confronting humanity. The inherent constraints of a states-system may, however, be a large part of the problem facing those who seek effective solutions to many contemporary issues.

The malign effects of a states-system on the attempted solution of many pressing problems fall under four interrelated headings.

The states-system enshrines and prioritises the **sovereignty of states**. This acts as an immediate and nominally absolute obstacle to solutions to many contemporary problems, where some substantial surrender of sovereignty would be entailed by the establishment of new, global, regulatory principles and institutions.

The persistence of sovereign states, and the related weakness of global authorities, encourages the operation of **free riders** in many areas of international life which undermines efforts to create, or sustain, mutually advantageous forms of international cooperation in many spheres of international interaction.[17] The current state of international maritime regulation is a shambles, with the registration of large numbers of ocean-going ships undertaken by pseudo-states, like Liberia and Panama, that are far from being able to able to manage their own internal affairs. International financial regulation, and the attendant maintenance of probity, is similarly beset by free-riding states.

The combination of sovereignty preservation and widespread free riding underlies a serious weakness in the **redistributional and compensatory capabilities** of the international system. The activities of such agencies as the World Bank, the International Monetary Fund and the United Nations' specialist agencies are much vaunted but have failed to attract significant portions of the wealth of the world's richer countries or, *on their own*, to materially improve the conditions of most of the countries towards which their efforts have been directed. The capacity of the states-system to mobilise adequate compensation for those who might have to accept the highest proportional burdens from many schemes for resource management and ecological preservation has thus been placed in serious doubt. Paterson's discussion of international justice and the global warming problem takes up some of the important issues here.

Sovereignty, free riding and the weakness of redistributional and compensatory capacities have also combined to reinforce the tendency towards **special pleading** amongst states facing substantial, or even disproportionate, costs in the pursuit of global collective goods. Many may be keen on desired outcomes, supportive of the sacrifices of others, but decidedly guarded about the exposure of their own societies to new or additional burdens for the collective good (help in coping with this problem would be one of the benefits of 'cosmopolitan democracy' identified in Holden's chapter).

The structural problems generated by a states-system are thus substantial. They may not, however, be fatal in all circumstances and on all issues. The possible solutions to the structural dilemma of a states-system will, however, be conditioned by the ultimate constraints exerted by such a system. The role of international 'regimes' and their varied fates demonstrates the limitations under which activity must take place in a states-system.

8. Regimes and Hegemons

A major mechanism for the constraint of disorder within the international system has been identified in international *regimes*, often under the guidance, if not coercive pressure, of dominant or *hegemonic* powers. Suitable international arrangements might overcome the impulses to disorder and sustain coordinated behaviour by states. Such arrangements might warrant the term *regimes*, if the term can remain sufficiently precise in the face of the breadth of its potential referents.[18]

The use of the concept of international regime has become extensive in contemporary studies of international relations. Indeed its breadth of application has reinforced many doubts about its analytical efficacy. In his introduction to the seminal survey of regime analysis Stephen Krasner defines the concept thus: 'International regimes are defined as principles, norms, rules, and decision-making procedures around which actor expectations converge in a given issue-area.'[19]

The existence of discrete issue-areas within international relations is, itself, a problematical matter. Hence the definition of regimes is so wide as to happily encompass a wide diversity of empirical conditions, from highly formalised treaty-based organisations, such as the International Monetary Fund and linked monetary institutions, to situations wholly lacking formal recognition or regulation, but with widely acknowledged 'principles'.

Given the range of possible international regimes, the paths to their formation may be highly varied. Three obvious avenues present themselves: spontaneous emergence, negotiated establishment and imposition.[20] A critical variable in determining the feasible paths to regime creation is likely to be the costs entailed by participation in, and support for, any potential regime. Where low costs are involved in a minimal regime, then spontaneous emergence is a clear possibility. Where costs to states are significant, but potential benefits considerable, then a negotiated path to regime creation may well be pursued. Where possible costs are considerable, and the temptations to free ride obvious, then it may be necessary to impose any regimes that may be created or underwrite them through the disproportionate contributions of one, or a small number of, *hegemonic* state(s).

The development and maintenance of valuable regimes in areas of costly international interaction are thus held to rest upon the efforts of the states that are dominant economically, and possibly militarily. *Hegemonic stability* thus arises and serves the needs of the entire membership of the international system, as in the heyday of British economic dominance in the late nineteenth century and the dominance of the United States of America throughout the non-Soviet world for the two to three decades following the Second World War.

Three questions, however, arise about the role of hegemonic powers in the states-system. The first concerns the influence actually exercised by the supposed hegemon, given the ease with which it can be exaggerated by enthusiastic analysts. Detailed studies of Great Britain's role in the nineteenth century certainly suggest that her role in the international financial system of that time was less that of a straightforward hegemon than has sometimes been claimed.[21]

Should a measure of hegemony exist, however, there is still the question of whether all members of the international system benefit equally. The clear danger is that the prime beneficiary of any regime, or set of international regimes, established under the influence of a hegemon will be the hegemon itself. Great Britain, and the group of 'core' industrial economies, was able to transmit the greater share of the costs of adjusting to trade imbalances to weaker economies through the operation of the gold standard during the later nineteenth century. The United States benefited considerably from the liberalisation of trade during the era of her economic dominance after the Second World War. In the political realm, the operation of the United Nations was dominated by the United States and her Western allies during the immediate post-war decades.[22]

In the extreme, the condition of international hegemony might reflect, and contribute to, the exploitative dominance of the international system by a small number of states and/or their economic and political leadership groups. Such a critical perspective upon international hegemony is offered by the neo-Gramscian analysis that has become popular in recent years. This approach identifies an insidious form of intellectual and ideological hegemony that has been generated by dominant capitalist interests and sympathetic state actors, and that subordinates the peoples of much of the world, mentally as well as materially.[23] As with most theoretical perspectives upon human activity this neo-Gramscian approach captures *something* of the nature of the contemporary international political economy; as a 'meta-theory',[24] however, it remains inherently untestable in any simple and straightforward manner and retains its force primarily as a critical perspective.

The third central question about hegemony and its effects is that of the durability of the conditions generated by hegemony, if and when the material basis of those conditions begins to dissolve. Two linked possibilities provide the specific regimes, and the general stability, generated by the previous hegemon with some prospects of survival.

Many specific regimes may be sustained, as Robert Keohane has been at pains to argue,[25] as a result of experience of those regimes themselves. In game-theoretical terms, the cost-benefit schedules faced by individual states when considering behaviour that might sabotage an established regime will differ in significant ways from that facing a state considering participation in the creation of a new regime. The diplomatic costs of destroying a valued regime will be far heavier than those of merely failing to join a new venture. Moreover the understandings and expectations of political decision-makers, business leaders, and citizens may all have been changed significantly by past participation in the regime. Finally material changes to production patterns and trade flows might have followed from participation in the regime which would now be costly to disrupt through withdrawal from, or destruction of, the regime. Self-interested behaviour may still prevail in an essentially Hobbesian world, but calculations of self-interest may have been substantially modified by changing institutional conditions and experiences.

The complications thrown up by international regimes and hegemons illustrate the structural difficulties that can arise from the 'realities' that human beings construct. Not all regimes will be internally consistent or coherent, either in the realms of basic principles or practical functioning. There may be incompatibilities between the fundamentals and effects of various regimes. The nature of some regimes may be such as to distribute advantages differentially. In part the dynamic dissonances within, and amongst, regimes reflect the differentials of 'power' amongst the actors that were involved in the initial creation of those arrangements and in defining their basic norms and principles.

9. Conclusions

This chapter has sought to develop a few points of particular pertinence to the discussion of change in international relations in general and to global adaptation to environmental problems in particular. It has sought to challenge approaches that veer too far to either extreme of the structure-agency and determinism – voluntarism debates. The view developed of the states-system, therefore, is that its constructed character renders it no less real in the constraints that it imposes upon human actions and possibilities. These constraints may not be immovable, but they are powerful.

The central difficulty created by the established states-system is its prioritisation of states, legally and ideologically. Action with a global focus and a cosmopolitan impulse is consistently obstructed by international institutions that are dominated by the agents of states, states that create innumerable obstacles to many forms of transnational activity and peoples who continue to be imbued with primary identities that focus at the level of states, nations, regions or even tribes.

The problems posed and confronted by a states-system, reflect the primacy of that system. A states-system contributes to some forms of conflict through the fragmentation of sovereignty and sentiment that it entails or encourages. The fragmentation of sovereignty, globally, also inhibits collective responses to common problems. The contradictions and constraints generated by a states-system do not, however, lock humanity into an inescapable prison, for they generate many of the tensions that may ultimately promote change.

A partial solution to the problem of fragmentation in the states-system has been sought, in neo-realist theory, in the role and influence of hegemons and regimes. The problems of such a solution, however, demonstrate the persisting problems of a states-system. Hegemons may decline, fail to act effectively, or be resisted by those who do not judge their actions to be benign or equitable, and remain an affront to the legal egalitarianism of a system of sovereign and equal states. Regimes continue to confront the problems of effective coordination and cohesion in the face of fragmentary pressures and free-riding temptations, whilst also requiring a substantial dilution of practical sovereignty if they are to prove effective. Complexity and potential contradiction thus continue to afflict some of the more promising solutions to the dilemmas of the states-system.

Change in human affairs may often reflect past problems. It does not, however, guarantee optimal adjustments. The complexity of the problems confronting humanity combines with a notable lack of prescience to sustain developments that are rarely ideal. New complexities and contradictions will accompany most innovations in the human condition and problems posed by the external environment will rarely be resolved comprehensively. The resultant tensions generate a persisting condition of structural dysfunctionality that sustains a constant pressure for further change in a world of increasing complexity and technological innovation.

At the level of international relations the dilemmas of a states-system will thus continue to colour ethical debate and decision. The complexities and complications of contemporary life are suggestive of much of the dynamism and potential change within human institutions, practices and principles as problems and tensions are encountered. Through the continuous effort to resolve persistent practical and ethical difficulties new principles and practices are adduced and adopted. None provides the final solution to the fundamental problems besetting humanity, or the difficulties generated by the institutions that they have chosen to adopt. Complexity, contradiction and change are thus endless and, in consequence, the sources of debate about international ethics are constantly refreshed and reinvigorated.

Notes and References

1   K. Waltz, *Theory of International Politics* (Reading, Mass.: Addison-Wesley, 1979).

2   On the concept of 'meta-theory' see F. G. Castles, *Politics and Social Insight* (London: Routledge, 1971).

3   See the contributions to M. Gibbons (ed.), *Interpreting Politics* (Oxford: Blackwell, 1987).

4   For the seminal discussion of which see A. Wendt, 'The Agent-Structure Problem in International Relations Theory', *International Organization*, 41 (1987) 335–70; see also: A. Wendt, 'Bridging the Theory/Meta-theory Gap in International Relations', *Review of International Studies*, 17 (1991) 383–92; and A. Wendt, 'Levels of Analysis vs. Agents and Structures: Part III', *Review of International Studies*, 18 (1992) 181–216.

5   For an effective discussion of this point see M. Hollis and S. Smith, 'Two Stories About Structure and Agency', *Review of International Studies,* 20 (1994) 241–52.

6   G. V. Plekhanov, *The Role of the Individual in History* (New York: International Publishers, 1940).

7   See P. L. Berger and T. Luckmann, *The Social Construction of Reality: A Treatise in the Sociology of Knowledge* (Harmondsworth: Penguin, 1991); and, for another development of this approach, see A. Giddens,

The Constitution of Society: Outline of the Theory of Structuration
(Cambridge: Polity Press, 1984).

8   R. O. Keohane, 'International Institutions: Two Approaches', *International Organization,* 38 (1988) 379–96.

9   See M. Hollis and S. Smith, *Explaining and Understanding International Relations* (Oxford: Clarendon Press, 1990).

10   Giddens, *The Constitution of Society.*

11   See on these: R. E. Jones, 'The English School of International Relations: A Case for Closure', *British Journal of International Studies,* 7 (1981) 1–13; and R. J. Barry Jones, 'The English School and the Political Construction of International Society', in B. A. Roberson, (ed.), *The English School Revisited* (London: Pinter, forthcoming).

12   M. S. Archer, *Culture and Agency: The Place of Culture in Social Theory* (Cambridge: Cambridge University Press, 1988), especially the Preface and Chapters 1 and 9.

13   On which see: H. Bull, *The Anarchical Society: A Study of Order in World Politics* (London: Macmillan, 1977); C. A. W. Manning, *The Nature of International Society* (London: G. Bell and Sons, 1962); M. Wight, 'The Theory of International Society', in M. Wight, G. Wight and B. Porter (eds), *International Theory: The Three Traditions* (London: Leicester University Press/RIIA, 1991), Chapter 3; H. Bull and A. Watson, *The Expansion of International Society* (Oxford: Clarendon Press, 1984); and A. Watson, *The Evolution of International Society: A Comparative Historical Analysis* (London: Routledge, 1992).

14   For a further critique of 'international society' theories see: Jones, 'The English School of International Relations: A Case for Closure', and Barry Jones, 'The English School and The Political Construction of International Society'.

15   A point made forcefully, if rather densely, by R. Ashley in 'The Poverty of Neo-Realism', *International Organization,* 38 (1988) 225–61, reprinted in an edited form in R. O. Keohane (ed.), *Neo-Realism and its Critics* (New York: Columbia University Press, 1986), Chapter 9.

16   For a further discussion of this conception of politics and political orders see Barry Jones, 'The European School and the Political Construction of International Society'.

17   See especially: R. O. Keohane, 'The Demand for International Regimes', in S. D. Krasner (ed.), *International Regimes* (Ithaca, NY: Cornell University Press, 1983) and R. O. Keohane, *After Hegemony: Cooperation and Discord in the World Political Economy* (Princeton, NJ: Princeton University Press, 1984).

18 See Susan Strange's critical comments on the concept, and attendant analysis: S. Strange, '*Cave! Hic Dragones*: A Critique of Regime Analysis', in Krasner (ed.), *International Regimes*.

19 S. D. Krasner, 'Structural Causes and Regime Consequences: Regimes as Intervening Variables', in Krasner (ed.), *International Regimes*, p.1.

20 See O. R. Young, 'Regime Dynamics: The Rise and Fall of International Regimes', in Krasner, *International Regimes;* and see also a number of chapters in V. Rittberger and P. Mayer (eds), *Regime Theory and International Relations* (Oxford: Clarendon Press, 1993).

21 See A. Walter, *World Power and World Money: The Role of Hegemony and International Monetary Order* (Hemel Hempstead: Harvester Wheatsheaf, 1991); and see also the earlier observations by K. Polanyi, *Origins of Our Time: The Great Transformation* (London: Gollancz, 1945).

22 See E. Luard, *History of the United Nations,* Volume 1, *The Years of Western Domination* (London: Macmillan, 1982).

23 For a full account of this perspective see S. Gill and D. Law, *The Global Political Economy: Perspectives, Problems and Policies* (Brighton: Wheatsheaf, 1988), especially Chapters 5, 6 and 7.

24 On the idea of 'meta-theory' see section 2 of this chapter above.

25 Keohane, *After Hegemony*.

3

Nothing Succeeds Like Success? Legitimacy and International Relations

*John Williams**

1. Introduction

What is and what is not 'legitimate' in international politics is becoming a more important question as the certainties of the Cold War disappear. The need to deal more thoroughly with a much wider agenda of issues renders old answers to the legitimacy question irrelevant or unsatisfactory. When is it legitimate to allow new states to come into existence, or old ones to dissolve? Is a global economy increasingly beyond the control of state-based institutions a legitimate development? Is the form of government within a particular state a legitimate area of concern to other actors? When and to what extent is it legitimate to protect human rights declared to be universal? Legitimacy is an important but largely neglected idea, a word used often by those in positions of authority but of dubious content.

The goal of this chapter is to examine the idea of legitimacy from the point of view of a broad understanding of international relations. Legitimacy is an idea that has suffered more than most from the prevalence of a domestic-international divide in theorising about politics.[1] Domestically, legitimacy has been dominated by Weberian approaches.[2] Internationally it has been largely ignored, and, when it has been considered, ideas of international law and the international system have largely monopolised the field.[3] There have been calls for a unified treatment of the idea but these too have largely been ignored.[4]

The idea has thus risked being subsumed in political expediency. I hope to rescue a potentially valuable reference point from this ignominious fate by looking at what legitimacy might mean from an international relations perspective that attempts to incorporate international and domestic aspects; and by looking at the growing importance of the international economy. Behind this lies one fundamental assumption about the nature of legitimacy. I argue it is a value judgement. This is partly because of the common sense understanding of the word: that which is legitimate is somehow right, good, desirable and in harmony with existing value systems. The need to link concepts such as legitimacy to their everyday meaning is emphasised by William Connolly in his discussion of Gallie's idea of 'essentially contested concepts'.[5]

This value-judgement approach is also a reaction to Weber's attempts to explain legitimacy as being why a particular social relationship is accepted by the parties involved.[6] Here it is 'value free' and a purely descriptive label. Thus the relationship in which a Mafiosi is able to maintain control of a peasant village through threats and violence is a legitimate one as long as the peasantry do not challenge it, even if the lack of challenge is simply the result of fear.[7] David Beetham has provided a thorough critique of this approach to legitimacy, stressing the impossibility of divorcing legitimacy from questions of ethics.[8]

Disputes over the theoretical make-up of legitimacy make it both tempting and sensible to try and limit its extent both in terms of content and application. This has clear practical advantages but risks creating a number of competing conceptions of the notion so that discussion between different groups, often using the same terms, becomes difficult. This chapter tries to avoid such problems with domestic and international versions of legitimacy.

The goal is to begin a process of reconciliation and unification of the concept of legitimacy by discussing the contradictions and the compatibilities between domestic and international conceptions. To do this, the chapter focusses on three major approaches: a realist understanding of the international system with its roots in the Europe of the *ancien regime*; the relationship between this system and an increasingly universal and cosmopolitan liberal conception of the state; and the growing importance of a liberal international economic order. Responsibility for much of the confusion over the idea of legitimacy lies in the different emphases and, more fundamentally, contradictory notions of what the term means to be found in these approaches.

Clearly there are other potential themes and frameworks that could be used in this quest. The most obvious include Marxism and Islam. These are not dealt with for a number of reasons. Firstly, and most practically, is a lack of time and space; secondly the three chosen approaches represent the most influential strands in each of their spheres – a theory of the states-system, a theory of the state and a theory of the economy. Therefore an examination of legitimacy based on these themes will establish an 'orthodox' position. This is not to deny the relevance or value of an approach to legitimacy that relies upon a Marxist or Islamic frame of reference; indeed the former continues to be particularly important in debates about the domestic legitimacy of states.[9] But setting out a framework for legitimacy derived from realism/neo-realism, political liberalism and economic liberalism will provide a target for these alternative viewpoints to aim at.

2. The European States-System and the Legitimacy of Order

The birth of the modern European states-system is often dated to the Peace of Westphalia of 1648.[10] Westphalia established many of the principles characterising the modern, global states-system. These include non-intervention in the domestic affairs of a sovereign state, mutual recognition of sovereign equality as the basis of relations between states, and the territorial integrity of states.[11] To all intents and purposes this reduced the previously multi-layered structure of the international system to a single one. Only recognised sovereign states were now legitimate players on the international stage. The formal power of the Holy Roman Empire and the Papacy to order territorial rulers to behave in certain ways and to interfere in their affairs ended.

The qualification for playing on the international stage, sovereignty, reflected the nature of the accepted players. The post-Westphalia system was largely one of territories governed by absolute monarchs.[12] They personified the sovereignty of the territory they ruled and claimed absolute rights within it. Their right to rule, the qualification entitling them to recognition by other monarchs in the system, was hereditary and rooted in the divine right of kings. The importance of this historical lineage, the historic right of a state to exist, continues into the modern day state system. It is exemplified in the construction of complicated historical genealogies for post-colonial states and their plundering of history for a shared national past.[13]

This historical approach to statehood and the need to fit in with a European states-system, made global by the expansion of European powers between the fifteenth and nineteenth centuries,[14] is important to legitimacy for two principal reasons: firstly the normative preference for order built into the Westphalian system; secondly it is historically prior to the development of political and economic liberalism, which thus bear its imprint and influence.

The structure of the states-system is a historical product. The establishment of the system of sovereign states we know today still reflects the concerns and needs of European rulers in the mid-seventeenth century following a period of immense turmoil and bloodshed stretching back two hundred years[15] and culminating in the decimation of much of central Europe.[16] Stability, predictability and clearer demarcation of responsibilities to avoid the kind of religious and political disputes that sparked the Thirty Years War needed to be at the centre of a settlement.

The Peace of Westphalia reflected these needs and created the basis of the international order we know today. Sovereignty, with its inevitable corollary of non-intervention,[17] and the doctrine of sovereign equality were established as the principles of the states-system with the goal of order in mind. The need to avoid the turmoil of the preceding era with its disputed authorities made the creation of an anarchic system attractive, paradoxical though this may at first appear. The evolving normative structure of the international system – its principles of sovereignty, sovereign equality, territorial integrity, political independence and non-intervention – are designed to create order. The goal of what today we would call an international society[18] was built into the anarchic structure of the European states-system from its inception. Bull's trinity of limitations on the use of violence (by constraining the permitted areas of dispute), sanctity of contract (by making the recognition of sovereignty mutual through continuing respect for the treaty), and property rights (by recognising the sole right of monarchs to rule their territory)[19] are at the heart of the European states-system that has come to provide the basis for international relations the world over. The highly conflictual and disorderly implications of an anarchic system have thus been mitigated from its inception, regulating power, security and competition in international politics.

The familiar neo-realist account of the way anarchic structure generates the realist pattern of international politics as a struggle for power and security[20] is thus useful but does not recognise the normative limits imposed by the system's order-seeking construction. This has obviously been refined and changed over time but the basic structure and goals have remained largely constant. The structure of the states-system is not an inevitable, value-free result of the existence of independent political units denying the existence of a higher authority, but a value-laden, normative and historical product. The value of the states-system and thus its legitimacy lies in its ability to generate order.

The system was created as an international society and has continued to develop in this direction on the basis of the furtherance of the goal of order. The methods of achieving order have changed, evidenced by the changing operation of the balance of power, the classic states-systemic management mechanism, and the effort to establish international institutions to manage affairs. The development of international law and its recent moves away from positivism, towards a more normative and Grotian version also reflect current refinements of the states-system's order seeking preference. The rise of the legal category of *jus cogens*, laws of special significance because they provide the inescapable basis for order,[21] is another aspect of the changes in recent years.

The idea of order as a prior value in international relations is hardly a new one. Hedley Bull's account of the need for order as prior to the attainment of justice[22] and John Vincent's defence of the principle of non-intervention in the name of order[23] are just two of the better known examples. Other realists have made similar points, for example Morgenthau's emphasis on prudence as a virtue among statesmen.[24] Debates within realism about the ability of the management mechanism of the balance of power to generate order and which sort of balance can do this most effectively are also familiar.[25] The source of the priority attached to order, the source of its legitimacy, has been less widely agreed on: the prudence of statesmen and women is seen as one possible source; the need for states to agree rules of co-existence within anarchy as a second; and a systemically determined requirement resulting from the distribution of capabilities within the system as a third (Morgenthau, Bull and Waltz respectively). This suggests a problem over cause and justification in relation to order, pointing to one of the reasons for confusion about legitimacy. For Morgenthau order is the product of prudent statecraft, thus the prudent statesman or woman is legitimate. For Bull and Waltz order is, at least partly, determined externally and its legitimacy comes via reference to the norms of an international society, for Bull, and its ability to contribute to state security, for Waltz. Statesmen and women are thus required to act in ways commensurate with the preservation of order. There is an overlap between the two: imprudent statecraft can threaten the wider systemic basis of order, but the distinction shows one way in which the international and domestic are umbilically linked with the potential to influence the issue of legitimacy in both spheres.

This analysis of the states-system attempts to isolate order as a legitimising value within the structure of the states-system by stressing the structure's normative character. This has roots in the needs and concerns of mid-seventeenth century European rulers. It was created and, as Adam Watson has shown, it is an unusual creation in the history of systems of independent political units.[26] Clearly a system of inflexible and iron bonds on states would not have been able to survive the dramatic and fundamental changes in the character of the units and the operation of relations between them. The flexibility of the understanding of statehood within the principles of the states-system is one of its most remarkable features. Because of this flexibility, the system has been able to cope with the shift from absolute monarchies to liberal democracies, the rise of nationalism and the development of an international economy whilst retaining its basic principles. This highlights the importance of order as a value and its prior status. In terms of the legitimacy of action and actors in international politics, their ability to contribute to the preservation and preferably furtherance of international order is crucial to their legitimacy. The states-system establishes order as a safety net for the legitimacy of actions and actors, especially states and international organisations. The basis of their legitimacy lies in their ability and willingness to contribute to the preservation of order, even if they are unable to pass any of the other tests of legitimacy.

The conception of order has changed and is changing. Order in the mid-seventeenth century was rather different to order today. These changes principally reflect the changing understanding of statehood, which in turn reflect the relationship between the type of states in the system and the nature of the system. Whilst the idea of 'statehood' implies common features among them they cannot be treated as 'like units', in the neo-realist manner, even as the result of interaction.[27] This ignores the way the shared common features have changed over time. It also ignores the way in which when states project their power they also unavoidably project the type of state they are and the different reasons for their power. As states have changed dramatically over the last three hundred years so has the nature of power; and so has the content of order as a value and thus what is legitimate in its name.

There are three key elements in considering the changing nature of statehood and how it has interacted with the states- system: the rise of the notion of the social contract; the evolution of political liberalism; and nationalism.

3. The Social Contract and the Domestic-International Divide

Alan James suggests that we should not trust those who include political philosophy in the study of international relations.[28] This is a mistake as the influence of the European states-system on political theory, and the influences of political theory on approaches to the states-system are important. It is inconceivable that the existence of the states-system did not have an affect on the development of political thought and vice versa. Traditionally, the two have remained separated except for the occasional approving quotation by realists of Hobbes's comment about life in the state of nature being 'solitary, poor, nasty, brutish and short.'

Hobbes, however, is also important for providing a classic statement of the social contract tradition that can be traced though political theory to the present day.[29] There is an interesting and potentially significant coincidence in the timing of the appearance of *Leviathan* and the Peace of Westphalia. The latter can be seen as trying to keep domestic politics, at least domestic religious politics, out of relations between the emerging states of Europe and concentrating power and responsibility in this area in the hands of monarchs and tiny circles of advisers. Three years later, in 1651, *Leviathan* portrays international relations as a kind of vacuum, a space in which states collide in lawlessness and war.[30] Consequently the international arena is not very interesting as far as explaining the growing domination of people's lives by centralised bureaucratic states is concerned. The domestic arena is Hobbes's primary concern, as it has been for just about every other subsequent major political philosopher on the syllabus of European universities' political theory courses.

It is possible to see two reasons for this. Firstly there are the fairly weak structures of order that followed Westphalia. The rest of the seventeenth and eighteenth centuries are not known for their international orderliness. Secondly is the way in which those who thought about the relations between states used the notion of the social contract in a way which reinforced the Hobbesian view of the state internationally, despite the growing salience of a much more restricted view of the social contract internally.

In the social contract tradition the creation of the state and its institutions aims to fulfil certain social goals. These regulate and limit the conduct of individuals in the interests of the greater good and at their most basic focus on issues such as limitations on the use of violence, respect for agreements and rights over property.[31] For Hobbes the horrific condition under which individuals must exist before their creation makes the appearance of such institutions inevitable and whilst Locke and Rousseau, for example, take a more sanguine view of the state of nature they also see considerable benefits in the binding together of individuals into a state mechanism.[32] Locke's more restricted social contract provides the basis for the development of the politically liberal tradition that has come to dominate thinking about legitimate forms of the state in Western Europe, North America and Australasia during the nineteenth and twentieth century and the rest of the world especially since the end of the Cold War.[33]

The state's contractual nature emphasises each individual is expecting to get certain benefits out of joining. Each is entering a relationship with all other members of the state and with the state's institutions. They place themselves under obligations to abide by the rules of the contract and in return they will have their rights respected by other individuals and receive protection from the state against those who attempt to breach them. The individual is the basic unit of analysis and the state exists to protect and enforce the rights and duties of the individual. The state owes its existence to the individuals who comprise it and they are therefore the source of its sovereignty. The state is a 'bottom-up' creation brought into existence by its population; it is also a purposive association, it exists to provide a secure environment within which individuals can act.

Provision of a secure environment clearly includes defence against external attack. Rousseau famously arrived at the conclusion that even in a world of ideal governments war would continue because of the obligation of rulers to promote and protect their populations in competition with other states.[34] This reflects the view of the international system as being a vacuum or state of nature. Rousseau is important in the development of Waltz's thought about the importance of anarchy as generating the power and security dynamic of international politics.[35] Rousseau is not alone in this positing of the duty of states to protect themselves. Vattel, perhaps the founder of the positivist tradition of international law, also argues for the right and duty of states to protect and pursue their interests; and in particular he argues for the right of the sovereign, as the embodiment of the state, to do this.[36]

In the way in which the tradition of the state as contract developed in the shadow of the Westphalian states-system it is possible to see how the idea of the state as contract can be fitted into a realist tradition of international relations. Morgenthau's inclusion of ideas of morality in his six principles of realism[37] rests on the creation of a form of state morality, different to that which applies among individuals inside the state and resting on the need to ensure survival. The doctrine of state as contract provides a conduit for the development of political liberalism to feed into international relations by establishing common ground. The creation of the anarchic European states-system rests on a contract among sovereigns. Because each state is the product of a contract among a group of individuals no state can claim to be morally superior to another, the basis of sovereign equality. Along with each sovereign being recognised as holding the monopoly of the legitimate use of force within his or her territory, they also have the right to employ force externally in pursuit of their interests, their freedom to act as they wish underpinning the realist assumption of states as unified actors. There is thus a tension between the Lockean and Hobbesian notions of contract which exist and operate side by side, providing the basis for disputes over the relation of the political form of a state and its legitimacy in the eyes of the states-system.

The importance of this contractual dispute also reinforces the need to portray the states-system not as Waltz does, as a neutral, value-free and inevitable product of the existence of multiple sovereign states, but as a historical and value laden construct, reflecting the passage of European history and the structure of European societies and their political thought. Where Waltz is so useful is in the way he concentrates exclusively on the systemic level. The enduring realist features of international politics and the continuing importance of questions of power and security are rooted in the structure of the states-system. The legitimacy of the behaviour to meet the challenges of these enduring realities is therefore also rooted in the states-system. Barry Buzan has tried to show how cooperation in the interests of coexistence can also be seen in states-systemic terms.[38] From what has been said already, reinforced by what is to follow, it should be clear the present writer feels Buzan's analysis to be of limited use in explaining the development of international society within Europe because it was created as an international society and has developed since because of political liberalism's revolution in the notion of legitimate statehood. The value of his account lies in the interaction between the European and non-European states-systems. However it tends to overlook the important restraints on the pursuit of power and security built into the foundations of the European states-system in the name of order.

One of the features of European politics was the very limited involvement in international affairs by anybody other than tiny political elites until this century.[39] This seems to have helped insulate the principles of the state-system from the effects of a radical transformation in the understanding of the basis of the state and the way domestic politics should be conducted. The power of the domestic – international divide means that in many ways we still work within the states-system created to serve the needs of the absolutist monarchies of the era of the *ancien regime*. Indeed the states-system may well be its last and greatest legacy.

The problem with realism and neo-realism is more the result of the invasion of the states-system by other issues, primarily social and economic issues. The mistake lies in assuming that the triumph of these 'domestic issues' will result in the end of international relations as we know it and, ultimately, the disappearance of the state. Rather, in the way the states-system is rooted in the contractual nature of the state so too are its challengers, thus suggesting a common basis for a mutually beneficial, if tense, interaction. These challengers also labour under the weight of the states-system which was in existence prior to their appearance and rise to dominance; and this can be seen in the way they deal, or do not deal, with the problem of a world organised around states.

4. Political Liberalism, States and Legitimacy

The idea of liberalism as a philosophical basis for the state has become an orthodoxy in both domestic and international politics.[40] It now provides the standard by which all others are judged.[41] Whilst this is not the place to present a thorough-going critique of the liberal conception of the state, it is necessary to examine some of its basic principles in order to understand the relationship between a liberally conceived state and the states-system.

The most important tenet of liberalism is its emphasis on the freedom of the individual within the rule of law.[42] Building on the contractual approach to the state classical liberalism posits the role of government as being to guarantee the maximum amount of liberty for each individual compatible with its equitable distribution. For what Gray calls 'classical' liberal[43] government establishes, monitors and enforces the framework within which the individual is free to do as he or she wishes. The restrictions are largely negative: they require individuals to refrain from doing things, such as killing one another, stealing property or breaking agreements, rather than imposing positive duties on the citizen. The state is a voluntary association, entered into because of the advantages it offers over the state of nature and as a voluntary association, the product of the free will of the individuals who comprise it, the state has no right to compel its citizens unless they breach the negative laws governing peaceful coexistence. Therefore, each individual remains the ultimate arbiter of his or her own fate, pointing to another basic tenet of liberalism, the self-ownership of the individual.[44] Citizens cannot be bought or sold as property because this breaches the fundamental principle of self-ownership. The relationship of the state with the individual defines its legitimacy.

There are some clear parallels between the freedom of the individual in an ideal classical liberal state and the position of the state in the realist states-system. Self-ownership can be seen as equivalent to sovereignty. The decision to join the state for the benefits it offers in terms of security is analogous to the voluntary accession of the state to international society. The negative nature of restrictions are also analogous; such as not killing one another and not invading one another. The relationship of the state to the states-system, especially the recognition of its sovereignty, determines the legitimacy of the state. These analogies are powerful contributors to realism's tendency to ascribe to the state characteristics of an individual and view the states-system as like that of the primitive state of nature for individuals. These analogies also show how structural principles of the states-system are not ahistorical, value-free constants, but are closely tied to a historical and philosophical tradition.[45] The social contract creates the over-arching authority of the sovereign domestically, establishing the basis of order. Internationally the principles of the European states-system do not create over-arching authority but they do establish basic rules and principles of conduct as the basis for peaceful coexistence and order. In the same way that order is the pre-requisite for the development of liberalism domestically so it is internationally. Order is the prior value, hence the concern of so many great thinkers in the contractarian and liberal tradition with the international goal of peace and the establishment of something akin to the social contract among states.[46] Whether or not this requires a world government, an international Leviathan, provides the core of the dispute between the reluctant realism of Rousseau and the historical optimism and faith in reason of Kant.[47]

For classical liberals, the minimal state provides true freedom because it allows individuals' more noble instincts to develop, free from basic worries about survival and the danger of attack. A liberal state creates true equality of opportunity for every individual opening the way for progress towards the full flourishing of man's rationality, reason and artistry. At this point there is a division between classical liberals and revisionist liberals, typified by T. H. Green but with the origins of the division dating back to the work of Jeremy Bentham.[48]

Revisionary liberalism challenges the purely negative role of the state, arguing those less well off in society must be helped to be free. The distribution of opportunity is uneven and the state must play its role in redistribution to give everybody a fair chance at success. This sort of argument underpins the provision of state schools to ensure everybody has a basic education enabling them to play an effective role in society; state health care to ensure basic fitness for work and life, and welfare provision to provide those with very little with a basic stake to play the poker game of liberty.

Again, there are some powerful parallels to be drawn between the revisionary liberal view of the state and international relations in the demands for distributive justice by Third World states and the calls for a New International Economic Order. Perhaps most interesting is the way in which Third World states have placed this within a framework which stresses sovereignty and non-intervention. This invites analogies between these constitutionally limiting principles of the international system and the principles of inalienable freedoms based on self-ownership (which is like sovereignty) and individualism (which is like non-intervention).

There is a chasm between the Hobbesian contractual view of the state with its emphasis on the need for individuals to bind together in order to escape the state of nature and the Lockean contractual view of the state as maintaining liberal order of maximum liberty equally distributed. Liberal critics of Hobbes recognised the potential for the abuse of power by state institutions. The means of restraining government thus became a central concern of liberalism with constitutional guarantees, a separation of state powers between different institutions, and a series of checks and balances becoming standard features of liberal thought.

The importance of this for the international system is that both liberalism and the international system of sovereign independent states share a common basis in a contractual view of the state. The rights and duties of the individual and the ruler are, however, radically different under these two conceptions of the contract and this helps explain the misleading nature of reification and analogies with the individual. From the international point of view the state is seen in Hobbesian contractual terms and has an absolute right to do whatever is necessary to maintain itself as the only means to avoid a return to the state of nature and as the manifestation of the purposive association generated by the contracting individuals. Legitimacy is vested firmly with the state as an institution – the state has rights. From the domestic point of view the state has overwhelmingly come to be seen in Lockean contractual terms, which imply a liberal view of the state. The classical liberal state is a minimal institution, placing as few restraints as possible on the freedom of the individual, and a revisionary liberal state incurs positive duties in the name of greater freedom for all. Legitimacy is thus determined in relation to the individual – the state only has rights insofar as it protects the prior rights of the individual. The international system sanctions an absolutist monarchy; liberalism a constitutionally limited, consensual and popularly accountable democracy.

This different understanding of the distribution of rights hints at a potentially fundamental dispute between political liberalism and the principles of the states-system. It may also suggest reasons why ascribing legitimacy is so difficult. On the one hand there is the point that liberalism is individualistic: 'Individuals have rights, and there are things no individual may do to them (without violating their rights),' says Robert Nozick, a modern classical liberal.[49] These rights are universal and a product of membership of humanity.[50] In realist approaches to the states-system, however, the rights of the individual are secondary and are the result of membership of the state that protects them from the outside world. Rights are thus the result of membership of a political community. Chris Brown has used this distinction between cosmopolitanism and communitarianism to suggest a fundamental and irreconcilable distinction between schools of theory in international relations.[51]

On the other hand efforts by Rousseau and Kant to transfer the ideas of civil society to the international level identified the problem of anarchy. Liberalism is inconceivable without the government that is clearly lacking at the international level. Those who support the development of some sort of global civil society continually run into the same problem.[52] The solutions they offer, the power of reason and public opinion or the development of some sort of global governance, are the same as those advocated by Kant and Rousseau respectively and are subject to the same difficulties they failed to overcome.

The significance of this lies not only in the ammunition it has provided for the realist critique of liberal approaches to international relations, but also in the limitations it sets on the development of liberalism itself. The states-system sets the limits of liberalism's ability to propose specific changes and make specific recommendations. Within the state there is faith in a consensus established by the social contract about the underlying framework of norms, values, practices and expectations within the state, backed by coercive power. Both the consensus and faith in it are less developed in the international realm. The aspects of civil society that do make it find themselves in competition with the alternative consensus of the state-system: it is not a case of one replacing the other, it is a case of the relationship between the two that is important.

Liberalism within the international realm, although limited by the states-system, is of growing importance because of its dominance as a value system against which state forms are legitimised. That need not mean the end of international relations as we know it but it will exacerbate the tension in the relationship between global civil society and the states-system. This will perhaps be most intense in the field of international law, which in the states-system protects the absolute freedom of the states and in the liberal view is designed to protect the individual from the state, guaranteeing freedom. Franck's primarily international legal approach to legitimacy demonstrates this in the way it divorces the issue of legitimacy among states from the individual.[53] The development of the international legal category of *jus cogens* containing principles necessary for the existence of international order also points to the importance of the states-system in containing and shaping the development of political liberalism.

This tension need not be destructive. It may indeed be highly creative. The prospect exists of greater humanity becoming a feature of international relations under the impact of social and political pressures from within liberally conceived states for liberal values to be more prominent and to receive greater protection at the international level. Indeed Franck has written of an emerging international legal right to democratic governance.[54] Liberal concerns are poking through into the states-system, altering the understanding of the basis of order and thus how states can seek to legitimise themselves and their actions by reference to their contribution to international order. International law bears witness to this with the growing body of international humanitarian law, especially within conflict situations,[55] and the recognition that the individual, as well as the state, can be a subject of international law.[56] There is growing concern about the implications of internal conflicts for international peace and security. Good governance criteria are being built into aid programmes. Even one of the traditional criteria of sovereignty, the state's monopoly of the use of violence, is under attack with growing concern about the use of force against domestic political opponents. Ideas of humanitarian intervention are more prominent now than ever before.[57]

The need for liberalism to seize control of a state in order to be effective on the international stage is an example of the power of the states-system. As Shaw points out, 'The fates of theoretical concepts in the social-sciences are intertwined with the development of historical reality.'[58] The historical development of the criteria for identifying legitimate rulers, from divine right monarchs towards leaders as spokesmen and guardians of the will of the people they represent, has provided one way in which liberalism's values have penetrated the states-system.

This can be seen in the modification of the classic realist goal of the protection of the national interest defined in terms of politico-military power and measured by the state's position relative to its main competitors and rivals in the states-system. The national character – the values, beliefs, principles, expectations, culture and heritage of a state – have become as important as territorial integrity. The national interest has become less mechanistic and more emotional, both straining and being constrained by the states-system. The system that has emerged is a product of both. The membership qualification shifted in the direction of the liberals, but the nature of action after admission continued to be along broadly the same lines of the old model. The unstoppable force of liberalism had met the immovable object of the international system: the force stopped and the object moved.

The resilience of the states-system will temper the tendency of this to result in some form of global government taking government away from the people and accelerating the cultural and political homogenisation of the world. Sovereignty may increasingly be under attack but it retains great power as a symbol of a political community and its right to control its destiny. This is not simply the result of the potential dilemma over the cosmopolitanism of liberalism and the communitarianism of realism, but includes the power of nationalism, something linked to both camps.

5. Nationalism and Legitimacy

The relationship between the states-system, nationalism and liberalism is a deep and complicated one. The goal here is limited to trying to show how the parallel rise of nationalism and liberalism in the nineteenth century reflected the pre-existing states-system and how they exacerbate the potentially irresolvable paradoxes for liberalism in its cosmopolitan form.

Nationalism, of course, is a difficult concept. There are perhaps three main schools emphasising philosophy,[59] history[60] and economics.[61] What they have in common is the importance of nationalism to the nineteenth and twentieth centuries and its basis as a form of identity. Nationalism undermines the idea of the abstracted individual behind the social contract and the cosmopolitanism of liberalism. Instead it creates ideas of community and belonging which underpin communitarian ideas of individuals as being products of the society they inhabit.[62] The nation becomes the well-spring of all that is good in human life and the achievements that set us apart from animals – language, culture, diverse civilisations and so on. Humanity is thus divided into nations as coherent and cohesive groups providing individuals with their identity. In terms of legitimacy, the value system against which this value-judgement is made becomes specific to each national group. The liberal ideal of universal human rights, for instance, or universal principles of justice rooted in our value as human beings, becomes untenable. An example of this can be seen in the criticisms made of Rawls' efforts to establish a theory of justice based on the notion of the veil of ignorance in which individuals are abstracted from their social milieu.[63]

In international relations the most notable difficulty arises over the idea of a universal right to national self-determination, which recognises the legitimacy of identifiable communities ruling themselves. This is an effort to grant cosmopolitan currency to a communitarian principle, perhaps partly explaining the resulting mess. The development of international law on national self-determination since the end of World War One is complicated and reflects the many problems this principle creates for older states-systemic standards of order, such as territorial integrity and non-intervention. The post-decolonisation compromise stressed the needs of order, generating such ideas as self-determination as a once-and-for-all right and the attachment of a rider to almost all UN declarations privileging territorial integrity over national self-determination.[64]

Stressing the chaotic consequences of the complete application of the principle of self-determination is hardly a profound or novel insight. However, it does help to show the way nationalism has been shaped by growing up within a states-system aimed at order. The single layer of membership of the states-system has made sovereignty the goal of almost all national self-determination movements. Only by controlling their own state can they be granted the protection of international law and the rules and norms of international society. Statehood and identity have become inextricably linked. The protection of identity rests on the achievement of statehood and once achieved the legitimacy of that state rests on its protection and promotion of the identity it embodies.

It has been argued this sort of communitarian basis for statehood is strongly reflected in realism, which assumes nation states and unified actors largely for these reasons.[65] The structurally induced problems of security increasingly focus around identity, especially in Europe.[66] This is a major problem for the legitimacy of liberal prescriptions for political development as they rest on cosmopolitan ideas of the value of human beings – universal principles of human rights, justice and so on – and standard forms of government represented by Western-style liberal democracy. The cosmopolitan versus communitarian divide threatens to hamstring the process.

6. The Semi-Detached Liberalism of the Economy and International Relations.

The picture is further complicated by the economic aspects of liberalism. At its simplest, it seeks the maximum freedom of movement of goods, capital and labour. This often comes into conflict with the goals of states. Wealth creation versus wealth distribution and utilisation is a central political issue, nationally and internationally, because of the competing demands of economic liberalism and political and social liberalism.

Economic liberalism is semi-detached because it has moved away from the state, the centre-piece of the states-system and political liberalism. Its position as a central aspect of classical liberalism declined during the nineteenth century to the point where it was no longer primarily concerned with the state. Classical political liberalism never lost this focus, even though its goal was to minimise the role of the state. Economic liberalism regards the state as a watchdog and guarantor of the basic legal framework within which individuals and economic entities can operate freely.[67] The operation of these actors is its principle concern.

Doctrines such as Adam Smith's 'invisible hand' – the notion that by pursuing individual interests people would also pursue the collective interest as well – seem to absolve economic liberals from being concerned about the international political system to any great extent. Individualism and the emphasis on liberty provide the links with the political liberal project, but the way in which liberty and maximum freedom commensurate with its equitable distribution, can be created are left up to the political liberals. Economic liberalism assumes it and asks what should be done with it.

The growing importance of an economically liberal model of the international economy has further complicated this relationship by attacking the legitimacy of state efforts at economic management thereby relegating the state to a secondary position. The value attached to interdependence and transcending and bypassing states helps explain the problems of attempting to reconcile international political economy with realist strands of international relations. The concerns of the two are very different and the frameworks of consensus they draw upon often incompatible or irrelevant to one another. The emphases they contain, their different conceptions of what is desirable and good in international relations inevitably colour the approach they provide to a value-judgement such as legitimacy.

The debates of the 1970s and 1980s over which is more important, with the interdependence and dependency schools sounding the death-knell of the state and Kenneth Waltz leading the neo-realist attempt to subordinate the multi-nationals in a revived states-system, demonstrate this well.[68] Whilst the problems of creating a unified theory of the international political and economic realms are now much more thoroughly investigated, a successful reconciliation has yet to be achieved.

The problems are deep ones because of the divergent historical development of economic liberalism and the states-system. In fact it is the challenge of political liberalism to the states-system which is the more concerted because of its similar state-centrism. The development of a truly international economy has taken place only over the last four or five decades, and is still continuing. This helps to explain why it, and its legitimising value system, has not come into conflict with the states-system in the way that political liberalism did much earlier. It remains to be seen whether or not the states-system will be able to accommodate it in the way it has accommodated liberal social and political concerns.

However the cosmopolitanism of economic liberalism, its basis in abstracted individuals leading to universal principles and relationships, is threatened by the communitarianism of nationalism and understandings of the states-system. The power of the idea of security, of both the state and identity, does not fit easily into an economic value system stressing competition and insecurity as the basis for success.[69] But economic liberalism remains powerful. Its legitimising of actions to cross borders and penetrate states, cultures and communities enables it to act as a transmission belt for the normative ideas about the states-system and the nature of statehood that more traditionally went along with the projection of power. This raises the international economy above being the result of a systemic feature like 'interaction capacity'.[70] It also offers a possible way in which the reconciliation between economic liberalism and the states-system may evolve.

The need to try and achieve some sort of balance between these competing value systems may see the international economy becoming the primary arena for competition but with competition being between political communities as well as firms. Seeing states and firms as both political and economic actors constrained by the needs of order and pursuing goals of prosperity and security of identity offers a possible compromise that sits within the value systems of both frameworks, attracting legitimacy to the system.

7. The International System and the Power of Ideas

The nature of the international system is one of the central questions in the study of international relations.[71] The notion of a system must logically involve some form of boundary. It is impossible to have an organisational principle, a framework in which to discuss action, without a degree of consensus on where that framework lies. Without some sort of agreed terms of reference, discussions of what is and what is not legitimate in international relations are worthless. So far this essay has tried to show there are three principal sets of possible terms of reference, although they are related to one another in a variety of ways.

Central to the *formal* boundaries within which international relations are played out are ideas of sovereignty, sovereign equality, non-intervention, reciprocity in respect of the recognition of rights and duties, and the territorial integrity of states. These are the classical principles of the states-system from Westphalia to the United Nations' Charter and their formal acceptance and relatively specific definition helps to account for their importance and legitimacy.

The framework for the international economy acknowledges these boundaries and especially the territoriality of the states-system and yet seeks to overcome them. Free movement of goods, people and capital as the ideal, the determination of prices based on the principle of supply and demand, the international division of labour through the mechanism of comparative advantage. These have dominated debates over the international economy and with the terminal decline of the communist challenge they are set to become ubiquitous, taking with them ideas about the nature of legitimate statehood and the relation between the domestic and the international.

The contradictions between some of the defining principles of the states-system and the international economic system are clear. Economic liberalism's notion of the harmony of interests does not square easily with an international system in which conflict appears to be a central feature and in which the state retains the right to resort to violence.[72] The integrative, harmonising, border-ignoring aspects of the international liberal economy have become an increasingly important feature of international relations since World War Two. Their importance cannot be denied and yet they continue to exist side by side with states recognising no higher authority characterised as pursuing a national interest dominated by power defined in terms of military might, political influence and perceived position in a competitive international hierarchy where the gain of one is usually at the expense of another. As Ian Clark put it:

> Indeed, it could be argued that it is the realists who are the truly successful utopians because they have created a world after their own image. Could there be any more wonderful tribute to the potency of ideas in human affairs?[73]

Turning to the political liberal ideal – a constitutionally limited state composed of a people with a coherent national identity, ruled by an accountable government reflecting the will of the population and respecting and protecting the rights of each member of the community – we can see it is not fulfilled but it undeniably provides a standpoint for judging the actions of states and their rulers. It provides a value system for judging legitimacy and one in competition with economic liberalism.

Political liberalism's effectiveness in providing a standard of judgement in international relations (witness the concern over human rights and the prominence of the question of redistribution of wealth) stems from the historical symbiosis between liberalism and the international system, rooted in a contractual view of the state. It has reinforced the realist emphasis on the idea of the national interest as the motive force in international politics and the state as the means to pursue it. Creating a 'hard-shell' – emphasising the territorial basis and integrity of the state; viewing other states as potential threats and competitors; meeting the demands of the people for security from external threat and for greater wealth, better social services and jobs; national pride – can be justified in terms of liberalism and in terms of the traditional, illiberal principles of the states-system. This is despite their very different normative frameworks which establish different conceptions of legitimacy. That this is so is further evidence of the power and resilience of the synthesis of the states-system with liberalism. It points to a further basis for international society's stress on cooperation on the basis of a sense of community and shared experience and concepts rather than simply coldly defined interest.

This appears to lead in the direction of the conclusion that whilst the rhetoric and the justifications may have changed, the game remains the same. There is mileage in this but it fails adequately to take into account the importance of the values and goals that liberalism necessitates for the state. A state cannot project its power on the international stage without at the same time projecting its values and form of society; hence the changing agenda of international politics; aid, humanitarian intervention, economic development, the environment.

Whilst there is a synthesis between the states-system and political liberalism (albeit one in which both are modified), international economic liberalism certainly sits unhappily with the international political system, although the two manage to coexist in some form of equilibrium. As in the classic game theory situation of the prisoners' dilemma, the tendency is for both to come off badly, although not as badly as might have been the case. The ability of states as the repositories of sovereignty to control access to territory means economic entities need their permission to operate within that territory. The governing authority may also need the economic actor because of the resources, technology, trade, expertise and money it may bring with it. It may disapprove of the reliance on foreigners this creates, but the foreigners may be equally unhappy with the restrictions on operations the governing authority is able to place upon them.[74] Compromise, consensus and a mutually acceptable outcome in which the benefits are split between both parties are the ways out of the potential impasse.

For this sort of bargaining to be successful, or even possible, both must share common terms of reference. Each must understand the goals of the other and the rights and duties each must aim to fulfil, whether to citizens or to shareholders. The divisibility of the two is proof of the failure to achieve this reconciliation. The very different set of values and principles each espouses, culminating in their very different views of the value of the state, means this would require a remarkable transformation.

Fulfilling the ideals that both neo-realism and economic liberalism profess requires a reconciliation ending debate about their meaning, compatibility and desirability. It would no longer be a question whether these principles represented the 'right' way to do things. Seeming contradictions between terms would disappear. It would no longer be possible to distinguish between the state and economic systems. Each would represent an ideology, but an ideology that was apolitical because unquestioned and accepted as 'self-evident truth'.[75] The chances of such a situation coming about are extremely low, in part due to the unavoidable social concerns that political liberalism puts firmly on the agenda; and, in any case, it would be undesirable. All three frameworks have a horror of absolute triumphs, whether they be world empire, a world state or a completely free global market with the risk of global economic monopolies. The end of history is more to be feared than welcomed.

The conceptions of the international political system as anarchic because of its lack of an overarching authority and the international economic system as interdependent because of the economic imperative to specialise appear to be incompatible. The former is positively against the institution of some sort of world government, the latter would appear to require it in order to safeguard the system of free trade and provide the regulatory mechanisms economic liberalism entrusts to a central authority. There is a clear tension and yet it is a creative tension, seeking ways to reconcile the two without allowing one to dominate the other, in the way political liberalism and the states-system coexist. Order exists not only in the sense of predictable, stable and regular conduct but also in the sense of the interdependence between one actor and another and the web of relations within, between and across states and the other institutions of the international system. World order, whether a 'new' one or not, is inconceivable without the interplay of anarchy, society and interdependence.

8. Conclusion

Where does this leave the issue of legitimacy with which we entered this maze? No clear, simple, single definition can be suggested but hopefully the reasons why this is the case, and why this is the case for other such value-judgements, are clearer. Whilst the answer 'well, it depends on how you look at it' is tempting, it is also inadequate. It is possible to narrow the field of search quite a lot as a definition of legitimacy that resides solely in one of the three possible frameworks will be weak. For example legitimate action as that which protects absolutely the principles of sovereignty and non-intervention is unacceptable. Bosnia, Somalia, Cambodia and South Africa provide ample proof of this. Alternatively, legitimate action as that aiming at global constitutionally limited government is both impracticable and unacceptable because it would require outside imposition, undermining the bottom-up nature of the liberal state. Finally, legitimate action as action which maximises profit carries unacceptable social consequences.

The end of the Cold War, with its emphasis on the concerns of the states-system – order, stability, power, security – has seen the standard of legitimacy move towards the concerns of liberalism. The calls for a broader definition of security are often specifically linked to the end of the Cold War[76] and include issues such as economics, human rights, the environment and the protection of cultural diversity. There is also a need for a broader definition of legitimacy than simply upholding the existing *status quo* and protecting the territorial integrity and sovereignty of the member states of the United Nations.

Nevertheless order remains the prior value domestically as well as internationally. An ability to contribute to the maintenance of order is a basic component of the legitimacy of actors and actions. The basis of international society in agreements about property rights, sanctity of contract and limitations on violence acts as a safety net. For some states their maintenance of these principles may be the only thing granting them legitimacy. International legal standards of statehood, such as the Montevideo Convention,[77] talk about the need for agreed borders, stable populations and a government able to control the territory as well as an ability to enter into diplomatic relations. In some cases, especially in the past, it seems as though the last of these has been enough to ensure continued international legitimacy for a state.

Since the end of the Cold War, however, this has shifted and the importance of political liberalism as a legitimising factor in its own right and the way it contributes to the understanding of order has grown. This is an acceleration of trends apparent for many years rather than something entirely new. Human rights, mass political participation, government within the law and accountable to the people, individualism: there can be no doubt these are now issues of legitimate concern in international relations;[78] yet the mechanisms remain largely those of the states-system – diplomacy, UN resolutions, international summits and occasionally threats of armed force or intervention. Order, stability, security and concern for the national interest remain strong. The balance has shifted, but the states-system is not dead and buried and should not be. It is ironic that some of the concerns of self-professed liberals – the 'Coca-Colaisation' of native cultures, cultural imperialism, the exploitation of the Third World and other 'North–South' issues – may in fact be best met through the maintenance of the states-system in all its order-fixated conservatism and distrust of change. Conserving the 'bad' of corrupt, brutal and repressive regimes in some places, may be the price to be paid for conserving and promoting the 'good' of cultural diversity, local people producing solutions to their problems and government close to the people in others.

This highlights the difficult question of success and legitimacy, something hovering in the background throughout this discussion. Can action that 'fails' when judged by the standards of liberalism, a philosophy that stresses 'development' and 'progress' as the measures of success, still be legitimate? The standards of capitalist liberal democracy have become the standards by which all political systems are increasingly judged and the failure to fulfil the expectations of their populations lies at the heart of the loss of legitimacy and ultimate collapse of the communist systems of Eastern Europe.[79]

For the economy the goals are different with progress measured in terms of development. Failure in either of these two liberal standards will not deprive a state or its ruling system and institutions of legitimacy immediately – it is even possible for a state to be temporarily extinguished without losing legitimacy – but they will induce a decline in legitimacy. A state must not only aim at, but be seen to have a reasonable chance of fulfilling, the aspirations of its people if it is to retain legitimacy, if it is to be able to exercise authority rather than power,[80] if its judgement is to be complied with voluntarily rather than imposed. This fulfilment of aspirations must include the broad issue of justice.

States cannot be seen as valueless abstractions, as 'like units' at the international level. Attempts to do so not only underestimate the importance of the domestic nature of the state and the relationship between domestic and international politics, but even ignores the importance of history in the principles of the states-system. The same is true for other international actors such as international organisations and transnational corporations. All must operate within an increasingly complicated value framework that not only surrounds but penetrates institutions. There is a great need to legitimate actions of institutions against a global standard that is partly the result of the power of the dominant states and their domestic political and economic philosophies. Despite this element of imposition, the standard of legitimacy binds great powers and is open to the modifications and changes of emphasis created by the need for coexistence with alternative views. Legitimacy, like the states-system and political and economic theory, is a living and evolving thing; the standard of success will change, as at the moment with the greater prominence of liberal standards.

International action cannot enhance legitimacy if it breaches the principles of the states-system which have evolved in order to provide a degree of peaceful coexistence and international cooperation and certainty; it cannot enhance legitimacy if it attacks the social purpose of the maximisation of equal freedom of the individual; it cannot enhance legitimacy if it destroys development. The relationship between these three, deliberately couched in the negative terms of classical liberalism as things which must be refrained from, is a delicate and complicated one ultimately judged in relation to specific circumstances. Nevertheless a contribution to order as the prior value can be seen as an irreducible minimum, with legitimacy enhanced if it also contributes to political liberalism – although these two are becoming more closely entwined – and to the promotion of an international and liberal economy. These gradations of legitimacy, the grey area at its heart, reflect the paradox of the cosmopolitanism of the two liberalisms and the communitarianism of the states-system, especially as it has been reinforced by nationalism. The working out of this paradox is part of the substance of the political process, domestically and internationally. Actors and actions need to promote what is deemed desirable by the community, comprising states, people and economic institutions, that inadvertently but inevitably establish the standards against which we judge.

Notes and References

*   I would like to thank Barry Buzan as well as the co-authors of this book for their valuable comments on earlier drafts of this chapter.

1   For an interesting discussion of the wider implications and declining relevance of this divide see H. Williams, 'International Relations and the Reconstruction of Political Theory', *Politics*, 14 (1994) 135–42.

2   For example J. H. Schaar, 'Legitimacy in the Modern State', in W. E. Connolly (ed.), *Legitimacy and the State* (Oxford: Blackwell, 1984).

3   T. M. Franck, *The Power of Legitimacy Among Nations* (New York: Oxford University Press, 1990); M. Wight, *Systems of States* (Leicester: Leicester University Press, 1977), pp. 153–72.

4   C. Navarri, 'Diplomatic Structure and Idiom', in J. Mayall (ed.) *The Community of States: A Study in International Political Theory* (London: Allen and Unwin, 1982), p. 17.

5   W. E. Connolly, *The Terms of Political Discourse*, 3rd ed. (Oxford: Blackwell, 1993) pp. 9–44.

6   M. Weber, 'Legitimacy, Politics and the State', in W. E. Connolly (ed.), *Legitimacy and the State* (Oxford: Blackwell, 1984).

7   J. Gow, *Legitimacy and the Military: The Yugoslav Crisis* (London: Pinter, 1992), pp. 17–18. At pp. 14–21 he attempts to establish a 'value free' concept of legitimacy.

8   D. Beetham, *The Legitimation of Power* (London: Macmillan, 1991). For a critique of Beetham's ideas see R. T. O'Kane, 'Against Legitimacy', *Political Studies*, 41 (1993), 471–87.

9   The most famous look at legitimacy from a Marxist perspective is J. Habermas, *Legitimation Crisis* (London: Heinemann, 1976).

10   For example T. Nardin, *Law, Morality and the Relations of States* (Princeton, NJ: Princeton University Press, 1983), p. 57

11   For example R. Lipschutz, 'Reconstructing World Politics: The Emergence of Global Civil Society', *Millennium* 21 (1992), p. 400.

12   Wight, *Systems of States,* p. 153.

13   A. D. Smith, *National Identity* (London: Penguin, 1991), especially pp. 112–16.

14   H. Bull and A. Watson (eds), *The Expansion of International Society* (Oxford: Oxford University Press, 1984).

15   J. Keegan, *A History of Warfare* (London: Pimlico, 1994), p. 13.

16   G. Parker, *The Thirty Years War* (London: Routledge, 1984).

17   R. J. Vincent, *Nonintervention and International Order* (Princeton, NJ: Princeton University Press, 1974).

18   H. Bull, *The Anarchical Society: A Study of Order in World Politics* (London: Macmillan, 1977).

19   Bull, *The Anarchical Society,* p. 5.

20   K. Waltz, *Theory of International Politics* (Reading, Mass.: Addison-Wesley, 1979).

21   G. Christenson, '*Jus Cogens*: Guarding Interests Fundamental to International Society', *Virginia Journal of International Law* , 28 (1988) 585–648.

22   Bull, *The Anarchical Society,* pp. 77–101.

23   Vincent, *Nonintervention and International Order.*

24   H.J. Morgenthau *Politics Among Nations,* 5th ed. (New York: Knopf, 1973).

25   For example Waltz, *Theory of International Politics,* pp. 102–29.

26   A. Watson, *The Evolution of International Society: A Comparative Historical Analysis* (London: Routledge, 1992), p. 251.

27   Waltz, *Theory of International Politics,* especially pp. 95–7.

28   A. James, 'Theorizing About Sovereignty', in W. C. Olson (ed.), *The Theory and Practice of International Relations,* 8th ed. (Engelwood Cliffs, NJ: Prentice Hall, 1991), p. 121.

29   M. Lessnoff, *Social Contract* (London: Macmillan, 1986), p. 45. In specifically international terms see D. R. Mapel 'The Contractarian Tradition and International Ethics', in T. Nardin and D. R. Mapel (eds), *Traditions of International Ethics* (Cambridge: Cambridge University Press, 1992).

30   T. Hobbes, *Leviathan* (London: J. M. Dent, 1973) p. 65.

31   Bull, *The Anarchical Society,* pp. 4–5.

32   Lessnoff, *Social Contract,* pp. 45–67, 74–83.

33 C. Brown '"Really Existing Liberalism" and International Order', *Millennium*, 21 (1992), p. 314.
34 F. H. Hinsley, *Power and the Pursuit of Peace: Theory and Practice in the History of Relations Between States* (Cambridge: Cambridge University Press, 1963), pp. 46–62.
35 K. Waltz, *Man, the State and War: A Theoretical Analysis* (New York: Columbia University Press, 1954), especially pp. 165–86.
36 P. F. Butler, 'Legitimacy in a States-System: Vattel's Law of Nations', in M. Donelan (ed.) *The Reason of States: A Study in International Political Theory* (London: Allen and Unwin, 1978).
37 Morgenthau, *Politics Among Nations,* pp. 4–15, especially pp. 10–11.
38 B. Buzan, 'From International System to International Society: Structural Realism and Regime Theory Meet the English School', *International Organization*, 47 (1993) 327–52.
39 E. H. Carr, *The Twenty Years Crisis 1919–1939: An Introduction to the Study of International Relations*, 2nd ed. (London: Macmillan, 1981) pp. 1–2.
40 Brown '"Really Existing Liberalism" and International Order', p. 314.
41 R. H. Jackson, *Quasi-States: Sovereignty, International Relations and the Third World* (Cambridge: Cambridge University Press, 1990), p.19.
42 This point is made repeatedly in J. Gray, *Liberalism* (Milton Keynes: Open University Press, 1986).
43 Gray, *Liberalism*, pp. 16–26.
44 Gray, *Liberalism*, pp. 62–72.
45 F. Kratochwil, 'The Embarrassment of Changes: Neo-Realism as the Science of *Realpolitik* Without Politics', *Review of International Studies*, 19 (1993) 63–80. A. Watson, *The Evolution of International Society*, especially pp. 120–5, 313–15.
46 Hinsley, *Power and the Pursuit of Peace*, pp. 33–113.
47 Hinsley, *Power and the Pursuit of Peace*, pp. 46–80.
48 J. Gray, *Liberalism*, pp. 28–30.
49 R. Nozick, *Anarchy, State and Utopia* (Oxford: Blackwell, 1974), p. ix.
50 For some discussion of the notion of cosmopolitan ideas in international relations see the chapters by Hutchings and Holden in this volume.
51 C. Brown, *International Relations Theory: New Normative Approaches* (Hemel Hempstead: Harvester Wheatsheaf, 1992), pp. 21–106.
52 For example M. Shaw, 'Global Society and Global Responsibility: The Emergence of Global Civil Society', *Millennium* 21 (1992) 421–34; Lipschutz, 'Reconstructing Global Politics'.

53   Franck, *The Power of Legitimacy Among Nations,* especially pp. 208–46.

54   T. M. Franck 'The Emerging Right to Democratic Governance', *American Journal of International Law,* 86 (1992) 46–91.

55   For example T. Meron, 'War Crimes in Yugoslavia and the Development of International Law', *American Journal of International Law,* 88 (1994) 78–87.

56   Franck 'The Emerging Right to Democratic Governance' p. 50.

57   See the chapter by Mason and Wheeler in this volume.

58   Shaw, 'Global Society and Global Responsibility', p. 421.

59   For example E. Kedourie, *Nationalism,* revised ed. (London: Century Hutchinson, 1985).

60   For example Smith, *National Identity.*

61   For example E. Gellner, *Nations and Nationalism* (Oxford: Blackwell, 1983).

62   Brown, *International Relations Theory,* pp. 52–81.

63   Lessnoff, *Social Contract,* pp. 130–48.

64   For the development of international law and practice on national self-determination see Y. Alexander and R. A. Friedlander, *Self-Determination: National, Regional and Global Dimensions* (Boulder, Colo.: Westview Press, 1980); H. Hannum, *Autonomy, Sovereignty and Self-Determination: The Accommodation of Conflicting Rights* (Philadelphia: University of Pennsylvania Press, 1990); Jackson, *Quasi-States;* M. Koskenniemi, 'National Self-Determination Today: Problems of Legal Theory and Practice', *International and Comparative Law Quarterly,* 43 (1994) 241–69.

65   R. P. Palan and B. M. Blair, 'On the Idealist Origin of the Realist Theory of International Relations', *Review of International Studies* 19 (1993) 385-400.

66   O. Waever, B. Buzan, M. Kelstrup and P. Lemaitre, *Identity, Migration and the New Security Agenda in Europe* (London: Pinter, 1993).

67   E. Roll, *A History of Economic Thought,* revised 5th ed. (London: Faber, 1992) pp. 129–30.

68   For example Waltz, *Theory of International Politics,* pp. 129-60. The idea of this debate is also represented in the structure of international relations theory text books and readers such as R. Little and M. Smith, *Perspectives on World Politics,* 2nd ed. (London: Routledge, 1992).

69   B. Buzan, *People, States and Fear: An Agenda for International Security Studies in the Post-Cold War Era* (Hemel Hempstead: Harvester Wheatsheaf, 1991), pp. 123–4.

70   B. Buzan, C. Jones and R. Little, *The Logic of Anarchy: From Neo-realism to Structural Realism* (New York: Columbia University Press, 1993), pp. 66–80.

71   Waltz, *Theory of International Politics,* especially pp. 18–37; Buzan, Jones and Little, *The Logic of Anarchy.*

72   Carr, *The Twenty Years' Crisis,* pp. 41–88.

73   I. Clark, *The Hierarchy of States: Reform and Resistance in the International Order* (Cambridge: Cambridge University Press, 1989), p. 89.

74   For example D. Leyton-Brown, 'The Roles of the Multi-National Enterprise in International Relations', in D. G. Haglund and M. K. Hawes (eds), *World Politics: Power, Interdependence and Dependence* (Toronto: Harcourt, Brace Jovanovich, 1990).

75   This bears a close resemblance to the ideas of the neo-Gramscian hegemony school. See R. W. Cox, *Production, Power and World Order: Social Forces in the Making of History* (New York: Columbia University Press, 1987); R. W. Cox, 'Gramsci, Hegemony and International Relations: An Essay in Method', *Millennium* 12 (1983) 162–75; S. R. Gill (ed.), *Gramsci, Historical Materialism and International Relations* (Cambridge: Cambridge University Press, 1993).

76   A good example is Buzan, *People, States and Fear.*

77   Hannum, *Autonomy, Sovereignty and Self-Determination,* p. 16.

78   See in particular the contributions by Holden, Hutchings, Dark, Paterson and Wheeler and Mason in this volume for discussions of these issues.

79   F. Halliday, 'The End of the Cold War and International Relations: Some Analytical and Theoretical Conclusions', in K.Booth and S. Smith (eds), *International Relations Theory Today* (Cambridge: Polity, 1995).

80   '... political authority represents a fusion of power with legitimate social purpose', J. G. Ruggie, 'International Regimes, Transaction and Change: Embedded Liberalism in the Post-War Economic Order', in S. D. Krasner (ed.), *International Regimes* (Ithaca, NY: Cornell University Press, 1983), p. 198.

PART 3

Is There a 'New World Order'?

4

Is There Any Moral Basis to 'New World Order'?

Peter M. Jones

1. Introduction

This chapter attempts to trace the origins of the concept of the 'New World Order' as developed by President George Bush at the time, and in the aftermath, of the Gulf War to liberate Kuwait. The author, however, does not make an assumption that there is a 'new moral world order' and accepts the view put forward by many theorists that such a concept is, at best, difficult to imagine in present circumstances. Indeed it might be better to argue that what is happening is that there has been a return to traditional realist principles, albeit tinged with some greater elements of moral awareness, than existed in the Cold War. On most occasions states will probably continue to act only when they feel their interests are at stake but may also feel an obligation to justify their actions and select their methods within greater moral limitations. This is not to argue that this is necessarily and invariably the case or that state interests have not changed since the end of the Cold War, it is merely to point out that for most states options and resources are limited. A number of other questions concerns the role that morality should play in international politics and the danger of oversimplification of moral positions so that there is a triumph of moralism over realism. The basic question, however, remains as to whether the existence of a New World Order will significantly affect the way in which states behave and determine policy or will it simply reflect a greater awareness of the need to *appear* to be more moral than before.[1]

The events of the late 1980s, particularly after the signing of the 1987 Intermediate Nuclear Forces (INF) Treaty and the increasing friendliness between the two former superpower rivals the USSR and the USA, had a number of important effects. Firstly negotiations were concluded that enabled a four-power peace treaty to be signed that ended the conflict with Germany. Secondly they witnessed the start of the process that was to lead to the end of the Cold War and with it the collapse of the Berlin Wall and ultimately the unification of the two German states; they also witnessed the end of the Soviet Empire in Eastern Europe and ultimately of the Soviet Union itself. Finally it could be argued that there was the possibility of an agreed set of values being applied to international affairs, thus replacing the ideologically-based values that had dominated the views of each side in the Cold War.

The changes that took place in the international system following the end of the Cold War and the subsequent collapse of the Soviet Union meant that the old bipolar order came to an end but it was by no means clear what the structure or rules of the new order would be. For many scholars the idea that there is a hierarchy of states in rank order is a commonplace; all systems throughout history have been dominated by some states and power relations were relative to an individual state's position in the hierarchy. The most obvious example of this has been the preoccupation of scholars and politicians with the balance of power. Much traditional and neo-realist international relations literature is concerned with the concept of balance of power.[2] Many such writers are less concerned with the moral value of the concept than with its practical impact that power relations will have on the ability of state to wage war. In other words traditional theorists have seen power in predominantly military terms and sought to proclaim the primacy of 'order', by which they appeared to mean stability, over justice; others have suggested that an unjust world order would not be either stable or peaceful.[3] Whilst military power will always be of great significance, in the latter days of the Cold War, and some might even argue from 1945 onwards, it could be said that the ranking of states became more complex. The reason for this was that there was a recognition that power did not just come out of the proverbial 'barrel of a gun' but had to be judged in other terms such as diplomatic, economic and political and that in these senses a different rank order appeared to apply depending on which index of power was being used.

An example of this would be the economic power hierarchy which clearly differed form the military hierarchy. The Cold War period had witnessed many changes in fortune among states: some of the Second World War victor nations, most notably Britain and France, had declined in power and status; whilst the defeated nations of Japan and Germany (particularly the Federal Republic) had made significant economic advances. Similarly it was obvious that the Soviet Union was no economic superpower and its eventual break up posed severe economic problems not only within its successor states and former satellites but for the international community as a whole.

In the sense that there always will be a hierarchical system it might be argued that the New World Order simply represented the new ranking of the great powers. This is not, however, to argue that there is an automatic balance of power, ordained by a 'law of nature', but simply to accept that there will always be some states at the top of any given index and others ranked below them.

The analyst of the 'New World Order' is thus struck by two different problems. The first is the theoretical concept of the 'New World Order' and its practical manifestation in international relations. The idea that there might be a unipolar world or even a multipolar world after the end of the Cold War had been discussed in the literature over the years.[4] Any world order that emerged after the Cold War had to take into account the many changes since 1945 as well as the rising political and economic significance of such regional blocs as the European Community. The European Union was, after the introduction of the Single Market in 1992, a larger economic unit than the United States, although its political unity was still in doubt. What was not clear was whether the proponents of the 'new world order' intended to refer to a system in which the United States *alone* played the leading role or whether it was meant to envisage a world in which power in its various forms was shared between different states or groups of states.

The second problem, which is the main focus of this chapter, concerns the idea of a 'new world order' as a system that would be transformed from one to which the traditional view of power politics applied into a morally superior system in which right and justice would prevail. This, to some extent, could be seen as the idealist politician's dream of a 'new world order'. However too often political leaders seize upon a big idea without fully grasping the meaning of what they are discussing. Furthermore they talk in grand terms without giving much consideration as to how to put their proposals into effect.

2. George Bush and the New World Order

This section sets out the background to, and development of, President George Bush's concept of the 'New World Order'. As international leaders gathered to declare the Cold War officially over few could have imagined the dramatic changes that were about to occur. Although there were many things that had been hard to accept about the Cold War, the old certainties of the period with its more or less stable bloc politics and nuclear stalemate had provided a consistent backdrop for international affairs. Each side in the Cold War conflict had dispensed its form of self-control and restraint over its allies and, however rough and ready a process this had been, it had proved to be an effective method of power management. With the exception of the 1962 crisis over the missiles in Cuba, the stable instability of the Cold War period and the nuclear stalemate that accompanied it had developed into a cosy familiarity, broken only occasionally by moments of heightened tension. In the more recent past examples of this heightened tension had been the 1973 Yom Kippur War and the 'Second Cold War' from 1979 until 1985. The arrival of Gorbachev as Soviet leader in 1985 had brought about a new era of détente and superpower cooperation. The logical progression of his policies both in regard to the Soviet Union and its relations with its Warsaw Pact allies had, by 1989, reached a crisis point and all the old certainties of the Cold War were about to be brought under severe strain.

On the other hand optimists were swift to point out that the very stalemate that had produced stability during the Cold War had effectively prevented international institutions such as the United Nations from performing their proper role in world affairs. The new post-Cold War period would give an opportunity to the superpowers to work together rather than in opposition. Although it was clear that the Soviet Union would have to expend much of its energy in rebuilding its shattered economy and developing its programme of political and economic reform, there was still some ground for optimism that the new-found superpower accord would prove to be a positive and not a negative feature.

Optimists were also able to point to the fact that even before the end of the Cold War had been officially confirmed the Soviet Union and the United States, along with the other veto-holding permanent members of the United Nations Security Council, had agreed to measures that contributed to the ending of the Iran-Iraq war. The sudden ending to that stalemated conflict had demonstrated that when the UN Security Council acted with unity and purpose and put aside Cold War games it could be effective in enforcing a conclusion to conflict. It was the hope of many observers that the end of the Cold War would bring about even greater activity on the part of the United Nations.

Secondly it became clear that the Soviet Union under President Gorbachev had no desire to retain its Eastern European allies by force and gradually the communist regimes collapsed and were replaced by non-Communist, democratic governments. While pessimists argued that vigilance was still essential because an empire in decline was always a dangerous animal, optimists believed that the time had come for overtures and assistance to be offered to President Gorbachev. The internal economic collapse and disarray in the Soviet Union was seen as a problem that needed to be addressed. The moral, economic and political triumph of liberal democracy had occurred and now it was possible to encourage the Soviet Union to abandon its former dictatorial, centralist and collectivist policies and espouse the causes of capitalist democracy. However in the grand tradition of linkage politics Western economic aid was conditional upon further Soviet concessions and agreements on arms control, greater liberalisation of the economy and significant reductions in Soviet conventional forces. Progress on these matters was being made, and by the early summer of 1990 President George Bush was able to announce that:

> As democracy blooms in Eastern Europe, as Soviet troops return home and tanks are dismantled, there is less need for nuclear systems of the shortest range.

> ... In the light of these new political conditions ... I've reviewed our plan to produce and deploy newer, more modern, short-range nuclear missile forces based in Europe ... I've decided, after consulting with our allies, to terminate the Follow-on to *Lance* program.[5]

Initially the Bush Administration seemed to concentrate its efforts on the implications of the changes in Eastern Europe on the role of NATO and the other European security institutions, such as the Conference on Security and Cooperation in Europe.

Most notable of these efforts, however, was the decision to revise NATO strategy. This was not an easy task nor was it likely to come about as a result of just one meeting. What was clear was that the Soviet threat had diminished, the former German Democratic Republic had been absorbed by the Federal Republic and a new relationship would have to be forged with the emerging democracies of the former Warsaw Pact. To this end the 1990 London Summit of NATO leaders declared in its final communiqué that whilst 'no-one ... can be certain of the future', the alliance should 'work together not only for the common defence, but to build new partnerships with all the nations of Europe'.[6] Even at the time of writing this chapter (May 1995), the full implications of the possible expansion of NATO and the basis on which it might be accomplished have yet to be finalised.

On the other hand it was clear that beyond the need to change NATO strategy in light of the changed conditions, there seemed to be a dearth of thinking about the broader implications of the end of the Cold War for world order. President Bush was accused by his critics of being too concerned with short-term issues, obsessed by the polls and lacking both any clear direction as to where he wished to go and any firm idea of what role he saw the United States playing in the future world order. One critic of the Bush presidency, Representative Richard Gephardt argued that his Administration was 'adrift; without vision, without imagination',[7] whilst another, a former member of the Reagan Administration, Elliott Abrams, commented that:

> after over a year in office, the Administration has yet to draw its actions into a logical whole ... We have neither defined the world we want to see emerge, nor said how we plan to get there.[8]

In response to these criticisms, George Bush himself indicated that he needed to work on what he called the 'vision thing'.

3. The Impact of the Invasion of Kuwait and the Second Gulf War

It was apparent that the post-Cold War world was beginning to take shape but in a somewhat haphazard fashion. All this changed dramatically and the focus of world attention turned to an area of activity that some had predicted would gain greater prominence in the new situation: regional conflict. On 2 August 1990, President Saddam Hussein invaded and occupied the small Persian Gulf state of Kuwait in what appeared to most observers to be an act of unprovoked aggression. For scholars and politicians this event provided the first real test of crisis management in the post-Cold War era. Firstly it provided an opportunity to find out whether George Bush would adopt the mantle of being the prime mover in the enforcement of order and justice in the new world order. Secondly it would be the first test for the UN Security Council in its presumed new role as the 'powerhouse' of that apparently revitalised institution.

Although the United Nations lost no time in asserting its authority in the crisis, passing a series of resolutions of increasing severity,[9] it soon became clear that the prime mover in this crisis was to be the American President George Bush. President Bush seemed to characterise the event as something of a personal duel between himself and Saddam Hussein. The US President clearly saw himself as holding the moral high ground, of defending the rights of a small independent state against the incursion of a bigger state ruled by an unfeeling and cruel dictator. Cynics on the other hand argued that President Bush was motivated more by his concern over oil supplies and the commercial interests of those that controlled them than the principle of Kuwaiti independence. Whatever the motive there were grounds for believing that the crisis had forced George Bush into a move towards an activist US role so that world stability would be maintained. Certainly the crisis had demonstrated that the United States was not preparing to return to isolationism as some had feared it might because of the huge burden of debt that had accumulated during the latter years of the Cold War. America appeared to be intent on playing the role of the last remaining superpower, willing to dispense its form of justice around the world with the help of others and through the medium of the United Nations. The fact that the United States was prepared to share the burden implied that it felt the need for any moral basis for action to be wider than just the American view. Or, on the other hand, was it just that military action shared with several powers reduced the risk, legitimised US actions and demonstrated a degree of international solidarity that was based on little more than a coalition of interests?

In an early response to the Kuwait crisis, President Bush, seeking to provide some moral basis for his policy, argued that all the gains that would flow from the ending of the Cold War would be placed at risk if aggression was allowed to flourish.[10] Such a view could be characterised as something of a commonplace and obfuscated the real American motives in taking strong action. As such it could hardly be described as a radical vision of a morally superior 'new world order'.

American foreign policy has continually oscillated between idealism and realism and between isolationism and involvement in world affairs.[11] Even during the Cold War there were constant attempts to offer some moral justification for the pursuit of what were in fact realist policies. Thus, American presidents sought to take the moral high ground not just in an effort to give their policies some kind of ideological or moral gloss but to appeal to the idea of widely-accepted moral principles that had universal application.

Over 30 years before George Bush proclaimed his desire to create a New World Order another president had sounded a 'call-to-arms', albeit within the context of the Cold War, that had appeared to be moralistic in tone:

> Let every nation know, whether it wishes well or ill, that we shall pay any price, bear any burden, meet any hardship, support any friend, oppose any foe to assure the survival and the success of liberty.[12]

President Kennedy went on to offer a moralistic overtone to his policy:

> To those people in the huts and villages of half the globe struggling to break the bonds of mass misery, we pledge our best efforts to help them

help themselves, *for whatever period is required – not because the Communists may be doing it, not because we seek their votes, but because it is right.*[13]

However high minded the sentiments, President Kennedy found it difficult not to temper this view by reference to American national interests. There were clearly limits to the hardships the American people were prepared to bear unless it was clear that obvious national interests were at stake as the war in Vietnam was to prove. It would seem that in the Cold War, and some would say after it as well, it was (and maybe is) very difficult for a President of the United States to deliver policies that are morally justifiable but not necessarily consistent with the generally perceived American national interest. This certainly was the experience of President Carter when he was in office. In his inaugural address he had placed human rights at the centre of his foreign policy, arguing that America's commitment to human rights must be absolute.[14] However, Carter was blamed by some opponents not only for his apparent softness in regard to the Soviet Union where he 'allowed' them to make significant military 'gains' despite the détente process but also because of his 'failure' to ensure the survival of governments, such as that of the Shah of Iran, that were friendly to American interests.

Other difficulties such as hostility from Congress may also come to haunt a president and frustrate his foreign policy intentions. One example of this could be provided by President Clinton if, as seems probable, the new Republican Congress seeks to reduce the president's flexibility in foreign policy and simultaneously reduces America's contribution to the running costs of the United Nations in general and the payments for its peacekeeping operations in particular.

Sometimes it could be argued that there has been agreement between those who approached the problem from an idealist perspective and those that approached it from a realist perspective, on the question of what American action should be undertaken in regard to a particular problem. An early case in point would be the response to the North Korean invasion of South Korea in June 1950 when proponents of each approach agreed that a military response was necessary, albeit for different reasons. The same could be said of the Iraqi invasion of Kuwait.

Nevertheless it was not until six weeks *after* the Iraqi invasion that President Bush began to articulate the view that the Gulf crisis might offer an opportunity for the achievement of a higher objective than merely the restoration of the independence of Kuwait and the renewal of stability to the Gulf region:

Out of these troubled times, our fifth objective – a new world order – can emerge: a new era – freer from the threat of terror, stronger in the pursuit of justice, and more secure in the quest for peace. An era in which the nations of the world, East and West, North and South, can prosper and live in harmony.[15]

To some this might be a Morganthau-like[16] attempt to justify the use of force for United States' national interest purposes rather than a real attempt to claim that a new moral order was at hand. Such a view would reflect the traditional realist approach that had dominated US foreign policy thinking since the early days of the nuclear age. On the other hand although Bush's comment could hardly be regarded as more than the adumbration of an idea which required considerable refinement if it was to have real meaning, here perhaps was a 'vision thing' that George Bush could at least start to convey to the American people and the world.[17]

Indeed with the bombardment of Saddam's forces in Kuwait well under way and Operation Desert Shield almost completed, Operation Desert Storm in progress and preparations for Operation Desert Sabre well advanced, George Bush began to refine the view of the New World Order he wished to see. Thus President Bush told Congress in his 1991 'State of the Union' Address:

What is at stake is more than one small country; it is a big idea: *a new world order* – where diverse nations are drawn together in a common cause, to achieve the universal aspirations of mankind: peace and security, freedom, and the rule of law ...

For two centuries, America has served the world as an inspiring example of freedom and democracy ... And today, in a rapidly changing world, American leadership is indispensable. Americans know that leadership brings burdens and requires sacrifices.[18]

Thus George Bush was able to suggest that the New World Order could to some extent be associated with the extension of American values throughout the world. The Bush Administration new world vision was to be backed up by a reassessment of America's strategic defence role in the world. Outlining his view of the world order and American strategic requirements for the future, Defense Secretary Richard Cheney told the House Armed Services Committee what the major elements should be. The first was 'Strategic deterrence and defense': 'America must continue to maintain a diverse mix of survivable and highly capable offensive nuclear forces'. The second was 'Forward presence': 'US forces must remain deployed overseas in areas of US interest'. The third was 'Crisis response': 'US conventional forces must be able to respond rapidly to short-notice regional crises and contingencies that threaten US interests'. Finally, there was 'Force reconstitution': '… we must maintain the ability to reconstitute a larger force structure if a resurgent threat of massive conflict returns'. Cheney concluded his testimony by arguing that all of these strategic objectives had to be considered within the broad context of American defence policy:

> Collective security remains central to US strategy as well … America must also sustain its support for constructive roles for the United Nations and other international institutions that contribute to a co-operative world order.[19]

Critics might argue that part of the hidden agenda of the New World Order concept was an attempt to justify the continuing high levels of expenditure on defence projects in the United States and thus avoid potential hostility from the powerful 'military–industrial complex'.

With the Cold War over many people had looked forward to a 'peace dividend', but the Bush Administration was now saying that in an uncertain world it was necessary to continue to spend large sums on defence because they would have to be prepared for any number of different threats to the new order. In other words, world leadership and American promotion and leadership of the New World Order would not come cheap, even if it could now expect to find greater levels of agreement and support for action within the world community in general and the United Nations in particular.

Certainly the United Nations could take some of the credit – if that is the right word – for the success of the campaign against Iraq; and the events in the Gulf had appeared to demonstrate that a united or near-united Security Council could take effective action to end acts of aggression. There was a clear international mood opposed to Saddam Hussein who was seen as a brutal tyrant who had scant regard for either his own fellow citizens or the rights of citizens of the countries working in Iraq. The use of innocent civilians as 'human shields' proved to be a good example of his attitude and his miscalculation of the effect such actions had on public opinion abroad. Caught in such a flagrant act of aggression and behaving in such a callous manner towards foreigners working in his country, it would have been difficult to find a more disliked or morally reprehensible character.

One effect of Saddam Hussein's international unpopularity was to make it all the easier for the United Nations to reach a consensus that action should be taken against him if the credibility of the organisation was to be established in the post-Cold War world. The despatch of a UN force to Saudi Arabia was a clear indication that it was possible for the United Nations to take decisive and effective action and to remedy the wrongs committed by 'guilty' nations. This was one of the principal features of an idealistic world order in which the weak would be helped by the strong, wrongs put right and evil punished by international collective action.

Equally it was clear that the Gulf conflict demonstrated a number of other factors. Firstly the presence of American troops in large numbers had been crucial to the success of the operation; indeed several observers found it hard to distinguish the role of the United Nations from that of the United States. Secondly despite all the talk of the emergence of new world powers to replace those that had been successful in World War Two but were now in decline, the main political, diplomatic and military action had been undertaken by the older powers. The newer powers, particularly Japan and Germany, partly for historical and partly for constitutional reasons, had been somewhat sidelined militarily (although they did still contribute much needed financial support). Thirdly it could be argued that the invasion of Kuwait was such a clear-cut case of aggression that it would have been difficult to ignore it and, in the first test case of the post-Cold War period, it was important that action should be taken and be seen to be effective. Finally, whilst the United States demonstrated its willingness and ability to act, the Gulf War continued to expose the real weakness of the Soviet Union. On the one hand the Soviet Union's former ally, Iraq, despite having one of the largest conventional armies in the world and using modern Soviet-supplied equipment, failed to make much of an impression against the US-led UN troops. Iraqi forces were overwhelmingly defeated in less than 100 hours of ground fighting, an apparent triumph of both tactics and advanced technological equipment. On the other hand the internal weakness of the Soviet Union prevented it from participating fully in the actions to liberate Kuwait. The outcome of the Gulf War was to confirm even more surely than before that there really was only one superpower left. The question that remained, however, was what kind of world did the United States wish to see?

It might be possible to argue that the UN action in the Gulf had been half-finished: Saddam Hussein was still in power and substantial military threats to the internal opposition such as the Marsh Arabs remained despite some international efforts to protect them. However it could be said that the action to liberate Kuwait had been successfully completed and that to have attempted to overthrow the regime and replace it with a more acceptable administration would have been to go beyond the UN mandate, thus breaking the consensus among the members of the anti-Iraq Coalition. Indeed there were some supporters of the UN action who believed that American forces had gone too far in doing what they had done and the legal justification for further action would have been severely in doubt as it would have involved intervention in the *internal* affairs of a sovereign state. This important principle, enshrined in Article 2.7 of the UN Charter, potentially remains a fundamental impediment to the further development of the UN role in accordance with the more idealistic view of collective security. Furthermore there have to be doubts as to whether there would have been domestic American support or international financial backing for a UN-led occupation of Iraq in support of a government that would be a replacement for that of Saddam Hussein whose internal popularity was difficult to measure. Thus whilst it was possible to paint the action to liberate Kuwait as a great victory, and in some sense it was, it also demonstrated the fragility of the consensus and the narrowness of the support within the United Nations for action by that organisation that could be regarded as threatening the sovereign independence of a member state even when that state was in breach of the Charter. The question in this context is the classic dilemma of collective security action as to where action to remove an aggressor from an illegal occupation should end and punishment begin.

It could therefore be argued that although he had begun to articulate some ideas concerning the New World Order, during the second Gulf War George Bush's approach was still rather vague. However with the success of the Gulf campaign and buoyed up in the polls, President Bush took a more optimistic view of the future, a future that he believed would be dominated by the principles espoused by the United States and which had been put into effect in the defeat of Saddam Hussein:

> The New World Order does not mean surrendering *our* national sovereignty or forfeiting *our* interests. It really describes a responsibility imposed by our success. It refers to new ways of working with other nations to deter aggression and to achieve stability, to achieve prosperity and, above all, to achieve peace. It springs from hopes for a world based on a shared commitment among nations large and small to a set of principles that undergird our relations – peaceful settlement of disputes, solidarity against aggression, reduced and controlled arsenals, and just treatment of all peoples.[20]

These were certainly fine words and principles, especially the references to peaceful settlement of disputes and just treatment of all peoples, and ones that almost all would agree are desirable. They were not very new or original but would be difficult to implement in an impartial and objective manner. Also, as can be seen, such remarks indicated a belief that American concepts of justice should apply and that they would continue to apply within the context of American national interests. Nevertheless it could be described as a movement away from the absolute amorality of Morganthau towards the more moralistic realism of Arnold Wolfers.[21]

What was becoming increasingly clear was that the translation of George Bush's New World Order vision into a reality was not going to be easy. If this ideal of a New World Order was to become a reality, it would be necessary that challenges to the principles George Bush was propounding should be met and matched with the same degree of determination that had been seen during the Kuwait crisis. Furthermore America might well have to demonstrate its willingness to involve itself in conflicts and crises where its direct interests were negligible if other states were to take its commitment to a 'new world order' seriously. As with nuclear strategy in the past, the new policy had to be not merely declaratory but also operational and believable.

There were a number of further complications. Firstly it soon became clear that not every member of the United Nations was enthusiastic about the idea of the United States imposing a *pax Americana* on the world. Nor was it always apparent that the American public themselves wished to play the role of policing the world especially in areas where their interests were not involved and with the national economy in recession. Being the leader of the remaining superpower, and being therefore expected to play the dominant role in the New World Order proved to be both politically costly for the Bush Administration as well as economically costly for the United States. The defeat of President George Bush in the 1992 election can, in part, be attributed to the belief that he was more concerned with foreign affairs and seemed to be indifferent to the domestic economic plight of many of his fellow Americans.

A second factor was that there were those in the United States who believed that it should not bear the burden of world leadership alone but share it with others, most notably the advanced industrial nations of Western Europe. In recognition of this factor and in response to the growing demands from its former enemies in the now defunct Warsaw Pact, NATO members had made moves to accommodate these desires by offering the 'new democracies' of east and central Europe the opportunity to join a wider North Atlantic Cooperation Council (NACC). In addition the possibility of belonging to a more ambitious security organisation, the Partnership for Peace (PfP), was also proposed. This proposal gave the former Warsaw Pact states some degree of support from NATO without the benefits of the security guarantee resulting from full membership. There were also some moves to establish a rapid reaction force within NATO, but this essentially Cold War institution was heavily engaged in the debate about its own future role and purpose and its relationship with other European institutions such as the Western European Union, the European Union and the Conference on Security and Cooperation in Europe. Nevertheless NATO remains the only organisation with a permanent and effective military organisation available to it and thus is still in a position to provide assistance either specifically to the United States or generally to the United Nations in a global role if such a requirement became necessary. NATO has indeed played such a role in regard to the UN action in former Yugoslavia[22] and NATO aircraft have, for the first time in the history of the alliance, fired their weapons in anger. However the experiences of this relationship have demonstrated that there are a number of difficulties that surround such actions. For example the interests of the UN troops on the ground and the wider political interests of the UN political leadership, anxious to negotiate a cease-fire as a prelude to a settlement, have not always coincided and have caused embarrassing public rifts. The lesson appears to be that the UN troops on the ground and NATO (if appropriate) must establish clear rules of procedure before the action starts and not leave it to *ad hoc* arrangements.

4. Enforcing the New World Order

Challenges to the new order have not been slow in coming. The withdrawal of the Soviet Union from world affairs and its subsequent collapse did not see the end of the regional conflicts it had previously supported through arms sales. Nor did the Soviet withdrawal make life significantly easier in terms of gaining international agreement about what to do over difficult cases. Two examples will be used to illustrate the difficulties of turning the concepts of the New World Order into a reality: Somalia and the various wars between and within the former states of Yugoslavia. In addition it seems that the post-Cold War world has been plagued by civil wars and military take-overs, as the examples of Rwanda and Haiti show.

Somalia in the Horn of Africa was a country that had been bankrupted by corrupt leadership and devastated by civil war and factional in-fighting. The dictator Siad Barre had ruled the country for more than twenty years until 1991, but his overthrow turned an already bad situation into a disaster. Whilst few could have hoped that Barre's overthrow would bring immediate relief, the events that followed were tragic as rival factions attempted either to seize power at the centre or to lead their supporters into secession and quasi-independence. A number of parties, including the United Nations, made attempts at resolving the problem and negotiating a settlement but without success.[23]

The failure to reach a settlement and the frustration of UN-led attempts to bring order out of the chaos and anarchy spurred the Security Council into further action. This action was, according to some critics, too little and too late and had only materialised once Boutros Boutros-Ghali had been appointed UN Secretary-General. In April 1992 the Security Council agreed to the establishment of a United Nations Operation in Somalia (UNOSOM) designed to monitor the agreed cease-fires but this proved ineffective and frustrating. Eventually the UN agreed to send a 40,000 strong American-dominated force – the unified Task Force (UNITAF) – to Somalia to attempt to ensure the distribution of humanitarian aid. More than twenty countries contributed forces to the task force and the action was authorised under the terms of Chapter VII of the UN Charter:

> The task force was the result of a temporary convergence of interests between Boutros-Ghali and former US President George Bush ... No doubt both felt something had to be done to alleviate the suffering, but they had other agendas as well. Boutros-Ghali sought an opportunity for the UN to demonstrate its interventionist capability, and Bush hoped to help protect the US defence budget after he left office by demonstrating the financial costs of US leadership of the 'new world order'.[24]

Although it is debatable whether UNITAF did more good than harm, it might well have proved to be a long and costly commitment for those participating in its activities. Evidence does suggest that there was some improvement in the humanitarian conditions in Somalia but orderly and civil government is still far from being restored. Patience soon began to run thin and the temptation to use military force to impose a settlement on the warring parties was never far from the surface. To do so might have been the understandable, if reprehensible, action of a superpower, but it would have been a far cry from the image of the New World Order that George Bush sought to create. Furthermore it would have gone beyond the UN mandate which had sanctioned a humanitarian mission rather than a collective security action, and action to impose a settlement or assign blame would probably not have enjoyed international support. However the lack of any clear US interest in Somalia also underpinned the desire for some 'quick fix' solution that would allow for an American withdrawal in circumstances in which it could be claimed peace and order had been restored. There was perceived to be a clear time-limit on the process and if necessary withdrawal would take place before the necessary conditions for long-lasting peace were in place. Others saw the

American withdrawal as a defeat for American interventionism, signalling an unwillingness to continue to commit troops in difficult situations. The whole episode has proved to be an embarrassment for the Clinton Administration which inherited the commitment from George Bush but seemed uncertain as to how to proceed. In May 1994 President Clinton issued Presidential Decision Directive 25 which dramatically curtailed American commitment to international peacekeeping. This followed the failure of an attempt the previous October to capture General Aideed a leader of one of he Somali factions during which 18 American servicemen lost their lives. The UN force in Somalia was scheduled to leave that country by the end of March 1995.[25]

It is certainly not obvious that President Clinton has any clear policy towards the concept of a 'new world order', although events surrounding Haiti did provide some clue as to his thinking on these issues. Bill Clinton argued that US 'policy on Haiti is not a policy for Haiti alone. It is a policy in favor of democracy everywhere.'[26] He later went on to expand this view by suggesting that the policy on Haiti had wider implications and reflected deeply held American interests:

> Now the United States must protect our interests – to stop the brutal atrocities that threaten tens of thousands of Haitians, to secure our borders and to preserve stability and promote democracy in our hemisphere and to uphold the reliability of the commitments we make, and the commitments others make to us.[27]

Tragic though the events in Somalia and Haiti were, the problems brought about by the breakup of Yugoslavia presented a rather different set of difficulties for the champions of the New World Order. It is representative of a feature that was feared would occur once the Soviet Union's grip over east and central Europe was relaxed. The world had already witnessed trouble within the former Soviet Union such as that between Armenia and Azerbaijan over Nagorno-Karabakh; and the Czechoslovakian republic had decided to dissolve itself, peacefully, into two separate republics; but nothing prepared the Europeans or the world community for the tragedy of the breakup of Yugoslavia.

Yugoslavia had been a federal amalgamation that straddled different nationalities and different religions and had been held together by a fragile thread and, because of its strategic position, the desire of the two superpowers to retain its neutralist stance. Once that element of superpower interest was removed the centrifugal forces which had been dormant but not extinct in the country began to tear it apart and various constituents of the federal republic began to put into effect their declared desire for independence. This was the prelude to a civil war in Europe, the first significant military action on that continent for nearly fifty years.

The problems in the Balkans brought into sharp focus a number of factors in relation to the New World Order. The first was the fragility of the consensus among the members of the European Community over foreign and defence policy and its overall weakness in that area. Whilst the Gulf War had not seen a triumph of unity among the Community, the Yugoslav crisis was to demonstrate even further difficulties. Several members came to regret the way in which the German government effectively 'bounced' its partners into the recognition of the breakaway republics, most notably Croatia and Slovenia. This action effectively destroyed even the remotest possibility that the Yugoslavian federation could be saved in some form.

The second factor that was demonstrated by the crisis was that the United States did not feel any great need to intervene. The United States believed that its interests were not directly affected and that it was 'doing its bit' in Somalia and that in any case Bosnia was a European problem. This was an example of what the United States meant by sharing its responsibilities in the New World Order with other states that it regarded as having a more direct interest and the necessary economic and military resources to undertake the necessary remedial action. This proved to be more difficult to put into effect than had been imagined and led to differences of opinion between the United States and the European allies as to what action could or should be taken.

The third factor was the failure of either the United Nations or the European Community, despite tremendous efforts, to broker a settlement of the civil war. Although a UN Protection Force (UNPROFOR) was eventually despatched to Bosnia to supervise the distribution of humanitarian aid, there was a general unwillingness on the part of most nations to get too involved. The terrain was difficult and the enemy hard to pinpoint, public opinion whilst believing that 'something should be done' was understood to be unwilling to support an operation of a size and duration that would probably be necessary; recent wars had been over quickly and involved the victorious side in relatively few casualties. This would be an unlikely scenario in Bosnia. Furthermore the recent action by the Bosnian Serbs in taking a large number of UN forces as 'hostages' in retaliation against NATO-led bombing raids has encouraged those critics of UN action to call for a speedy withdrawal of UNPROFOR. Although these calls have so far been resisted, the likelihood of renewed fighting around Sarajevo and its possible escalation into a more general war, makes the enforced and humiliating withdrawal of UN forces increasingly probable.

The fourth problem was one that has already been noted. Despite a considerable overlap in their membership and influence, there was a high degree of buck-passing between the United Nations and NATO, with the latter arguing that it was willing to help but needed to be told what to do; whilst the UN seemed incapable of reaching an agreement. The United States seemed to favour more active military involvement and the arming of the Bosnian Muslims but this approach was resisted by leading European states such as Britain. This division of opinion was clearly based on the fact that those on the ground and thus facing the greatest danger of counter-measures and reprisals were less willing to agree to such proposals than were those operating from the comparative safety of the skies. The effect of this indecision was to lead some nations to charge that the West was uninterested in assisting the Bosnians either directly, or indirectly by lifting the arms embargo, because the Bosnians were Muslims and because Bosnia had no oil. Although the example of Kuwait suggests that religious concerns are not significant, such critics had a point as it began to appear that the principles of the New World Order only applied where there were strong collateral interests as well as a moral imperative.

Whilst public opinion might be outraged at the thought of 'ethnic cleansing' and other atrocities, at the sight – not for the first time – of great and historic cities being reduced to rubble and the seeming acceptance of the principle that the use of force pays, governments were acutely aware that actions taken might make matters worse and could involve their troops becoming casualties in a war in which they had a limited interest. Although it should not be exaggerated these issues raised serious questions over the effectiveness of peace enforcing in the New World Order, especially where the direct interest of the great powers were not involved.

In Africa, too, the events in Rwanda brought disturbing and horrific examples of suffering, death and disease to the attention of the world public in a civil war in which many thousands were killed or maimed. Once again the cry went up that something should be done. Appeals for money, food aid and medical help were made and responded to but once again the world appeared willing to stand idly by as the civil war raged on. The outcome of the fighting was that one side eventually triumphed but it has not yet led to the resolution of the problem: thousands of refugees continue to live in camps unable or unwilling to return to their homelands for fear of reprisals or death. Indeed many seemed to prefer to face death in the refugee camps than to return home. Although the situation has improved slightly and a semblance of order has been restored, fears of reprisals and the possibility of trouble spreading more widely within the region remain strong.

Even within what it has traditionally regarded as its own hemisphere, US policy has not been decisively in favour of the principles of the New World Order. The American government attitude to Haiti is a final example of where it took a long time to act: it took a long time for any positive action to reinforce sanctions against the military regime or to convince the American people that the United States had any real interest to defend in that island. The reaction of Congressional leaders to President Clinton's proposed invasion was quite negative. However, as noted earlier, the Clinton Administration attempted to justify its actions in moral terms by taking a strong line against the Haitian military leaders and arguing that America had a moral and national interest in seeing the junta overthrown and President Aristide restored to power. The operation code named Uphold Democracy had all the hallmarks of moral rectitude but critics hostile to the Clinton presidency have pointed out that since Haiti has hardly ever known democracy, upholding democracy was a rather fanciful title for the operation. Other critics thought that President Clinton's desire for action was as much motivated by his internal political difficulties as by any strong feeling of devotion to the cause of the exiled President Aristide. On the other hand these views should not necessarily be seen as critical of the idea that it is desirable to seek to expand the frontiers of democracy in this area of the globe as much as any other. After all this is (and perhaps should be) one of the main planks of the New World Order. Furthermore President Clinton could argue that the objective of his policy was achieved following negotiations and American military action was bloodless and merely sought to facilitate the return of the legitimate government and the peaceful hand over of power to the democratically elected leadership.

5. Conclusion

It is clear that since the end of the Cold War there has been a reluctance on the part of many states to accept the idea that the United States should dominate international affairs and set up a *pax Americana*. It is equally clear from the evidence above that the other states in the international system are reluctant to take action in conformity with some 'generally accepted' code of international morality partly because there is still no agreement on what that should be or when it should be applied. But this reluctance is also because states only seem willing to act where it can be demonstrated that in addition to the moral issue at stake there are also some 'reasons of state'. Where this cannot be adequately demonstrated action is often slow in coming, lacks domestic and sometimes international support and is likely to be short-lived.

A second phenomenon brought forth by the end of the Cold War has been the high expectation that many issues of international concern could be resolved. It was certainly the case that some people thought it likely that the demise of the Cold War alliance system would lead to the elevation of the United Nations to a position of prominence in world affairs which it had never before had. Such a view might be regarded as both premature and unrealistic but the cause of the United Nations was greatly enhanced by the events following the invasion of Kuwait. UN action proved to be successful in the sense that the invasion was repulsed. However the issue of what the United Nations should do after that was left unresolved as the coalition did not agree on the lengths to which Saddam Hussein should be pursued and punished; and this left open the possibility that he might try again.[28]

Since the end of the Cold War, the United Nations has been faced with the consequences of the breakdown of the system imposed by the United States and the Soviet Union and has faced frequent demands for UN peace-keeping forces to be sent to trouble spots. Not all of these demands have been met. This is a further reflection of the fact that few states are prepared to endorse a policy of supporting any cause because it is right: most still adopt a far more realistic and hard-nosed attitude. With regard to calls from the United Nations for action, states are prepared to act where they see their own direct or indirect interests at stake, but they are not prepared to risk the possibility of high loss of life for a cause that they find remote or not directly relevant to themselves. Even where UN forces have been provided, the United Nations has been forced into humiliating powerlessness as is evidenced by the experience in Bosnia and Somalia. The irony of the situation is that whilst public opinion seems to be as concerned as ever over the issues of humanitarian aid and support for those in need, it is adjudged to be reluctant to support military action in circumstances where national interests are not at stake, where the conflict may be prolonged and the possibility of high casualty rates is great. Differences of opinion seem to arise between those states with troops 'on the ground' and those offering air cover or financial support. Furthermore it is clear that the financial burden of the costs cannot fall on the same few states every time and that it has to be shared, thus raising further issues concerning the reform of the UN Security Council. These issues, as yet unresolved, centre on the question of whether the current permanent members accurately reflect the realities of the 1990s or whether they should reflect the economic and political changes that have taken place over the last fifty years. This might suggest that the Security Council should reflect a wider geographical balance or that some of the current permanent members should be replaced by other economically stronger states. Another possibility would be to eliminate the veto power altogether whilst still retaining some method of qualified voting within the Security Council.

Finally it would seem that wars, if fought at all, have to be short and sharp and involve minimal casualties if public support is to remain strong. If this view is correct then the ideals of a New World Order as set out by President Bush will be difficult to achieve and most states will continue to operate on the basis of the past principle of 'might is right' whilst attempting to give their policy decisions a semblance of moral rectitude. Or to put it another way, for the majority of states it will be 'business as usual' and power politics and national interests will remain the strongest influences motivating states in the conduct of their foreign policy. The final conclusion must, therefore, be that a New World Order based on general moral principles is much easier to propose than it is to be put into effect.

Notes and References

1   Some of these issues are explored more extensively in other chapters of this book, such as those by Coates, Williams and Mason and Wheeler.
2   Among the many important books dealing with the subject are I. L. Claude Jnr, *Power and International Relations* (New York: Random House, 1962); K. Waltz, *Theory of International Politics* (Reading, Mass.: Addison-Wesley, 1979) and A. F. K. Organski, *World Politics,* 2nd ed. (New York: Alfred Knopf, 1968).
3   For a discussion of this point see for example: H. Bull *The Anarchical Society: A Study of Order in World Politics* (London: Macmillan, 1977) and A. Mazrui *Towards a Pax Africana* (London: Weidenfeld and Nicolson, 1967).
4   For example R. Rosecrance, 'Bipolarity, Multipolarity, and the Future', *Journal of Conflict Resolution,* 10 (1966) 314–27.
5   President George Bush, Oklahoma State University Commencement Address, 4 May 1990 (Washington DC: United States Information Service (USIS), May 1990).
6   London Declaration on a Transformed North Atlantic Alliance (Brussels: NATO Information Service, 6 July 1990).
7   Quoted in M. K. Albright and A. E. Goodman, 'US Foreign Policy After the Gulf Crisis', *Survival* , 23 (1990), p.538.
8   Albright and Goodman, 'US Foreign Policy After the Gulf Crisis' p.538.

9   UN Security Council Resolutions 660 (2 August); 661 (6 August); 662
     (9 August); 664 (18 August); 665 (25 August); 666 (12 September);
     667 (16 September); 669 (24 September); 670 (25 September); 674 (29
     October); 677 (28 November); and 678 (29 November).
10   Televised speech by George Bush, *The Financial Times*, 9 August
     1990.
11   For a discussion of this process, see G. E. Rainey, *Patterns of Ameri-
     can Foreign Policy,* (Boston: Allyn and Bacon, 1975). For a good his-
     torical account of contemporary American foreign policy, see S. E.
     Ambrose, *Rise to Globalism*, 7th ed. (London: Penguin, 1993).
12   John F. Kennedy's Inaugural Address, 1961, reprinted in R. D. Heffner,
     A Documentary History of the United States (New York: Mentor Books,
     1965), p.320.
13   Heffner, *A Documentary History of the United States*, p.321 (emphasis
     added).
14   Quoted in Ambrose, *Rise to Globalism*, p.282.
15   President George Bush's Address to Congress, (Washigton, DC: USIS,
     11 September 1990).
16   H. J. Morganthau, *Politics Among Nations*, 5th ed. (New York: Alfred
     Knopf, 1973).
17   For a discussion of the argument that there need not be a conflict between
     the national interest and moral purpose, see the chapter in this volume
     by Coates.
18   President George Bush's State of the Union Address, 29 January 1991.
     Excerpts published in *Survival*, 33 (1991), p.183 (emphasis in the
     original).
19   Secretary of Defense Richard Cheney, testimony to the House Armed
     Services Committee, 7 February 1991. Excerpts published in *Survival*,
     33 (1991), pp.538-9.
20   President George Bush, Speech at Air University, Maxwell Air Force
     Base (Washington DC: USIS 13 April 1991) (emphasis added).
21   See A. Wolfers, *Discord and Collaboration* (London: Johns Hopkins
     Press, 1971), particularly Chapter 4 'Statesmanship and Moral Choice'.
22   A factual account of NATO activities in regard to Operations Sharp
     Guard and Operation Deny Flight is published weekly by the NATO
     Information Service.
23   For a full summary of events following the overthrow of Siad Barre,
     see the IISS *Strategic Survey, 1991-1992* (London: Brassey's, 1992),
     pp.178-81.

24   IISS *Strategic Survey, 1992–1993* (London: Brassey's, 1993), p.186. The *Strategic Survey, 1992–1993* also contains a discussion of the major events in Somalia during the period in question, see pp.185–8.

25   IISS *Strategic Survey, 1994–1995* (London: Oxford University Press, 1995) p.210.

26   President Clinton's Press Statement on 4 June 1993 (Washington DC: Office of the Press Secretary).

27   President Clinton, television remarks on September 15, 1994 (Washington DC: Office of the Press Secretary).

28   This is indeed what he is rumoured to have attempted during 1994.

5

Realist Objections to Humanitarian Intervention

Andrew Mason and Nick Wheeler*

The issue of humanitarian intervention attracted considerable attention after the Cold War came to an end. Many believed that new possibilities of cooperation were opening up between the major powers, and humanitarian intervention was one of the items near the top of the agenda. Events since the Gulf War have not borne out that optimism, but nor have they shown it to be wholly misplaced: at worst they have demonstrated that if there is a genuine opportunity for increased international cooperation, then that opportunity has not yet been properly seized, and there is a need for more rigorous thinking about the conditions under which humanitarian intervention might be justified.[1] This paper is a contribution to that on-going debate. It argues that it would be morally desirable to legitimise a practice of humanitarian intervention, but that this should only be done in vivid awareness of the dangers inherent in such a practice. It maintains that there is an important battery of arguments contained in the realist tradition which are not always fully appreciated, and which count against sanctioning humanitarian intervention unless it is tightly constrained and properly regulated.

1. Some Preliminaries

Let us begin by stipulating that humanitarian intervention occurs when, and only when, one or more states (or perhaps an international body) intervene with military force, or the threat of such force, in a territory that is beyond their jurisdiction, where a weighty and non-instrumental part of their reason for doing so is to end the suffering or oppression of some group who live in it. So in order for an intervention to count as *humanitarian*, at least part of the basic reason for intervening must be to end suffering or oppression, though there might be other reasons which also motivate, for example national interest. Cases of humanitarian intervention may therefore involve mixed motives: there may be genuine examples in which the motive of national interest is the stronger of the two, and where humanitarian considerations, though significant, would not by themselves be sufficient to lead to action; there may also be instances where neither sort of considerations on its own is enough to motivate, but they are jointly sufficient to do so.

Although the definition is stipulative, it is intended to be reasonably sensitive to two considerations: ordinary usage and empirical applicability. A definition which required that humanitarian intervention be motivated solely by humanitarian motives would run the risk of being irrelevant to the understanding of actual events.[2] On the other hand if the definition were widened so that it referred only to the effects of state actions rather than the intentions which informed them, thereby allowing any outside intervention to count as humanitarian provided that its success would mean the ending of some form of suffering or oppression, then this would violate ordinary usage since it would admit cases where the sole ground for intervention was national interest. The proposed definition restricts the use of the expression 'humanitarian intervention' to cases where military force is involved or threatened. This may depart from ordinary usage to some extent for it excludes cases where intervention takes the form of supplying food or medicine without any military force being used, but it is a legitimate departure since it allows attention to be focussed on the kind of measures which are hardest to justify.

The discussion which follows will concentrate on realist objections to humanitarian intervention: although these are not the only objections to it, they are very powerful. There is another class of objections which arises from those who argue that humanitarian intervention is a violation of communal autonomy and that just as the state should respect individual autonomy, so too states should respect communal autonomy.[3] Once this approach has been adopted, however, it provides the resources to argue that humanitarian intervention is morally permissible in some extreme circumstances. First when a community has broken down irretrievably, leaving a power struggle between a number of competing factions, considerations of respect for communal autonomy are irrelevant to the issue of intervention. Second the most plausible case for respecting communal autonomy appeals to the way in which the rights or interests of individuals require that the communities to which they belong be self-determining. When the rights or interests of a group of individuals within a community are seriously threatened, then the case for respecting the autonomy of that community (if indeed any genuine community can be said to exist under such circumstances) is undermined. Michael Walzer, for example, sanctions intervention in cases of massacre and enslavement.[4] So the hard question for theorists who defend non-intervention on grounds of respect for communal autonomy is not 'Can humanitarian intervention be justified?', but 'What forms of suffering or oppression justify humanitarian intervention?' In contrast, the realist objections to humanitarian intervention that will be considered here are designed to count against it even in extreme circumstances such as massacre, and even when a political community has broken down irretrievably.

Realism, however, is a diverse tradition and a number of different varieties of it need to be distinguished. Perhaps the most basic distinction is between what will be called interpretive and prescriptive realism.[5] Interpretive realism argues that states always pursue only their national interest. According to this view humanitarian intervention will never occur because it requires a humanitarian motive, which (for various reasons) is absent in international politics. Interpretive realism has no moral objection to humanitarian intervention. It is just sceptical about the possibility of its occurring, and for that reason regards discussions about whether it is morally justifiable as pointless.[6] Prescriptive realism, in contrast, assumes that humanitarian intervention is possible, but maintains that it is unjustifiable because humanitarian considerations never provide a legitimate reason for intervention. This form of realism engages in moral argument, advocating the view that states ought to pursue the national interest and only that interest.

Interpretive realism is difficult to assess because there is considerable latitude for re-interpreting state behaviour which apparently conflicts with it: there are few 'hard facts'. Defenders of it at least owe an account of why states will always refrain from intervening on humanitarian grounds in two sorts of cases, however: when national interest coincides with humanitarian motives, and when even though intervention is not in the national interest, it does not seriously compromise it. It is hard to see what plausible explanation the interpretive realist could give for why humanitarian intervention is always ruled out in these sorts of cases.[7]

2. Functional Realism

An evaluation of interpretive realism raises a number of difficulties, much debated, about what is meant by 'the national interest'. These difficulties also beset prescriptive realism, a normative position according to which the state ought to pursue the national interest and only that interest. Prescriptive realism, in the forms of it which will be considered here, tries to clarify the issue by identifying 'the national interest' with 'the interests of the citizens of the state'.[8] Of course this still leaves many questions unanswered, but it does provide a framework within which debates over the national interest can be conducted, and allows the possibility of an important distinction between vital and non-vital national interest, drawn in terms of the vital and non-vital interests of citizens. Then the prescriptive realists position is that, given the costs of military intervention, the state should use military force only when this is required to further its own vital national interests, and that this provides the only legitimate reason for such intervention.

Prescriptive realism can take different forms. For the purposes of this essay, the most important varieties are what will be called functional and consequentialist realism. These differ in terms of the explanations they give for why the state should pursue only its national interest. Functional realism says that the state should pursue only its national interest because this is the proper role or function of the state, and then offers a story about why the state has only that legitimate role. Consequentialist realism says that the state should pursue only its national interest because if each state does so this will produce the best consequences, considered impartially and globally. It is hard to find unambiguous examples of these forms of realism in the international relations literature: indeed it sometimes appears as if realists oscillate between interpretive and prescriptive realism, maintaining that moral judgements should be avoided but then making them, and also between functional and consequentialist realism. The fact that realists cannot be neatly classified along the lines that have been drawn does not undermine these distinctions since it will be argued that they are important in understanding the different objections that are made to humanitarian intervention. In this section functional realism will be the focus of discussion.

The clearest examples of functional realism are to be found in the social contract tradition.[9] According to Hobbes in order to gain security each person contracts with every other to obey the state, provided that the others enter into such a contract as well. Even though the contract occurs between future citizens rather than between future citizens and the state, the state nevertheless has a duty to look after their interests because this is what it is authorised to do.[10] The state is not entitled to act on behalf of the citizens of other states because it is not authorised to pursue their interests.

Hobbes's account has notorious difficulties, however. As Hobbes is aware, most have not expressly entered into such a contract. He tries to avoid this difficulty by arguing that people nevertheless subject themselves to the sovereign and, even if they do so through fear, that is sufficient to constitute a binding contract.[11] But the idea that people consent to obey the state merely by, say, conforming to the law through fear of the consequences of breaking it, is deeply suspect. Some latter-day Hobbesians argue that even if no one has really entered into a contract of the kind Hobbes described, it nevertheless would have been reasonable for them to do so. But that fact (if indeed it is a fact) has no clear moral weight, for hypothetical contracts have no binding force.

It might be thought that the essence of Hobbes's account does not depend upon the metaphor of a social contract. For example John Gray (influenced by Michael Oakeshott) takes the view that the proper role of the state is to nurture the institutions of civil society. He argues that civil society provides the best way of respecting human dignity in states which have a certain set of historical traditions, committed to a concrete ideal of freedom.[12] But it is unclear how this position can underwrite what has been called functional realism, for it would seem that a state might maintain a robust civil society whilst nevertheless sometimes intervening on humanitarian grounds outside of its borders. It is implausible to suppose that engaging in a practice of humanitarian intervention, however limited, will have consequences which threaten civil society at home. (In response it might be argued that, globally speaking, the best consequences will be brought about by each state nurturing only its own civil society, but then functional realism will collapse into what has been called consequentialist realism, which will be discussed in the next section.)

The account of the state's obligations given by functional realism competes with an alternative which maintains that citizens have positive obligations to aid those beyond their borders, and that a legitimately constituted government is entitled to act, without their express consent, to fulfil these obligations. Such an account can agree that the state has stronger obligations to its own citizens than it does to the citizens of other states, and that it should give greater weight to its own citizens' interests, but argue that when confronted by the more urgent needs of outsiders, it is entitled, and perhaps even sometimes obliged, to act to meet those needs.

Impure forms of functional realism are possible, and these are much more plausible than functional realism it its purest manifestation.[13] But their plausibility is bought at the cost of making it highly unlikely that they can justify a blanket opposition to humanitarian intervention. These forms of functional realism maintain that the state's proper role is to give priority to the interests of its own citizens, but that it is nevertheless permissible for it to give some weight to the interests of the citizens of other states. So, for example, unlike pure functional realism, impure forms allow the permissibility of giving foreign aid in order to meet urgent needs abroad. Once the concession has been made that the state is entitled to give some weight to the citizens of other states, however, it becomes unclear how it can rule out the permissibility of humanitarian intervention (which, according to our definition, necessarily involves the use of military force) in some cases. Suppose, for example, that by engaging in military intervention a state could save millions of lives whilst only subjecting its soldiers to minimum risks. If the state is entitled to give some weight to the interests of those outside its borders, surely it is entitled to intervene in such cases. Furthermore suppose that the relevant army is made up of volunteers: soldiers who joined in full awareness that they might be asked to put their lives at risk for outsiders. Even though a volunteer force would use public funds, impure functional realism would be hard pressed to explain why humanitarian intervention is impermissible when it is just the lives of volunteers that are put at risk. It is only by maintaining that the state should give absolute priority to its own citizens, and that the distinction between volunteers and conscripts is irrelevant, that impure forms of functional realism could justify a blanket opposition to humanitarian intervention. And then, in practice at least, they would start to become indistinguishable from pure functional realism, and would lose much of their plausibility.

There is a position closely related to functional realism, but distinct from it, which merits consideration at this point, and which derives from the Lockean rather than the Hobbesian tradition. Robert Nozick, for example, would argue that persons have rights which place absolute moral side-constraints on the actions of others, including the state.[14] In his view these rights are such that individuals can acquire full private ownership of external resources, and the state is not entitled to intervene to prevent them from using their justly acquired resources as they see fit, provided that they do not harm others. Nozick argues that for this reason taxation by the state is a violation of individual rights because it deprives people of resources to which they are entitled, except when the state's purpose is simply to provide protection for its citizens and their property.

Strictly speaking Nozick's view is not an example of functional realism, for functional realism says that the state ought to pursue its national interest, come what may, whereas Nozick holds that there are moral constraints on the legitimate pursuit of national self-interest: the state is not entitled to violate the rights of outsiders any more than it is entitled to violate the rights of its own citizens. But Nozick's view does stand opposed to humanitarian intervention, for in practice such intervention requires taxation in order to provide the resources to fund it, and according to Nozick's theory taxation is illegitimate unless the state's purpose is to protect its citizens and their property.

Nozick's account raises large questions about the nature of justice, and about the justification of taxation. It offers a historical theory of justice according to which we have to examine how a particular distribution came about in order to determine whether it is just. In Nozick's view a person is entitled to what he has if its original acquisition was just, and subsequent transfers involving it were just: original acquisitions are just on the condition that no one is made worse off by them; transfers are just provided that they are voluntary, and they do not violate the condition placed on original acquisition.

Nozick's account has been much discussed and it has not stood up well to criticism: the theory of original appropriation which provides its core is deeply problematic. As G. A. Cohen has pointed out, in asking whether anyone is made worse off by an appropriation, Nozick compares only the situation in which the object (or piece of land and so on) goes into full private ownership with the situation in which it remains unowned.[15] But there are a host of alternative possibilities, and other people, wherever they happen to live, may be made worse off by an object's entering full private ownership by being deprived of these possibilities. The alternatives here would include the object's entering partial private ownership, so that others (including those beyond the boundaries of any state with jurisdiction over it) were entitled to some of the fruits of using it. If a theory such as Nozick's could be defended, it would provide the basis for an objection to humanitarian intervention. But the prospects for such a theory do not look good. Indeed, as Raymond Plant argues, rights-based approaches are more likely to justify humanitarian intervention in some cases than to rule it out altogether.[16]

3. Consequentialist Realism

Consequentialist realism is the view that the best consequences, globally considered, would be created by each state pursuing its own national interest. Like all forms of consequentialism, consequentialist realism maintains that at the most basic theoretical level people should be treated as equals, that is to say their interests should be considered impartially, regardless of race, sex, nationality or religion.[17] It argues, however, that global well-being will be maximised by each state taking into account only the interests of its own citizens when it comes to forming policy; in decision-making statesmen should not aim to maximise global well-being directly, but instead should consider only the interests of their own citizens.

Consequentialist realism is best understood as based upon rule consequentialism, rather than act consequentialism. Act consequentialism says that the right act or policy is that which produces the best consequences; in contrast rule consequentialism (as it will be understood here) maintains that an act or policy is right if it accords with a moral code which, if generally accepted, would produce the best consequences.[18] Since consequentialist realism says that states should follow their national interest because the best consequences will flow from each state doing so, it coheres well with rule consequentialism. (If consequentialist realism were founded upon act consequentialism, then it would have to hold the implausible view that, on every occasion, the best consequences would be created by powerful states pursuing only their respective national interests even when weaker states were practising genocide.)

What arguments might be given in favour of consequentialist realism, and the idea that the best consequences would follow from each state accepting the principle that it ought to pursue only its national interest in foreign policy? A number of arguments are possible but only the four strongest will be considered.[19] First it is argued that there is no agreement on what counts as injustice or oppression, and hence no agreement on when humanitarian intervention would be justified, or indeed on what counts as humanitarian intervention, since it is defined in terms of the attempt to end oppression. Because there is no such agreement, allowing humanitarian intervention would be likely to undermine world order. Second even if agreement could be reached on what counted as oppression or injustice, whatever rules are devised to govern humanitarian intervention will be abused. Third in practice it is impossible to know whether humanitarian intervention will be successful; even if it is likely to be successful, it is difficult to know whether it will lead to an unacceptable level of casualties. The outcome of intervention is always highly uncertain and therefore it is unreasonable to embark upon it. Fourth, even if an intervention is successful in the short term, it is likely that the same oppression will occur again in the future, or that some other form of oppression will take its place.

The first argument informs some of Hans Morgenthau's reflections upon state behaviour. Morgenthau warned against crusading in the international arena, and maintained that pursuit of the national interest, when it was conceived in an enlightened way, would be conducive to a better world. Moral crusading will always rest upon controversial commitments, and for

that reason will lead to conflict between states that do not share these commitments. Pursuit of the national interest, provided that the national interest
is properly conceived, is more likely to preserve a modicum of world order.[20]
In a similar vein George Kennan also argues that idealism and moralism
undermine world order:

> It is a curious thing…that the legalistic approach to world affairs, rooted
> as it unquestionably is in a desire to do away with war and violence,
> makes violence more enduring, more terrible, and more destructive to
> political stability than did the older motives of the national interest. A
> war fought in the name of high moral principle finds no early end short
> of some form of total domination.[21]

Kennan argues that (in the period 1900–1950) if American statesmen had had
a better understanding of the realities of power, and had avoided idealistic
crusading and moralistic slogans, then the world would have been a better
place.[22]

Hedley Bull, though not a realist, appeals to some of the same considerations, emphasising that there is no agreement on what human rights there
are, and suggests that this underwrites the reluctance of many statesmen to
sanction a right of humanitarian intervention.[23] Bull's rejection of humanitarian intervention rests on moral grounds, for he sees the provision of international order as a necessary condition for the protection and promotion of
individual well-being. Bull's argument seems to be that aggregate well-being
is better served by upholding the principle of non-intervention than by allowing humanitarian intervention in the face of disagreement about where and
when it is justified.[24]

The second argument really makes two different points, although they
are sometimes run together. The first point is that states will intervene simply
in order to further their own national interest whilst claiming a humanitarian motive. Thus Thomas Franck and Nigel Rodley argue that the principle
of non-aggression enshrined in Article 2.4 of the United Nations Charter is
vulnerable enough to states abusing it in the name of self-defence, without
a legal right of humanitarian intervention providing yet further scope for
abuse.[25] Given the possibilities of abuse, humanitarian intervention may just
become a new form of imperialism and constitute a threat to world order.[26]
It is worth distinguishing this point from another: that states will apply the
rules governing humanitarian intervention selectively, intervening only
when they can also further their own national interest. On this ground, it
might be argued that humanitarian intervention is likely to be destabilising
in other ways. It will occur unexpectedly because it is impossible to foresee

where states will perceive an interest in intervening. It will lead to grievances because one state will complain that it has been unfairly targeted or made an example of, whilst others are equally guilty. This point differs from the first because it maintains that even when an intervention is genuinely humanitarian, abuse will occur because the practice of intervention will be selective, and will not occur in all cases when the need for it arises.

The third argument, that in practice it is impossible to know that an intervention will be successful, or whether it will lead to unacceptable casualties, can be supported by a number of observations.[27] First it is very hard to gather the information necessary to make a prudent judgement about what kind of difficulties will be encountered, for the political context in which an intervention takes place is complex and unfamiliar. Second the success of an operation is frequently dependent upon a multiplicity of factors that are out of one's control: since advocates of humanitarian intervention want to distinguish it from imperialism, they suppose that successful intervention will involve providing an oppressed group with the means to protect itself, but in practice that will often involve helping to install a government that is friendly to that group. Whether that is possible is much more out of the intervening force's control than, say, simply defeating an oppressor. Third it is hard to intervene successfully without destroying the institutions of government, and without alienating a section of the population large enough to make effective non-military government impossible.[28]

The fourth argument, that even if an intervention is successful in the short term it is likely that the oppression which has been countered will re-emerge later, or simply be replaced by a new form of oppression, was defended in one form by John Stuart Mill. Mill produced the argument in defence of the principle of non-intervention, restricted in its application to so-called civilised societies, but it could equally be deployed more generally as part of what has been called consequentialist realism. Mill argues that where a people, or some portion of them, is being oppressed by their government there is no point in liberating them, for unless they are willing to liberate themselves it will only be a matter of time before their liberty is taken away again.[29] The direct attempt to free a people is likely to be self-defeating in the long run, since unless a people is willing and able to free itself it is unlikely to remain free.[30]

4. A Response to the Consequentialist Realist's Case Against Humanitarian Intervention

The consequentialist realist's arguments against humanitarian intervention are very powerful, but they do not show that a properly regulated and limited practice of humanitarian intervention cannot be justified, or that world order would be threatened by such a practice. It is true that any rules governing humanitarian intervention will be open to some abuse, but the scope for abuse could be seriously constrained by imposing the following conditions:

(i) Humanitarian intervention should be permitted only in extreme cases, perhaps just to end mass murder.[31] Although it is possible to disagree over the definition of 'mass murder' (for example can letting a group of people starve constitute mass murder?), and to disagree over the application of any agreed definition to particular cases, with some small measure of good faith agreement should be possible in many cases.[32]

(ii) A state (or group of states) should be required to obtain the permission of the Security Council of the United Nations before it acts. Unilateral action would be permissible but only if it was authorised by the United Nations.[33]

(iii) The Security Council should work within a definite framework when considering whether humanitarian intervention ought to be permitted in a particular case. It should specify that an intervention will not be authorised unless the following conditions are met:[34] the intervention does not threaten international peace and security (for example by causing disruption in neighbouring countries); the intervention must have a reasonable chance of success, and there must be good reason to believe that casualties will not be disproportionate; less drastic measures must have been tried already, or there must be a good reason for thinking that they would fail and that there is no time to try them out.

No doubt states would undertake humanitarian intervention selectively. It is likely that states would intervene only when they could further their national interest by doing so. (Of course if these were to be genuine instances of humanitarian intervention, humanitarian motives would nevertheless have to be a weighty part of the reason for intervening.) It is not clear, however, that selectivity is likely to pose a threat to world order. By and large it would be clear where national interests were at stake, and hence where interventions were likely to occur. In any case the interventions, if they were to be legitimate, would have to be authorised by the United Nations, so they would not be wholly unpredictable.

It is also not clear that selectivity is objectionable in itself. Only if humanitarian intervention were morally required in all cases where it was morally permissible would it follow that selective intervention was always objectionable. Although we cannot argue the point here, it is plausible to suppose that humanitarian intervention is morally required only in some of the cases where it is morally permissible. If intervention were selective in those cases where it was morally required, then it would not be the selectivity itself that was morally suspect, but rather the absence of humanitarian intervention in some circumstances in which it should occur.

The argument that in practice it is impossible to know that an intervention will be successful and not involve unacceptable casualties also has considerable weight, but overstates the case. There are many dangers attached to humanitarian intervention. Forces may become unwilling participants in a bloody conflict from which they cannot extricate themselves. It is very hard to intervene with sufficient force to be successful without at the same time alienating a sizeable proportion of the population, or without destroying the institutions which are necessary for government of any sort. But surely in practice there can be cases in which we know that humanitarian intervention has a reasonable chance of success, and that the potential gains are such that the risk is worth taking.

Mill's claim that if a people is to remain free for any length of time then they must free themselves – because unless they want their liberty sufficiently strongly for them to be prepared to win it for themselves they are likely to lose it again in the future – also seems to overstate the case against intervention: a love of liberty is not always enough to enable a people to escape tyranny, especially when that tyranny takes the form of mass murder. In these cases intervention would be justified not so much on the grounds that it is needed to liberate those who are being oppressed, but on the grounds that it is required to prevent their extermination.

A number of counter-objections to these proposals might be made.[35] First it might be argued that no principled reason has been given for restricting intervention to cases of mass murder. Why draw the line there rather than to include enslavement (as Walzer does) or widespread torture? This is not a genuine objection to the proposals, however, though it does draw attention to their incompleteness. No attempt has been made to distinguish all the cases in which humanitarian intervention would be legitimate; the aim has been more modest, viz. to show that there is at least one class of cases where it would be justified, provided certain other conditions were met. It is not clear anyway that it is possible to resolve this issue by appealing to a principled reason for drawing the line in one place rather than another. Further progress on the matter requires a balanced judgement concerning the consequences of allowing a more extensive practice of intervention: there are considerable grounds for caution, since the consequences could be quite grave for the reasons given by consequentialist realists.

Second it might be argued that even if humanitarian intervention is morally legitimate in some cases, it is better not to institutionalise it as a practice, or give it the sanction of international law. (This argument is similar in form to one which is sometimes presented in the debate over euthanasia: although euthanasia is morally permissible in some cases, it is better for it to remain illegal given the possibilities of abuse.) The appropriate response to this objection is to maintain that the institutional arrangements described would minimise the scope for abuse, and create a state of affairs better than the one in which all humanitarian intervention is ruled out by the United Nations and regarded as a violation of international law.

No attempt has been made to answer all the objections that might be raised to legitimising a practice of humanitarian intervention. A number of realist objections have been considered, in the belief that these provide the strongest case against doing so. Despite their power, however, they are unable to show that a properly regulated and suitably constrained practice of humanitarian intervention would be morally impermissible, or create a worse world than the one we currently live in. It has been argued that allowing humanitarian intervention in some cases – when it is authorised by the United Nations, and when mass murder is involved – would promote overall well-being. So far from forbidding humanitarian intervention, consequentialist reasoning will support it in some cases.

Notes and References

*   We would like to thank John Andrews, Ken Booth, John Cottingham, Roger Crisp, Brad Hooker, Robert Jackson, Justin Morris, and Howard Williams, as well as contributors to this volume (especially John Williams) for their helpful comments. Earlier versions of the paper were presented at the Seminar on International Political Theory at the London School of Economics and Political Science, and the Nuffield Political Theory Workshop, and were much improved by the comments received.

1   Of course there is often good reason to be sceptical about the rhetoric which promised a New World Order: see P. M. Jones's contribution to this volume.

2   As Michael Walzer noted several years ago, it is hard to find cases in which purely humanitarian motives are involved: see M. Walzer, *Just and Unjust Wars* (Harmondsworth, Middlesex: Penguin, 1978), p. 101. Nothing has changed in this respect since he wrote the first edition of the book. Why not hold, however, that an intervention counts as humanitarian only if the *primary* reason for it is to end oppression? It would be more difficult to apply such a definition in practice, for it is harder to determine the primary reason for an intervention than it is to determine which considerations were weighty.

3   For example Walzer, *Just and Unjust Wars*, p. 58. For a good discussion of this kind of argument, see J. McMahan, 'The Ethics of International Intervention', in K. Kipnis and D. Meyers (eds), *Political Realism and International Morality* (Boulder, Colo.: Westview Press, 1987), pp. 78–91.

4   Walzer, *Just and Unjust Wars*, pp. 90, 101–8.

5   This distinction, or a related one, has been drawn by others. See especially J. Thompson, *Justice and World Order: A Philosophical Inquiry* (London: Routledge, 1992), pp. 27–8, but also: S. Forde, 'Classical Realism' in T. Nardin and D. Mapel (eds), *Traditions of International Ethics* (Cambridge: Cambridge University Press, 1992), p. 62; M. Smith, 'Ethics and Intervention', *Ethics and International Affairs*, 3, (1989), pp. 8–9.

6   Interpretive realists sometimes hold the implausible view that moral considerations do not apply to the international arena, on the grounds that obligations can exist only when they are enforceable.

7   Like 'extreme holism', interpretive realism drifts dangerously close to a form of determinism which allows no scope for individuals, or even groups within a state, to influence state behaviour: see Barry Jones's contribution to this volume.

8   Not all forms of prescriptive realism make this move. For example some forms think that the national interest is wholly independent of the interests of its citizens.

9   There are also some fairly clear examples of functional realist arguments in the media. See for example A. Tonelson, 'If You Want to Help, Volunteer' (*International Herald Tribune*, 30 December 1992); C. Krauthammer, 'In Bosnia, Partition Might Do' (*International Herald Tribune*, 9 September 1992).

10   T. Hobbes, *Leviathan*, ed. C. B. Macpherson (Harmondsworth: Penguin, 1968), pp. 227–8 (Part 2, Chapter 17). Strictly speaking, according to Hobbes the sovereign cannot have *obligations* towards his subjects: for Hobbes obligations are created by contracts, and the sovereign makes no contract with his citizens. Indeed Hobbes could not allow the possibility of a valid contract between the sovereign and his subjects because in his view contracts are valid only if they are enforceable, and any contract between the sovereign and his citizens would be unenforceable. However the sovereign has *duties* towards his subjects since he is authorised by them to protect their interests. See Hobbes, *Leviathan*, p. 230. D. Gauthier, *The Logic of Leviathan* (Oxford: Oxford University Press, 1969), p. 139, attributes a distinction between obligation and duty to Hobbes.

11   Hobbes, *Leviathan*, p. 252 (Part 2, Chapter 20).

12   For example the essays in J. Gray, *Beyond the New Right: Markets, Government and the Common Environment* (London: Routledge, 1993).

13   It is, we think, much more plausible to suppose that the state should operate with a principle of giving priority to the interests of its own citizens, rather than with a principle of equal consideration of interests which, for example, Peter Singer recommends: see P. Singer, *Practical Ethics*, 2nd ed. (Cambridge: Cambridge University Press, 1993), especially Chapter 2, and p. 260. Many ethical theories can allow that it is permissible for the state to give greater weight to the interests of its own citizens in forming policy, for example consequentialism (see R. Goodin, 'What Is So Special about Our Fellow Countrymen?', *Ethics*, 98 (1988) 663–86) and Kantianism (see A. Gewirth, 'Ethical Universalism and Particularism', *Journal of Philosophy*, 85 (1988) 283–302).

14   R. Nozick, *Anarchy, State, and Utopia* (Oxford: Blackwell; 1974).

15   See Part Two of G. A. Cohen, 'Self-Ownership, World-Ownership and Equality', in F. S. Lucash (ed.), *Justice and Equality Here and Now* (Ithaca, NY: Cornell University Press, 1986).

16   See R. Plant, 'The Justifications for Intervention: Needs before Contexts', in I. Forbes and M. Hoffman (eds), *Political Theory, International Relations, and the Ethics of Intervention* (London: Macmillan, 1993), pp. 104–12.

17   Some would regard this as a cosmopolitanist form of realism: see Thompson, *Justice and World Order*, p. 28. Certainly if cosmopolitanism were simply defined as the view that human beings ultimately

have equal status, regardless of race, sex, nationality and religion, then this would follow.

18 See B. Hooker, 'Rule-Consequentialism, Incoherence, Fairness', *Proceedings of the Aristotelian Society*, 95 (1994) 19–35, for a recent defence of rule consequentialism, and of the idea that it does not collapse into act consequentialism but is nevertheless coherent.

19 See C. Thomas, 'The Pragmatic Case Against Intervention', in Forbes and Hoffman (eds), *Political Theory, International Relations, and the Ethics of Intervention*, pp. 91–103, for a recent presentation of some of these arguments. She maintains on the basis of past interventions that 'most of the time intervention will do more harm than good' (p. 92). See also Coates's discussion of realism in his contribution to this volume.

20 H. Morgenthau, *In Defence of the National Interest: A Critical Examination of American Foreign Policy* (Washington, DC: University Press of America, 1982), especially pp. 38–9.

21 G. Kennan, *American Diplomacy 1900–1950* (Chicago: University of Chicago Press, 1950), p. 101.

22 It is hard to read *American Diplomacy* without supposing that Kennan believes America and others morally ought to pursue the national interest, properly conceived, because this will maximise global well-being. Consider, for example, his plea that we view 'the tragedy of Russia as partly our own tragedy, and the people of Russia as our comrades in the long hard battle for a happier system of man's coexistence with himself and with nature on this troubled planet', (Kennan, *American Diplomacy*, p. 147); and his comment elsewhere that 'we in the end are compelled to consider the security of our people, ... because unless they can enjoy that security they will never be able to make any useful contribution to a better and more peaceful world' (quoted in J. L. Gaddis, *Strategies of Containment: A Critical Appraisal of Postwar American National Security Policy* (Oxford: Oxford University Press, 1982), p. 32). This provides some support for the idea that Kennan is a consequentialist realist.

23 See H. Bull (ed.), *Intervention in World Politics* (Oxford: Clarendon Press, 1984), p. 193.

24 Bull's argument draws attention to the possibility of attempting to justify the principle of non-intervention, rather than consequentialist realism, on consequentialist grounds. Bull could be seen as appealing to the very same arguments that some consequentialist realists do, but in defence of the idea that the state should intervene only on grounds of self-defence. Consequentialist realists, in contrast, would argue that

the best consequences would be brought about by each state following
its own national interest (properly conceived), breaking the principle
of non-intervention when national self-interest required it to do so.

25   See T. Franck and N. Rodley, 'After Bangladesh: The Law of Human-
     itarian Intervention by Force', *American Journal of International Law*,
     67 (1973) 275–305.

26   See McMahan, 'The Ethics of International Intervention', p. 92, for (in
     our view) a much too hasty dismissal of considerations of this sort.

27   This argument is presented most forcefully by G. Graham, 'The Justice
     of Intervention', *Review of International Studies*, 13 (1987) 133–146,
     see especially p. 143, although he defends a position within the just
     war tradition, rather than a form of realism.

28   See T. G. Weiss, 'UN Responses in the Former Yugoslavia: Moral and
     Operational Choices', *Ethics and International Affairs*, 8 (1994), p. 5.

29   J. S. Mill, 'A Few Words on Non-Intervention' in his *Collected Works*,
     Vol. 21, *Essays on Equality, Law, and Education*, ed. J. M. Robson
     (London: Routledge, 1984), especially pp. 122–3.

30   See Walzer, *Just and Unjust Wars*, pp. 87–8, for a somewhat different
     reading of this argument.

31   'Mass murder' is not restricted to cases of genocide, for the notion of
     mass murder does not imply any racial or ethnic connection between
     those killed. Those who defend a principle of non-intervention by
     appealing to the value of communal autonomy or self-determination
     would also allow intervention to stop massacre.

32   Whether the necessary good faith exists will, of course, depend upon
     specific historical circumstances. Whether it exists now is a matter of
     dispute.

33   There might also be a case for the United Nations directly to recruit a
     volunteer force which could be used for the purposes of humanitarian
     intervention: see B. Urquart, 'For a UN Volunteer Military Force', *New
     York Review of Books*, 10 June 1993, for this proposal.

34   Compare C. Beitz, 'The Reagan Doctrine in Nicaragua' in S. Luper-
     Foy (ed.) *Problems of International Justice* (Boulder, Colo.: Westview
     Press, 1988), pp. 182–95.

35   Both of the objections considered here are anticipated in J. Slater and
     T. Nardin, 'Non-Intervention and Human Rights', *Journal of Politics*,
     48 (1986) 86–95.

PART 4

Aspects of Cosmopolitanism

6

The Idea of International Citizenship

Kimberly Hutchings

1. Introduction

The argument of this chapter has two aspects to it. On the one hand I want
to make a case for using a conception of 'international citizenship' as one
way of articulating issues of ethico-political identity and agency in relation
to rights and responsibilities within the international arena. On the other
hand, in parallel with this argument, I want to address the broader question
of what are the most useful philosophical frameworks for making judgments
about ethical issues in a global context. The former part of my argument
overlaps considerably with the concerns of Holden's chapter in this volume
on the possibilities of global democracy. Like Holden I would argue that it
is possible to think of 'rule of the people' beyond the constraints of the nation
state and without the attainment of world government. Thinking about the
idea of international citizenship is another way of raising the question of who
'the people' are or might be in different kinds of trans-state political, and
potentially democratic, processes. There are, however, peculiar difficulties
with defining 'the people' in this context, most notably the fact that the international arena is full of actors who are not individual persons, even though
they may be bearers of rights (as well as responsibilities) in a way analogous
to the individual citizens of a domestic state. Through a discussion of recent
work on the idea of citizenship in the domestic context and of an article by
Linklater, 'What is a Good International Citizen?',[1] I examine some of the
issues involved in articulating a concept of international citizenship, given

both the different ways in which citizenship can itself be defined and the different sorts of entity constituting 'the people' in the international realm.

The second aspect of my argument touches on issues which underlie the concerns of all of the contributors to this volume. The fact that there are ethical dimensions to global change is patently obvious, but what is less obvious is the appropriate way to theorise the ethical in a global context. The resources of traditional liberal normative political theory are put to the test by questions of justice and intervention beyond state borders (see the chapters by Paterson and by Mason and Wheeler in this volume). For Linklater Kant's idea of the connection between 'republican' states and perpetual peace, and Habermas's communicative ethics and notion of collective 'moral learning' provide a background frame of reference within which ethical judgment can be framed in the international sphere in order to answer the question of what a good international citizen is. I will be arguing that there are difficulties both with an over-reliance on states as the medium of international progress and with a commitment to ethical universalism. Instead I suggest that an alternative vocabulary for thinking about global ethical issues may be found in the work of Hegel and Foucault. As Barry Jones points out in his chapter in this volume, the options for discussing ethics in the international sphere are too often polarised between structure and agency, state and individual. One result of this is that readings of history tend to become fixed into either perpetual pessimism or perpetual hope. In conclusion I will suggest that the more fluid conception of citizenship implied by my argument in the first part of the chapter represents a way of thinking about global ethico-political life (in a way that mirrors developments in thinking about citizenship in the domestic context) without either despair or unwarranted optimism.

2. Why Focus on Citizenship?

Before going on I should perhaps explain why I choose to focus on the notion of 'citizenship' at all, given that it is traditionally the concept of a political and legal status which is state-bound. What I find useful about the concept of citizenship is the way in which at the same time as it expresses a purely formal, abstract status it is also necessarily tied to specific forms of political identity and agency. The idea of citizenship suggests the accomplishment of a mediation between the realms of concrete particularity and abstract universal right, something which must also be accomplished in any adequate account of global moral and political rights and obligations.

The notion of 'international citizenship' is a paradoxical one. The term 'international' captures a particular vision of the global order as the space between territories. The distinguishing mark of the international is the absence of any overarching authority. According to traditional liberal accounts of political obligation generated by contract or consent, the international becomes defined as an inherently non-legitimate sphere, a perpetual state of nature. Unlike the terms 'global' or 'world', the idea of the international expresses an absence of location. In contrast to this conceptions of the citizenship, however contested they may be, tend to have in common the understanding that citizens are individual persons owing allegiance to a specific political authority, with the latter typically conceived in modern times in terms of the nation state. Thus, while the international cannot be identified with any particular sphere of authority, citizenship is seen as restricted within state boundaries. Given these orthodox conceptions of the scope of 'international' and 'citizenship' there appear to be two obvious ways of making sense of the bringing together of these two concepts.

The first option is what I will refer to as the 'citizen-state' option. According to this account an analogy, though not a strict one given the differences between national and international law, can be made between the position of citizens within the domestic state and the position of states in international society. On this reading international citizens would be states, bearers of rights and obligations in relation to international law. The problem with this option is that it relies on the idea of states as beings with integrity in the sense both of being unitary agents analogous to individual human beings and in the moral sense, and both of these claims are contestable. The second option for making sense of the notion of the international citizen I will refer to as the citizen-human option. According to this account what is relevant to the idea of international citizenship is the fact that humans as a species inhabit the same community and that in regard to certain issues (in particular issues of the environment, peace and human rights) all individuals existing in the world are citizens of the world, bearers of rights and responsibilities which may well transcend the existing scope of international law or the institutional structures available for global political rule. The problem with this option is that it seems a long way removed from the actualities of global political life in which prudential state interests continue to dominate. If the first option might be seen as liable to lapse into a pessimistic realism about interstate relations, then the second option can be accused of an unrealistic optimism about the possibilities of international politics. In my exposition of Linklater's account of the good international citizen below it will be seen how he attempts to find a way between these two options, but to some extent remains haunted by the terms of the choice between them. First, however, I will examine the concept of citizenship itself.

3. Changing Ideas of Citizenship

It has become a commonplace to identify two strands to the history of the concept of citizenship in Western Europe, the strand with its origins in the ancient Greek polity which is often labelled 'civic republicanism' and the decisively modern liberal strand.[2] The first of these involves an active and participatory model of citizenship, in which the political identity of the individual citizen is bound up with the constitution and protection of the polity of which he/she is a member. The second, liberal-democratic, strand involves a model of citizenship more in terms of the citizen as a bearer of rights over against the state. According to this account citizenship becomes identified with a set of civil and political entitlements for which the subjects of the state qualify according to criteria which are universal in scope (a degree of rationality or responsibility abstractly measured by the age of consent). In Marshall's famous account, the civil and political rights constitutive of citizenship within the liberal-democratic polity have to be supplemented by social rights which ameliorate the real inequalities underlying the apparent equality of all citizens in relation to the state.[3]

In recent years there has been something of a revival of theoretical interest in the concept of citizenship and the comparative strengths of the civic republican and liberal accounts. The strength of the former account is often seen to lie in its linkage of citizenship to the involvement of the individual in political life and its radical democratic potential. The weakness of the civic republican tradition, on the other hand, can be seen to lie in the fact that it is compatible with a totally non-democratic allocation of citizen status (consider the narrow range of the population counting as citizens in the Greek *polis* or Italian city-state), in the question of its workability in complex and large scale polities and in the close tie it establishes between individual identity and the state. The latter point is important for contemporary political theorists anxious to make room for plurality in the political identities which form part of citizenship.[4] In the case of the liberal conception, its strength lies in the centrality of the idea of equality of entitlement in which protection for individual citizens is entrenched and rights are held equally by all subjects of the state who have reached the age of consent. The liberal citizen is, as it were, defended from the state by a series of rights which enable a plurality of ways in which individuals can live their lives within the private sphere and civil society. On this model the emphasis is much more on what the state owes the individual subject than the other way round. It is precisely this latter point which for some commentators also marks the weakness of the liberal account of citizenship. It is argued that the liberal concept of citizenship encourages political passivity and the increasing detachment of individual identity from the public realm of the state.[5]

One consequence of the discussion of the concept of citizenship within the modern liberal-democratic polity, given the problems with both civic republican and liberal models, has been to encourage an 'enquiry into the extent and characteristics of modern social citizenship'.[6] This enquiry focusses attention both on how citizenship is established and sustained in practice in modern societies and on what the ideal model for citizenship within such societies should be. Frequently such discussions aim to blend elements of the civic republican and liberal models, retaining the idea of participation and the significance of political identity from the first model and the notions of plurality of interest and entrenched rights from the latter.[7] Two implications of these developments in the theory of modern citizenship are of particular interest to anyone trying to articulate a concept of international citizenship.

Firstly, whereas traditionally the notion of the basis of modern citizenship right tended to be treated as a matter of natural right or abstract principle, recent discussions have focussed on the ways in which acquisition of citizenship has invariably been the outcome of struggles for political recognition in which both the extent of the citizen body and the nature and extent of citizen rights are constantly contested and changing. The nature of citizenship within the liberal polity has been marked by a dialectical relation between the abstract equality of right represented by citizenship and a series of exclusions of subjects from the citizen body which have been overcome through political action on the part of the excluded. Secondly, following on from the latter implication, the notion of citizenship becomes defined more flexibly as a political identity which may be formed in various ways and which may be legitimated by reference to communities other than the state, on the basis of which recognition by the state is demanded. In addition to this Norman points out that the necessity of a link between citizenship and the nation state becomes open to question once an account of citizenship is historically contextualised:

> Citizens do not have to be citizens of a nation-state. It came to be the primary form of political community by a specific historical process in which new forms of organization grew up, and in due course we may likewise become citizens of new political communities, of Europe or of the world, to the extent that we come to constitute ourselves as such. [8]

Whereas in the past the idea of citizenship was conceived as an achieved status with its meaning necessarily attached to the political community of the state, these new accounts of citizenship associate citizenship with the political identities and practical struggles which underwrite the acquisition of rights recognised by the state. Such accounts involve the central claim that the idea of citizenship has in fact always been inseparable from, and dependent upon, conceptions of political identity and agency both in principle and in practice.

It is interesting that, for some thinkers, this re-thinking of citizenship encourages a theoretical shift from the resources of liberal political theory precisely because the latter does tend to operate with a notion of citizenship as achieved, rather than always in process, and as defined at the level of moral principle or legal recognition rather than at the level of the formation and sustenance of political identity and agency. For example in a recent collection of essays on pluralism, citizenship and community Walzer draws on the idea of civil society derived from Hegel's work to rethink the question of political identity in liberal-democratic polities, and argues for the mutual dependence of membership of civil society and citizenship of the state.[9] In the same volume McClure claims that post-structuralist contributions to political theory may be the most adequate resource for thinking about political identity and rights in the modern era because they do not close off potential sites of political action in the way that liberal political theory and its emphasis on the public sphere of the state does, nor do they make political identities depend on recognition of claims by the state alone.[10] From both Walzer's and McClure's accounts one gains the impression that the ideal of modern citizenship they are implying combines a dimension of political agency, nourished through solidarities with different communities and interest groups and a dimension of radical democracy, in which practices of citizenship are essentially practices of self-determination.

4. International Citizenship

As Linklater notes the analysis of citizenship within current theory may have challenged traditional and more rigid conceptions of citizenship but by and large the analysis has remained focussed on political life within the nation state. However he points out that even so 'several writers have added that the current internationalisation of modern economic and political life requires, and might very well generate, the further transformation of citizenship'.[11] Linklater then goes on to follow through this suggestion and to examine answers to the question of what counts as a good international citizen.

According to Linklater the idea of international citizenship is ambiguously related to the notion of citizenship within the state. In so far as the latter indicates membership of a bounded political community, as noted above, international citizenship appears to represent an impossibility outside of the framework of a world state. On the other hand Linklater argues that the politics of domestic citizenship, in which citizenship becomes a weapon against exclusionary practices within the political community, has an implicit logic (reliant on a basic human ethic) which extends to exclusionary practices beyond the bounds of the state. In the history of citizenship the distinction between insiders and outsiders is always contestable. The difficulties of formulating a conception of citizenship within the international context are therefore counteracted by the usefulness of a concept which can be used to challenge boundaries as well as enforce them. For Linklater, thinking about citizenship in an international context is part of both an analytic and a normative agenda. On the one hand political rights and obligations clearly function at a transnational level in contemporary world politics and there therefore needs to a be vocabulary to capture the idea of globally contextualised political membership. On the other hand Linklater traces the same tension he perceives in domestic citizenship (between a fundamental ethic of justice, which involves a commitment to universal rights, and the particularistic legitimation of these rights within the state) to the idea of international citizenship. The latter is seen as undermining unjustifiable distinctions between insiders and outsiders, humans and citizens, just as citizenship within liberal polities has been the vehicle for extending the rights of all subjects of the state:

> Judged accordingly, the idea of the good international citizen can be a means of weakening the exclusionary character of the modern state and of overcoming an ancient tension between the rights of citizens and duties to the rest of humanity.[12]

Linklater identifies three dimensions of citizenship, which he summarises as 'rights before the law; rights of participation in major political processes; and the duty to promote the widest social good'.[13] In the context of the discussion of the idea of international citizenship the three dimensions are linked to three theoretical traditions which have framed analytic and normative thinking about international relations: realism, rationalism and cosmopolitanism/universalism.[14] In 'What is a Good International Citizen' the first of these dimensions becomes that of the recognition of collective responsibility of states for the maintenance of international order. This dimension is derived from realist contributions to ways of thinking about the international which emphasise the importance of finding mechanisms for stabilising interstate relations (p. 28). The second dimension, derived from the rationalist tradition (drawing on Bull's work in particular), is now that of a commitment to the society of states. This second dimension involves the encouragement of international regulation, peaceful ways of settling disputes and the pursuit of international consensus politics (p. 29). Linklater suggests that this second dimension of international citizenship, in which citizenship rights are identified with state rights within an international society, increasingly tends towards the extension of the idea of citizenship rights within the international context to entities which are not states. Linklater quotes Bull's claim in *The Anarchical Society* that new kinds of political organisation at a sub-state and trans-state level may well come to undermine the state's claim to exclusive sovereignty and therefore its parallel claim to be the only legitimate international actor:

> This formulation encapsulates the idea that states should permit the development of multiple forms of citizenship: sub-national, national and trans-national in character. The proposition that they should permit the growth of sub-national and cosmopolitan loyalties which have previously been foreclosed is the third theme in good international citizenship (pp. 30–1).

The third dimension of good international citizenship is claimed to follow on from the second, and is what Linklater refers to as the universal moral principle of the right of self-determination (p. 33). This principle is associated with the cosmopolitan/universalist perspective and is designed to capture the idea of a moral imperative to respect the rights of other international citizens in the same way as a state should respect the rights of its own citizens. The third dimension of international citizenship would require the issue of the justifiability of privileging insiders above outsiders to be addressed and operates on the assumption that it can be addressed at a universalist level (p. 33).

It is in the introduction of an element of ethical universalism that Linklater's third dimension of international citizenship departs distinctively from the previous two dimensions. Although the universalist dimension is said to follow on from the international society dimension, the sense in which it does so does not explain the introduction of a universalist moral framework as a necessary corollary of the idea of good international citizenship. The logic of the link between the rationalist and universalist viewpoints appears to lie in the historical development of different political agencies within the international sphere. In itself, however, as Linklater acknowledges, these developments would not convince either realist or rationalist theorists of the viability of the idea of a cosmopolitan world order or a universalist ethical theory (p. 31). The explanation of Linklater's claim as to the significance of his third dimension of citizenship in fact takes us back to his initial analysis of the notion of citizenship in the domestic context and its problematic relation to both universal and particularistic rights claims. As indicated above Linklater sees traditional concepts of citizenship as caught between universal and particularistic legitimation. In his view it is the universalist dimension of citizenship rights which has been the catalyst for the extension of rights to excluded groups within the polity. It is in this context that Linklater introduces the question of the grounds of such universal rights claims and refers to the ways in which Beitz and Habermas invoke the idea of universal contract, consent or consensus as being at the root of moral thinking:

> Both theorists universalise ideas about consent and dialogue which are intrinsic to citizenship in the domestic domain, enlarge the meaning of citizenship by conferring rights of participation on every member of the species, and maintain that every individual is obliged to widen the sphere of moral responsibility to embrace the entire species (p. 32).

Linklater acknowledges that the kind of moral universalism involved in his third dimension of good international citizenship is as problematic in the international as in the domestic context. Just as the apparent fairness of legal status may mask real unfairness for citizens in the domestic context, so ethical universalism can be a guise for the imperialistic imposition of Western values on other cultures and communities (pp. 32–3). At the same time Linklater also acknowledges the pragmatic difficulties of actualising the idea of cosmopolitan citizenship within an international context which continues to be dominated by the interests of states and where the equality of the state-citizens who make up international society is still in question (pp. 34–5). He responds to both of these difficulties by turning in his conclusion to Kant's account of the three axes of citizenship in his essay on perpetual peace. In this essay Kant distinguished between the constitution of states, interstate law and the constitution of a cosmopolitan state. A different concept of citizenship can be correlated with each of these levels of political association, but they are linked together both by a particular conception of right and of historical development. In all of his political writings Kant operates with the idea of there being a dual spur to the development of state and interstate

relations. On the one hand politics is governed by the requirements of morality to make human behaviour consistent with the moral law. On the other hand
the means by which politics brings about consistency with the demands of
the moral law are through external coercive influences operating on human
fears and desires.[15] What connects the different axes of citizenship together
is both a claim that in reinforcing each other, each of the levels of political
association is ultimately fulfilling the requirements of the categorical imperative and a claim that history develops in the direction of the cosmopolitan
ideal through the manipulation of human self-interest:

> The central question which Kant's philosophical history sought to answer
> was whether the advancement of multiple citizenships – required by
> Reason itself – was likely to take place in practice. Kant doubted whether
> anything straight could ever be made out of anything as crooked as
> human nature; however, he believed that three developments in the
> modern world provided some optimism. These were the growth of inter-
> national commerce, the increasingly destructive role of modern economic
> warfare given economic interdependence, and the advance of moral
> consciousness.[16]

Immediately after the above quotation Linklater points to the fact that for
Kant the third of these reasons for hope is tied to the development of specific
kinds of states, what Kant termed 'republican' states. In Linklater's revision
of Kant's account of citizenship 'moral consciousness' comes to be seen as
advancing through the kind of collective learning processes which Habermas sees as driven by the logic of communication,[17] and Kant's 'republican'
regimes are identified with liberal democratic ones. Linklater points to Doyle's
work on the interrelation of liberal-democratic states as substantiating Kant's
point that there are certain kinds of state which will promote interstate cooperation and thereby forward the cosmopolitan/universalist dimension of
international citizenship.[18]

5. State-Citizens and Human-Citizens

At the beginning of this chapter I suggested that the idea of international
citizenship seems most obviously linked to two possibilities: the idea of the
state-citizen and the idea of the human-citizen. Linklater's discussion of the
idea of the good international citizen combines both of these possibilities in
the three dimensions he discusses, but particularly in the second and third
dimensions. The result of this is a concept of international citizenship which

is composed of two layers, an international society layer in which state-citizens interact, and a cosmopolitan layer in which human-citizens recognise each other's rights. Both of these layers are necessary according to Linklater. The first layer reflects the political actualities of an international realm in which states remain identified as the primary actors; the second layer incorporates the critical dimension of ideas of modern citizenship which enable claims to citizenship to function as a weapon in political struggles for the recognition of rights. Linklater acknowledges the tensions between the two layers in his discussion of the problems of striking a balance between universal and particularistic claims, but argues that this tension may be managed if not resolved through the development of the right kind of state-citizens. Although Linklater refers to the growth of non-state and non-individual international actors in his discussion of the ways in which international society is developing, his key reference points throughout the discussion remain states and individual humans.

There are two problems which I would argue are raised by Linklater's account. Firstly because the state-citizen is identified as the route through which the third dimension of international citizenship will be encouraged to emerge, international citizenship appears to depend on the idea of the state-citizen, with other notions of political identity and rights effectively only developing via the *permission* of the state. Secondly Linklater's analysis of the possibility of international citizenship at the level of the species rather than the state depends on reading history in terms of a story of moral evolution at the level of the state and on the viability of a universalist ethical discourse. I will now go on to examine why I see these two aspects of Linklater's argument as problematic and how one might reformulate the concept of international citizenship to take account of the difficulties I have identified.

It might seem that to tie the conception of the good international citizen to the state is a completely obvious and unproblematic move. After all it is states that are the most crucial international actors; and international law and international intervention work at the level of regulating state behaviour and involve the mutual acknowledgement of both state authority and its limitations – taking us into the vocabulary of rights and responsibilities which is central to accounts of modern citizenship – and it is not as if Linklater is denying the idea of sub- or trans-national political loyalties, rights and obligations. However in making the recognition of international citizenship beyond the idea of the state-citizen depend on the development of particular kinds of states, it seems to me that Linklater becomes committed to a dualism between states as specific, particular, self-interested actors and states as keepers of a collective moral conscience. Unless we can be sure that state-citizens can be identified with the latter as well as the former then it is unclear how the third dimension of international citizenship can develop. Moreover an account of international citizenship which relies in this way on the idea of the state-citizen risks both an oversimplification of the nature of the international realm and international political relations and the abstraction of the concept of citizenship from the question of political identity which has been so central to recent work on the idea of citizenship in the domestic context. It risks the former because, as much recent work in international relations has demonstrated, the international realm involves political actors who are neither states nor individuals. It risks the latter because the discussion of international citizenship becomes defined in top-down terms – a matter concerning the rights which the society of states will come to recognise because of their internal constitution (and because they are morally right), rather than one concerning the outcome of political struggles which mobilise the idea of membership of different kinds of collectivity in order to claim particular rights or identify particular duties for international actors.

If we accept Linklater's account of international citizenship then much depends on the link he (following Kant) establishes between liberal democratic states and ethical universalism. On Linklater's account it is precisely because of the element of ethical universalism at work in concepts of citizenship within the liberal polity that liberal polities will promote international citizenship in all of its dimensions. Linklater draws on Habermas's notion of the discursive validation of moral claims and the kind of 'moral learning' which is enabled through identification with the conditions of communicative action.[19]

In order to accept Linklater's account one needs to accept both the validity of universal ethical theory and the idea that historical development operates in accordance, at least partially, with the logic of communicative rationality. It is impossible to deal with the former fully in the context of this chapter but it is worth noting that the claims of ethical universalism have been subject to considerable attack in recent years, as Linklater himself notes, from communitarian, feminist and postmodern points of view. One of the central issues at stake in debates between universalist and contextualist ethical theory has been the difficulty of substantiating the grounds for universal ethical claims without invoking abstract and hypothetical criteria of moral judgment, an argument made by critics of Habermas among others.[20]

Even if a universalist moral theory can be defended, however, there is still the difficulty of tying the notion to the development of particular kinds of states within international society. Linklater acknowledges that the evidence is both complex and contradictory; the degree of what he calls 'moral openness and closure' between different states is difficult to judge, particularly since the language of universalism can itself mask purely prudential concerns. However Linklater sustains his claim by reference to two things: firstly the fact of the growth of international consensus within the society of states about the 'need to dismantle illegitimate forms of exclusion' in world politics;[21] and secondly the ways in which, in spite of the amoral nature of state intentions, the calculation of interests which underlies commercial and military activity itself results in increasing international interdependence and cooperation and challenges to existing patterns of inclusion and exclusion within the global context.[22] What remains uncertain in Linklater's analysis is the ways in which the latter point is connected to the former. Linklater embraces the Kantian paradox according to which moral progress is brought about by non-moral motivation in the political realm. However by doing this Linklater raises two related questions. Firstly can progress brought about through self-interest count as real progress in the moral sense? Secondly if moral progress can be brought about by non-moral means does one need the third dimension of international citizenship at all, or can one simply trust in the hidden hand of providence to bring about the cosmopolitan ideal?[23] Linklater's idea of international citizenship in all of its dimensions appears to have become uneasily balanced between pessimism and optimism about the possibility of moral progress.

6. A Multiplicity of Political Forms

It could be argued that all Linklater is doing is reflecting international polit-ical realities. Perhaps international citizenship is inevitably a poorer and weaker thing than domestic citizenship, offering some hope but no certainty of a future of international cooperation and equality of right. What I want to go on to argue, however, is that it is possible to take a different approach to thinking about international citizenship which is less reliant both on the citizen-state and on the idea of citizenship as intrinsically linked to a kind of universalism which is in perpetual tension with the acknowledgement of particularity.

In *The End of Sovereignty* Camilleri and Falk explore the ways in which contemporary world politics can no longer be adequately described in terms of the centrality of sovereign political authorities:

If they persist, the twin trends of globalization and its corollary, domestic fragmentation, are likely to weaken the conceptual and practical foun-dations of sovereignty: first, by challenging the notion that state authority is exercised exclusively or even primarily within clearly demarcated boundaries; secondly by calling into question the claim that within its territory the state's authority is unlimited and indivisible; thirdly by suggesting a growing disjunction between state and civil society, between political authority and economic organization, and between national identification and social cohesion.[24]

Although they do not dismiss the continuing significance of the state as an international actor, Camilleri and Falk stress the ways in which the state stands in an increasingly uneasy relation to a variety of other sub-state, inter-state and trans-state actors. They suggest that world politics may be moving towards the growing importance of global civil society as the context in which a complex of state, sub-state and trans-state authorities and allegiances overlap and conflict. They also suggest that in this context in which identities are multiply grounded, opportunities may arise for new emancipatory social and political movements which are neither confined to the state nor carried through by the state, in the sense that Linklater's good state-citizen carries the requirements of justice forward. This possibility is seen as derived in part from the failure of the state to protect national integrity in the face of a world market and the concomitant development of new forms of solidarity which bypass national identity:

> One possible consequence of such a disjuncture is a gradual transition to a new conception of civil society, a new polity cultivating a renewed sense of wholeness, with no clearly demarcated boundaries set by state territoriality or statist notions of national identity. Civil society may come to acquire a richer meaning grounded in the multiplicity of overlapping allegiances and jurisdictions where the traditional, the modern and the postmodern coexist, where local, regional and global space qualify the principle of nationality and redefine the context of community. The recovery of local and regional identities may encourage new expressions of autonomy and democratic practice and at the same time facilitate the emergence of a cosmopolitan global culture.[25]

Setting aside the viability of Camilleri and Falk's speculation about the future of international relations, I would like to focus on the difference between their account and Linklater's reading of history. Two things distinguish Camilleri and Falk's account: firstly they separate political identity and democratic practice from any necessary link with the nation state; secondly they make no claims about the operation of a dynamic of ethical universalism within the development of global political relations. As far as the former claim is concerned, Linklater also argues for a conception of international citizenship which would transcend state borders. However in Linklater's case this 'cosmopolitan' dimension to citizenship depends on the development of particular sorts of states which will legitimate broader conceptions of international citizenship. For Camilleri and Falk, on the other hand, the connection between conceptions of political identity/agency and the state, whatever its political complexion, is always contingent.

It could be argued at this point that Camilleri and Falk are actually concerned with notions of political identity/agency that are rather different from conceptions of citizenship. However, as the discussion of recent work in the theory of citizenship in the domestic context earlier in this chapter indicated, the idea of citizenship has always been inseparable from and dependent upon conceptions of political identity and agency both in principle and in practice. What Camilleri and Falk's analysis suggests is that one does not need to have reached a particular stage of development of citizen-states making up international society in order to actualise the promise of the cosmopolitan dimension of citizenship. Rather than the latter being incorporated in an ethical universalism which is latent in concepts of liberal-democratic citizenship, it becomes located in the actual interrelation and interaction of both individuals and collectives in what Camilleri and Falk refer to as this 'shrinking and fragmenting world'. Examples of international political citizenship on this account would not be confined to a series of achieved state or human rights correlated to obligations underwritten by international law. Rather attention would be focussed on the ways in which different political agents within the international arena struggle for the recognition of rights not only by international law or by particular states but by other entities such as transnational corporations or other individuals:[26]

> Effectively, transnational social movements scramble the distinction between national and international politics that grounds the Westphalian system. Their struggle, in short, may be viewed as an active and important refusal to live in a Hobbesian world, a refusal to suffer the consequences of a politics founded on fear, which, by definition, is a politics not of participation, but of resignation.[27]

For Linklater the ethical universalism involved in the third dimension of international citizenship is both necessarily linked to the state and necessary to counteract the particularity of state interest. What Thiele (quoted above) suggests is that the possibility of transcending the particularity of states may not need to rely on a universalist counterweight. Even prior to the achievement of a cosmopolitan ideal in history the everyday economic, environmental, moral and political interests of individuals, corporations, international organisations and states necessarily transcend borders in the contemporary world. If this is taken into account in the formulation of conceptions of international citizenship, then Linklater's vision of a bridge between domestic identity, international society and a community of mankind in a sense becomes something we always already have. If arguments about rights and responsibilities in a global context are to be articulated through the idea of international citizenship, then to root such an account in global actualities rather than transcendental principles makes it more difficult for international actors of all kinds to refuse to recognise mutual obligations on the grounds that the world remains too imperfect. At the same time the detachment of conceptions of international citizenship from over-reliance on the state-citizen reminds us that the benefits and dues of citizenship are always inseparable from the question of how citizens become identified as such and gain recognition within a given political arena.

7. Particularity and Universality

I have suggested that an account of international citizenship would be better off being oriented by the multiple political identities and agencies which operate in the international realm than by the transcendental promise latent in liberal-democratic models of citizenship. This immediately raises the question of whether I am not in effect repeating Linklater's move of positing a cosmopolitan direction to history, a move which I had earlier claimed to be problematic. Surely I am not claiming that we can rely on the implications of current world political developments to deliver an ideal world? It seems obvious not only that the world is not developing towards an ideal end of history but also that one aspect of responses of international actors to the growing interrelation of the world is a reassertion of particularistic solidarity through the medium of the nation state. Articulating global rights and responsibilities in relation to multiple particularistic identities might equally be seen simply as repeating the logic of realism, in which the increased complexity of international relations simply confirms the way in which international politics are always driven by the demands of agents' self-interest (prudentially understood). As Camilleri and Falk point out, globalisation and fragmentation are developing hand in hand. What this could be taken to imply is that more than ever a universalist impetus is needed to encourage identification of different entities with each other across very different kinds of boundaries, not all of which are coextensive with the state. What is at stake here is the status of the kind of discourse about international citizenship which I am suggesting may be more adequate than the one offered to us by

Linklater. I argued that Linklater's account was caught between pessimism on the one hand and optimism on the other when it came to assessing the future of international citizenship. Is this also going to be the fate of the alternative model I have begun to articulate?

In recent years debates in ethical theory have been marked by a logic of the mutual exclusiveness of particularity and universality. Arguments between liberal theorists and feminists, communitarians and postmodernists have centred around the divide between accounts of ethical judgment which claim a transcendent or universal basis and those which claim that such judgment can only be legitimated by reference to specific contexts or forms of life.[28] In the context of international relations the distinction between the specificity of states in the domestic sphere and their universal sameness in the international sphere, which is foundational for realism, complicates the effect of the particularity/universality dichotomy in relation to international ethico-political questions. It appears that in order to engage in critical moral and political judgment within the international sphere one must adopt a voice from nowhere, because the international is in principle unlocatable. Even for thinkers such as Linklater who would challenge the realist model a universalist moral dimension is necessary to counteract the particularity of state and local interest if ethical judgment is to be possible in a global context.

Any attempt therefore to discuss rights and responsibilities in a global context by reference to current global political relations needs to address the question of whether this is in effect to abandon the possibility of critical moral and political judgment in the contemporary world. Another way of posing this question is to ask whether there needs to be a latent moral universalism in the concept of citizenship to underwrite struggles to allocate global rights and responsibilities. It is at this point that I will call upon ideas in the work of Hegel and Foucault to argue that there may be ways of discussing international citizenship which do not return the theorist either to realist cynicism or cosmopolitan naivety. It is impossible to do more than sketch out what appears to me to be valuable in the ethical and political theorising of these thinkers, so I will confine myself to drawing attention to one aspect of Hegel's work and one of Foucault's. I will then return specifically to the idea of international citizenship.

In Hegel's work it his concept of 'ethical life' (*Sittlichkeit*) which suggests a useful way of thinking about ethics in an international context. Ethical life is the term Hegel uses to refer to the contexts of mutual recognition available within a given social formation. In the modern era he identifies the family, civil society and the state as the crucial elements in the constitution of ethical life. It is possible to read Hegel's conception as harking back to a Greek ideal, in which the citizen recognises himself within the social and legal order of the *polis*, and there are clearly 'civic republican' elements to Hegel's idea. However in the *Philosophy of Right* it is clearly not the case that ethical life is either simple or harmonious. Instead ethical life is constituted through a pattern of relative identities in which there are constant tensions between the different spheres of ethical life, and between the individual and the private, economic, social and legal relations in which he/she is caught.[29]

The conception of ethical life is not a moral ideal, it is an essentially descriptive term, in line with Hegel's restriction of political philosophy to consideration of what is rather than what ought to be. But this does not mean that the conception of ethical life is without evaluative implications. Hegel draws attention to the way in which within ethical life there are different kinds of potential for development. His task as a political philosopher, though, is to understand how those potentials arise and how they might develop, rather than to pass judgment on which ones are ethically acceptable and which are not. However to say that it is not the business of the moral or political theorist to pass judgment on different moral possibilities in a way that claims general validity is not to say that theorists should not or cannot pass judgment at all. As participants in ethical life theorists necessarily make moral judgments and decisions all the time. In passing such judgments, however, theorists are in the same position as any other international actor, a position which mediates the particular/universal distinction in the sense that the identity of the political judge and actor is neither static nor confined to any one particular sphere and is also one in which the possibilities of the present and the future meet. It is the specific task of the political theorist to articulate the ground of political judgment and action. But on Hegel's account this ground is not identifiable either with a set of universal criteria or with the resources of a particular way of life. Instead it is identified with the dynamism and complexity of actual patterns of recognition and lack of recognition within ethical life. On this account ethical and political judgment follow a logic of transcendence which does not require the notion of a transcendent obligation to drive it and which is unlikely to be unidirectional.

Like Hegel, Foucault is well known for his refusal to offer prescriptions for how people ought to live. However in his late work on ethics Foucault focussed his attention on the question of what ethics might mean if prescriptivism and universalism are both abandoned. Foucault's answer hinged on the idea of posing the question of identity: 'Maybe the target nowadays is not to discover what we are, but to refuse what we are.'[30] The context in which Foucault makes this suggestion is one in which he is discussing the simultaneous individualising and totalising effects of the construction of subjectivity in modern times. Foucault is fully aware of the complex processes through which subjective identity is constructed and rejects the invocation of any abstract essence or principle as a means through which identities might be transformed. Instead he draws attention to the concrete possibility of challenging given identities through political action by playing on the necessary double-sidedness of given limitation – the way in which limits articulate the idea of what one is not as well as what one is. Foucault argues that all limits are both constructed and reversible, and that recognition of limits is linked to the possibility of working on those limits, changing and transcending them. Refusing given identities is not a matter of theory but of practice.[31]

What I would suggest is that while Hegel's account of ethical life reminds us of the way in which both limitation and transcendence are built into our situation as international actors and judges, Foucault's notion of ethics as self-creation can help us to understand how international actors can be international citizens without invoking either a transcendental ideal or a philosophy of history. As Linklater acknowledges, the history of citizenship in the domestic sphere is one in which new kinds of recognition are fought for by different individuals and communities. These struggles centre around the possibility of redefining the given constraints on who is to count as a political actor with acknowledged rights and responsibilities in the public realm. The rewriting of given identities is what underlies the possibility of actual citizenship. Good citizenship is less a matter of living up to certain ideals once you have been admitted to the public realm, than of the fight for recognition in which your identity as a subject is constructed. Camilleri, Falk and Thiele draw attention to the role of new social movements in world politics. In these kinds of movements individuals and collectivities do not ask admission to the circle of international citizenship, they assert and fight for their claim to be already within that circle – a claim which is crucially substantiated by reference back to the ways in which different individual and collective identities are also always internationally mediated.

8. Conclusion

Whilst I recognise that the above claims are extremely sketchy, I would argue that the approach to thinking about international ethical and political issues, which I suggest is implicit in the work of Hegel and Foucault, is very much in line with some of the more worked out arguments in recent literature on citizenship in the domestic context (for instance the arguments of Turner, McClure and Walzer mentioned above). If we are to think about the idea of international citizenship we need to do so in a way that reflects the fact that we inhabit neither an anarchic state of nature in the international sphere nor an ideal end of history. It is this actuality which Linklater acknowledges in his invocation of different dimensions and axes to modern international citizenship. I have argued that the way between realist pessimism and cosmopolitan optimism which Linklater follows tends to repeat rather than resolve the problem of choosing between these two options, but nevertheless it is undoubtedly right to argue that we are unlikely to progress in thinking about ethical issues in an international context unless the terms of this choice are transcended.

Notes and References

1 A. Linklater, 'What is a Good International Citizen?', in P. Keal (ed.), *Ethics and Foreign Policy* (St Leonards, NSW: Allen and Unwin, 1992). It should be noted that Linklater's essay was written in the context of a discussion of Australia's role as an international citizen and that the emphasis on the state within this essay is not necessarily representative of Linklater's approach to international relations in other examples of his work.

2 This is exemplified in Mouffe's discussion of debates about citizenship in C. Mouffe (ed.), *Dimensions of Radical Democracy: Pluralism, Citizenship, Community* (London: Verso, 1992), pp. 4–6; see also R. Norman, 'Citizenship, Politics and Autonomy' and R. Plan, 'Citizenship and Rights', in D. Milligan and W. W. Miller (eds), *Liberalism, Citizenship and Autonomy* (Aldershot: Avebury, 1992).

3 For a discussion of Marshall's account of citizenship see B. Turner, 'Outline of a Theory of Citizenship', in Mouffe (ed.), *Dimensions of Radical Democracy*, pp. 34–40.

4 See C. Mouffe, 'Democratic Citizenship and the Political Community', in Mouffe (ed.), *Dimensions of Radical Democracy*, pp. 226–8.

5 The argument that modern conceptions of citizenship in terms of entitlement have encouraged political passivity and discouraged civic responsibility is one which has been taken up from very different points of the political spectrum. See T. Skillen, 'Active Citizenship as Political Obligation', *Radical Philosophy*, 58 (1991), pp. 10–13.

6 Turner, 'Outline of a Theory of Citizenship', p. 34.

7 This is a recurring theme in recent scholarship, see, for example, Norman, 'Citizenship, Politics and Autonomy' and M. Walzer, 'The Civil Society Argument', in Mouffe (ed.) *Dimensions of Radical Democracy*.

8 Norman, 'Citizenship, Politics and Autonomy', p. 39.

9   Walzer, 'The Civil Society Argument', p. 107.

10   K. McClure, 'On the Subject of Rights: Pluralism, Plurality and Political Identity', in Mouffe (ed.) *Dimensions of Radical Democracy*.

11   Linklater, 'What is a Good International Citizen?', p. 22.

12   Linklater, 'What is a Good International Citizen?', pp. 26–7.

13   Linklater, 'What is a Good International Citizen?', p. 36.

14   Linklater discusses these three traditions at greater length in his book, *Beyond Realism and Marxism: Critical Theory and International Relations* (London: Macmillan, 1990).

15   For a more detailed account of Kantian political theory see K. Hutchings, 'The Possibility of Judgement: Moralizing and Theorizing in International Relations', *Review of International Studies*, 18 (1992) 51–62.

16   Linklater, 'What is a Good International Citizen?', p. 36.

17   For an account of Habermas's ethical theory, see J. Habermas, *Moral Consciousness and Communicative Action* (Cambridge: Polity Press, 1990). Another example of the way Linklater uses Habermas's idea of communicative ethics can be found in A. Linklater, 'The Question of the Next Stage in International Relations Theory', *Millennium*, 21 (1992) 77–100.

18   Linklater, 'What is a Good International Citizen?', p. 38; M. Doyle, 'Liberalism and International Relations', in R. Beiner and W. J. Booth (eds), *Kant and Political Philosophy* (New Haven, Conn.: Yale University Press, 1993).

19   Linklater, 'What is a Good International Citizen?', p. 35.

20   This point is made very clearly by Benhabib in her discussions of contemporary debate in ethical theory, see S. Benhabib, *Situating the Self: Gender, Community and Postmodernism in Contemporary Ethics* (Cambridge: Polity Press, 1992).

21   Linklater, 'What is a Good International Citizen?', p. 35.

22   Linklater, 'What is a Good International Citizen?', p. 37.

23   I. Kant, 'Perpetual Peace: A Philosophical Sketch', in H. Reiss (ed.), *Kant's Political Writings* (Cambridge: Cambridge University Press, 1970), p. 108.

24   J. A. Camilleri and J. Falk, *The End of Sovereignty?* (Aldershot: Edward Elgar, 1992), pp. 254–5.

25   Camilleri and Falk, *The End of Sovereignty?*, p. 255.

26   On this account it would become possible to think of international citizenship as involving 'horizontal' as well as 'vertical' dimensions. In other words international citizenship would be conceived as a complex web of entitlements and obligations, which would hold between

different non-state actors as well as between non-state actors and states and between both of the latter and international law.

27 L. P. Thiele, 'Making Democracy Safe for the World: Social Movements and Global Politics', *Alternatives*, 18 (1993) p. 278.

28 See Benhabib's formulation of the problems posed for ethical universalism by communitarian, feminist and postmodern arguments: Benhabib, *Situating the Self*, p. 3.

29 G. W. F. Hegel, *Elements of the Philosophy of Right* (Cambridge: Cambridge University Press, 1991), pp. 189–198.

30 M. Foucault, 'The Subject and Power', in H. L. Dreyfus and P. Rabinow (eds), *Michel Foucault: Beyond Structuralism and Hermeneutics* (Hemel Hempstead: Harvester, 1982), p. 216.

31 The examples Foucault draws on to illustrate transcendence of given identities include feminism and the anti-psychiatry movement; see Foucault, 'The Subject and Power', pp. 211–12.

7

Democratic Theory and the Problem of Global Warming

Barry Holden*

1. Introduction

One of the key areas of global change, involving associated changes both in the physical world and in ideas and practices, is in the field of the environment. This topic is taken up in the chapters in this volume by Dark and by Paterson; and Paterson in particular shows how what is perhaps the most critical set of (actual and postulated) changes in this field – those relating to global warming – have an important ethical dimension. In this chapter some other changes will be discussed which link up with those associated with the global warming problem. Here again there is an ethical dimension that is of importance, partly linked to that discussed by Paterson.

The problem of global warming[1] – or, more precisely, the problem of responding to the threat of global warming – clearly involves deep-seated moral, conceptual and practical difficulties concerning the possibility and desirability of effective global action.[2] Understanding these difficulties and acting to overcome them is both assisted and complicated by changes in the nature of the international order. At the same time there are developments in democratic thought and practice that have considerable interconnections with these changes. And an aim of this essay is to point towards an analysis of how such developments might be related directly to the global warming problem (the analysis itself must await another occasion).

Such an analysis will involve consideration, on the one hand, of the extent to which developing and nascent democratic ideas and practices might contribute to overcoming difficulties in responding to global warming; and, on the other hand, of the ways in which the need to overcome the difficulties might in turn stimulate and sharpen theoretical analysis and contribute to the development of democratic ideas and practices. But also involved is the general issue of the relative merits of democratic and non-democratic responses to environmental problems. And one of the aims of the eventual analysis will be to assess the extent to which consideration of the global warming problem can support the case for a democratic response.

2. Democracy and Environmental Problems

Let us begin with a glance at this general issue of the suitability or desirability of democracy for tackling environmental problems. There is a line of thought according to which environmental problems can only be solved, if at all, by non-democratic means. To an extent this is a manifestation of traditional anti-democratic strictures concerning the selfishness and irrationality of the mass of people and/or their general inability to know what is good for them. But there can also be more particular arguments. Some anti-democratic strands in green political thought have focussed on the non-viability of democratic political responses to environmental problems because of the sheer urgency of the need for action and because these problems so often involve prisoners' dilemma-type situations which can be especially intractable. When there is added to this the environmentalists' account of the indisputable rightness of, and absolute necessity for, particular solutions to environmental problems then there can be generated a rationale for authoritarian action or, at least, a stance that is in fundamental conflict or tension with democracy.[3] However the dominant trend in green political thought is pro-democratic; indeed it is ideas of participatory democracy that are most commonly embraced.[4] And this espousal of democracy is certainly entering into responses to global warming: Agenda 21 (one of the 1992 'Earth Summit' agreements) 'is strongly oriented towards "bottom up", participatory and community-based approaches'.[5] Nonetheless the issues remain, and the case for democracy still needs to be argued. Establishing the merits of a democratic response to the global warming problem could be a crucial part of such an argument. This is partly because global warming can be seen as the most fundamental and important of environmental problems. But it is also because it may be regarded as the least amenable to attempts at a 'democratic solution': if democracy can work here it can work anywhere.

3. Democracy and the International Realm

This perception of the especial unsuitability of democracy is partly a matter of the especial scale and complexity of the problem. But there appears to be another, and overlapping, basic difficulty: whilst combating global warming must be a matter for action which is global, and therefore international, it appears that democracy only occurs *within* states. Only the actions *of* a (democratic) state can be democratic, not the interactions *amongst* states: democracy is unsuitable because it cannot be applied.

However all is not necessarily what it seems. In fact for various reasons the traditional idea of democracy as only an intrastate phenomenon is being undermined and new thinking is called for. Indeed there is something of a conjuncture of significant developments here.

The source for one set of such developments actually stems from the status now achieved by democracy as traditionally understood, that is democracy within the state. Recent dramatic events have involved what has been seen as the 'triumph' of liberal democracy. This view has been criticised, but whether or not one should talk of a 'triumph' it is difficult to deny the extent to which the *idea* of democracy – the idea that democracy is the best form of government – is now unchallenged.[6] Indeed it is arguable that the international pre-eminence of the idea of democracy has been established and that it is now being reflected in the development of an international norm of democracy, manifested, for example, in an 'emerging right to democratic governance'.[7]

It is, however, nascent further developments, both of this international norm and developments associated with it, that are of especial interest here. It is arguable that the 'triumph' of democratic notions 'may well prove to be … the fulcrum on which the future development of global society will turn.'[8] The key point is the way in which the international pre-eminence of 'intra-state democracy' (democracy as traditionally understood) is now beginning to flow over into international norms and practices – which later may become established processes and structures. That is to say the democratic idea, because of its primacy *within* states, is now beginning to extend and to develop an important role in the structure of the environment within which states operate. The pre-eminence of the traditional form of the democratic idea within components of the international order is contributing to the democratic idea becoming incorporated within that order itself.

On one understanding, and in one of the forms it might take, such a process is simply one of democratisation of broadly the existing international system. This – for some the only possible – interpretation will be referred to later. However there are crucial difficulties in giving an account of what 'democracy' and 'democratisation' can mean under this interpretation. There remains a key conceptual disjunction between states themselves and the system within which they operate; and because of this – and because democracy has hitherto been understood as a form of *state* – it is difficult to know what 'democratisation' of the *international system* can mean. Moreover there are developments, to be discussed below, which may be generating an outcome which is more complex and which involves changes that are more extensive. Understanding these changes can lead to a new interpretation of the idea of the democratisation of the international realm. On this interpretation there are, or may be, developing changes to democracy and to the international order that prefigure a democratic 'international' realm that is importantly different from the existing international system. It is not so much a case of democratisation of an international system distinct from the states which are its components – a process additional and different to the democratisation of those states – as the prefiguration of a new democratic realm subsuming democratic states. Thus, for example, a recent essay sees in the spread of democracy an unmistakable 'long-term trend ... towards the sovereignty of an embryonic world public.'[9] However this is to anticipate; and it is also to oversimplify since, as we shall see, this is not the only way in which a new democratic realm can be seen as developing.

4. Cosmopolitan Democracy

It can be argued, then, that we may be witnessing the beginnings of a trans-mogrification of democracy from an intrastate to an interstate phenomenon. (This convenient way of putting it is actually rather misleadingly rooted in the *status quo* since the kind of democratic realm indicated above in fact involves a dislocation of the states-system.) But *how* can there be such a change? As already indicated there is a conjuncture of factors; and to answer this question we must look at further developments fuelling this potential transmogrification.

There is both an empirical and conceptual dimension to these further developments and they require, and are already beginning to involve, some fundamental rethinking of the nature of democracy. Already there is developing a theory of 'cosmopolitan democracy'.[10] To sum this up, one could say that the core idea of democracy, rule by the people, needs – and is starting – to be rethought because of changes in the world that may be rendering obsolete received notions of 'rule' and 'the people'. The traditional idea of democracy centres on the state. The state gives content to 'rule by the people'. It does this by specifying 'rule' as 'that which is done by the state', 'the people' as 'those who are citizens of the state' and accordingly 'rule by the people' as 'control of the state by its citizens'. Now changes are afoot that are undermining this account.[11] For various reasons states are becoming less pivotal. We shall be commenting on this 'top-down' change below, but the key point here is that 'rule' is perhaps ceasing to be confined to what is done by states.[12] And who constitutes 'the people' is ceasing to be specified only by citizenship of a state.

To some extent this latter is a separate, 'bottom-up', development, and it is to this that we shall turn first.

The Idea of 'The People'

It could be said that there has always been a hiatus in democratic theory when it comes to specifying 'the people'. As just indicated, under the traditional view the specification is supplied by the idea of the state. However the rationale for this has been assumed rather than made explicit (and of course it is precisely such a rationale that is now at issue here). In fact it can be said that until now the problem of the rationale has been beyond the province of democratic theory. It has been seen as 'insoluble within the framework of democratic theory'.[13] And the 'solution' has been supplied 'from without' by presuppositions about the world supplied by nationalism and the prevailing states-system. 'The "sovereign people" came to be identified with the nation'[14] and 'until recently, at least,' liberal democratic theory has 'accepted as a given a world divided into nation-states'.[15] But it is now being asked whether, in a changing world, this is any longer 'the given'. There is both a questioning of the presumed coincidence of existing nations and states and some dissolution of the division of the world into watertight compartments. There are important interrelationships, but broadly we can say there are two sorts of reasons for this. Changes in the international system are the top-down reasons. But first we shall focus on bottom-up reasons: the emerging salience of other bases for specifying 'the people'.

There are, in fact, two somewhat contradictory developments here. The first is the resurgence of disruptive nationalism – disruptive, that is, of established states (civic nationalism is not by nature disruptive in this way but the current resurgence involves mainly ethnic nationalism). From Quebec to the Balkans and the former the Soviet Union nationalisms are threatening – or have already caused – the undermining of established states. In other cases (Northern Ireland, for example) nationalism has been a cause of bitter dispute about the territories of states. These are all instances of (or disputes concerning) the delineating of a state by reference to an antecendently specified people, in contradistinction to the specifying of a people as those who are citizens of a state. It is not the prioritising of peoples to states that is new[16] but its current salience, and the corrosive force of its validity being freshly reasserted against what, according to the established conception, already are nation states. This established conception had bred the idea that states *are* nation states, which had obscured the potential difference between specification of a people by reference to the nation and specification by reference to the state. Exposing the difference sunders the tight connection between the state and the definition of the people, thereby highlighting non-state conceptions of the people. The importance of such non-state conceptions is further reinforced by the decreasing saliency of states themselves, the top-down factor discussed below.

The second development is the growing significance of the idea that the 'logic' of democracy points to the desirability of governmental decision-makers being accountable to all those affected by their decisions. We may call this the 'all-affected' principle. As Whelan[17] points out this principle has frequently been supported by recent democratic theorists, and May[18] actually builds this into his definition of democracy, so that 'rule by the people' becomes 'necessary correspondence' between governmental acts and the wishes of 'the persons who are affected by' them.

Now, it is claimed there are crucial difficulties with this idea.[19] One such difficulty, it can be argued, is that the theory and practice of democracy assume and require the specification of a single entity or collection of individuals as 'the people' rather than the marking off of varying sets of individuals who happen to be affected by the acts of a particular government. An associated difficulty is that of deciding in what ways and to what degree individuals need to be affected to qualify as being members of 'the people'. (In the traditional conception this difficulty would appear not to arise precisely because 'the people' is specified without explicit reference to individuals being affected by governmental decisions. But this may be misleading: an individual's membership of a state, for instance, is such an important matter in large part *because* this means he is subject to the decisions of the state's government.) Very important issues are raised by these claims, aspects of which are taken up below but which cannot be fully discussed in this essay. In particular the issue of the way in, and degree to, which individuals are affected raises some fundamental questions which cannot be properly addressed here. Suffice it to say that in answering them John Burnheim's account of 'legitimate material interests' and his critique of the usual notions of the common good would provide much illumination.[20]

The importance of these issues may, indeed, provide a stimulant for fresh thinking and support for the all-affected principle. Indeed some of the 'difficulties' may be seen, in the present context, as ideas that are fruitful and illuminating. The point is that one of the main 'difficulties' discerned is the fact that the decisions of the governments of particular – especially the more powerful – states clearly affect persons beyond the boundaries of that state. And this is not just a reference to the field of foreign policy where, by definition, the actions of the government of one state affect other states and persons within them.[21] Perhaps more important is that what are regarded as the domestic actions of a government can also crucially affect those outside its state. (Again there is an interconnection with top-down factors: this is also an aspect of the increasing interdependence that is considered below.) Sometimes the non-domestic effects are specific and direct, as in the trans-boundary environmental effects of domestic governmental policy – such as acid rain in other countries caused by a government's policies on power generation. In other cases the effects are more general and diffuse: for example actions of the American President and Congress in the field of domestic economic policy can have profound effects on the economies of other countries and, indeed, the global economy. But in all these cases the important point is that the 'all-affected' principle brings in persons *outside* the state of the government in question and thereby includes them amongst those to whom that government should be accountable. And it is this that is seen as the crucial difficulty with the principle: indeed it is seen as an absurdity. However a key ingredient of this absurdity verdict is the presupposition that there already exists a self-evidently and uniquely valid delimitation of those to whom a government should be accountable, that is to say 'the people', as traditionally understood.[22] But of course precisely what is at issue here is the validity of this traditional notion of 'the people': and arguably a crucial weakness of the notion is that it no longer captures the realities of who is importantly affected by acts of governments!

There are, then, four important aspects of the 'all-affected' idea of democracy that emerge from the argument of the previous two paragraphs. First there is the notion of control by an 'extended' people. This involves both extending[23] (to all those that are affected) the range and number of persons that it is relevant to consider in relation to the acts of a government and maintaining that these persons, like 'the people' of orthodox democratic theory, should control[24] that government. Second there is the notion of multiple populations: rather than the single entity or collection of persons that constitute the people of orthodox democratic theory we have the varying sets of persons who are affected by the various different acts of government. In these two notions, then, we have the translation of the central idea captured in the traditional conception of 'rule by the people': it is translated into the conception of 'control of governmental activity by the various sets of persons affected by that activity'.

It is worth noting that there are some connections here with the work of Burnheim and Hirst.[25] They have developed important unorthodox analyses of democracy, a key feature of which is a rupturing or modification of the link between democracy and the state. We shall remark on aspects of this below but here we should note the dissolution or modification of orthodox ideas of 'rule by the people'. Instead of a traditional notion of rule by 'a people' Burnheim substitutes fragmented decision making by those whose interests are affected,[26] whilst Hirst focusses on dispersed governance by a pluralised civil society.

What we have then is an emerging conception of who should control acts of government. And this leads us to the third aspect of the all-affected idea – that it involves a revision of, rather than an alternative to, the concept of the people. It is true a contrast has just been drawn between the notion of differing populations and that of the 'single' people of orthodox democratic theory. However the fact that *the* central democratic value – mass control of governmental activity – is re-embodied in this emerging conception gives it a definitive importance such that it can be said to re-define 'the people'. The question of who constitutes 'the people' comes to be answered by reference to a fresh specification of which sections of the masses should do the controlling.

This brings us to the fourth, and most important, aspect of the all-affected idea of democracy: the notion of a spread beyond state boundaries. Under the redefinition, the people spread beyond state boundaries (but see also note 23). And crucially, as already indicated, rather than a difficulty it can be seen as a feature of the all-affected idea that it posits control of a government's activities by populations that include those outside the boundaries of the state in which the government is located.[27] This notion, to the extent that it becomes influential, will in turn downgrade the importance of those boundaries and hence the importance of the state itself. And this will reinforce, and be reinforced by, the changes in the international system to be referred to in a moment.

The developments relating to disruptive nationalism and to the all-affected idea of democracy clearly suggest, then, that important new ideas about the nature of 'the people' may be emerging. As noted earlier the two types of development are in some ways contradictory, since nationalism stresses the importance of communal entities in contradistinction to the all-affected idea's focus on diverse sets of individuals – this point will be taken up below. Nonetheless both converge on the undermining of the traditional state-specification of 'the people'.

Globalisation and Interdependence

The above are the key 'bottom-up' reasons for a questioning and undermining of traditional state-centred identifications of the sovereign people of democratic theory. But, as already remarked, there is interaction and mutual reinforcement between these and important 'top-down' reasons. These latter, of course, concern changes in the nature of the international system that are summed up by the terms 'interdependence' and 'globalisation',[28] various dimensions which are of central importance for the cosmopolitan democracy argument.

The first point to note is the way in which emergent and possible dilutions of the states-system complement, reinforce and are reinforced by the factors disruptive of the traditional notion of 'the people' just discussed. The central point here is the extent to which processes of interdependence and globalisation potentially involve the diminution of state autonomy and perhaps, in the long run, the undermining of state sovereignty. Clearly such developments dilute the importance of the state and, besides any wider implications, by subverting a key part of its *raison d' être* the traditional state specification of the people is further undermined. This is because (a) the idea of states as constituting *the* key divisions of humanity is challenged and (b) the role of the state as *the* agency for action is compromised. In other words what is subverted is the notion that the state is uniquely the means whereby a people is (a) constituted and (b) enabled to act. (Because it derives from factors in the external environment of states this amounts to an external critique of the idea of the state as the instrument of the people's will. Our concern here is in fact with such a critique but there is naturally an overlap between external and internal critiques.)[29]

Let us focus for a moment on the compromising of the role of the state as *the* agency for action. The processes of interdependence and globalisation are diminishing, sometimes drastically, the extent to which states are effective agencies of control. This is most evident – and most often commented upon – in respect of the global economy where states are becoming increasingly enmeshed in, rather than in control of, events and processes.[30] But it is true of other fields too. Of especial relevance in the present context, of course, are environmental problems although here 'interdependence' and 'globalisation' apply to the situations, rather than to the processes, in which states find themselves, and to the nature of the problems producing those situations.[31] Here the failure of states to be effective agencies of control derives from an inability to act singly, together with an incapacity for acting collectively, to deal with trans-boundary problems. As John Dunn puts it (after suggesting the threat to the welfare state from the global economy is the central challenge to the viability of the state):

A less immediate, but potentially more profound, threat to state viability is already beginning to arise from the challenges of environmental degradation. In the sphere of economics the threat to the political standing of the nation state comes essentially from the tension between a national framework of sovereign authority and an uncompromisingly international field of economic causality. In the sphere of ecology, the national framework of sovereign power and governmental responsibility is also in some tension with ecological causality. (Acid rain, the ozone layer, still more global warming, are no respecters of boundaries.) But the principal residual obstacle to effective action in the face of ecological hazard ... is ... a difficulty in [governments] cooperating effectively. Their problem ... is not a deficiency in domestic power but a disinclination or incapacity for collective action.[32]

The central point that arises from this is that the erosion of states' capacity for control means an erosion of the capacity for popular control, as this has formerly been conceived by democrats. (The reference is, of course, only to what are seen as *democratic* states; but it is these that are the subject of this analysis and our question here concerns the relationship between these and potential cosmopolitan forms of democracy. In any case the establishment of an international norm of democracy means, in effect, that the democratic state has become the archetype.) To the extent that there has been this diminution of control by states, the masses are unable to control events via states. If there are events, processes and problems that transcend states and that require popular control then there must be means of popular control that transcend states.

Popular Control in an Interdependent World

This positing of the need for new modes of popular control suggests three questions. First there is the fundamental question of why in fact the issue of popular control should be raised at all – why should control by the masses of these kinds of events and processes be desirable? We shall return to this question later. Second, supposing popular control of this kind is desirable and possible how does this relate to orthodox democratic theory: how does it relate to traditional conceptions of 'rule by the people'? This is partly a question about the idea of 'the people' but it is also about modes of control; and here there is an overlap into the third question – how might popular control of this kind be achieved?

Let us turn to the second question. Part of what is at issue here is the viability of the alternative conceptions of the people thrown up by the undermining of traditional conceptions. How satisfactory are the principles generating the alternative conceptions that we have just been discussing?

Currently the national identity principle is prominent. Its salience may increase; and if it does it will undermine the globalising trends presupposed by the argument of this essay. On the other hand it may well be undermined by precisely such trends. An aspect of this is the fact that it falls foul of the all-affected principle; and, since the growing importance of this latter principle is a presupposition of this essay the national identity principle will not be further considered. (This is not to deny that the presuppositions *might* be wrong; nor is it to deny the contribution already made by the national identity principle to undermining the traditional conception of the people.)

The national identity principle, however, has a crucial ingredient apparently lacking in the all-affected principle, which seems deficient because it appears that no communal identity is postulated amongst sets persons who happen to be affected. Communal identity is crucial because it converts a mere collection of dissociated individuals into what a people as conceived by any notion of democracy must be – a group in which those individuals are supplied with a rationale and motivation for collective action.[33] There is a need, then, to combine the all-affected principle with some kind of communal identity criterion to obtain a satisfactory account of 'the people'.

Before we look at this, however, there is an additional complicating factor to consider. This in fact relates to the diminution of control by states that has just been discussed. In our consideration above of the all-affected principle it was assumed that it was simply to acts of governments that accounts of the people needed to be related. Arguably, however, the logic of the principle implies that accounts need to be related to more than this: we have just seen that there is the need to provide popular control of events and processes that are beyond the control of single states and this seems to imply an account according to which 'the people' ought to contain those who should be included in this popular control. The all-affected principle surely implies that those included should be persons affected by the events and processes in question, besides those affected by acts of governments. (In their effect on people such events and processes are as important as acts of government; moreover part of what is implied by a concern with their being beyond the control of governments is precisely that they should nonetheless be controllable by those who are affected by them.) The all-affected principle now brings in even wider spreads of persons, since 'events and processes beyond the control of single states' often cover wider areas than simply the 'acts of government' of the previous interpretation (the question of *how* the wider people, once identified, can have control of matters that are beyond the control of states will be taken up below).

'International' and 'Global' Conceptions of the People

Let us now return to the underlying question of formulating a satisfactory account of the people. The question concerns the possibility of identifying as communities, in some sense, the wide spreads of 'affected persons'. And here there are two broad approaches, although they can overlap. One, which will be referred to in a moment, in a sense retains a key aspect of the sense of community in traditional conceptions of the people – the notion that a community embraces a fixed, territorially delimited set of individuals and potentially incorporates any of their concerns and activities. The other recognises the ways in which there can be communities including diverse and varying sets of individuals, which are identified by criteria other than territory and which incorporate only certain of their members' concerns and activities. There are two issues here. First there is the general question of whether and how any such sets of individuals can be constituted as communities. On this Burnheim is again illuminating with his account of how people could be seen as 'being part of many diverse social activities and functional communities rather than any simple inclusive community.'[34] Second there is this question as it arises in an international context, where identifying communities by criteria other than territory means indentifying communities that are unconfined by – that spread beyond – states.[35] But given the previous argument about the decreased importance of states there is perhaps little substantial difference between this and the first question. In any case possible answers continue the same theme, focussing on the communal potential of persons having the shared situation of being affected by the same acts, events and processes: the common factor of 'being affected' can itself be important in relating persons together as a community. Certainly modern communications can readily bring affected persons into mutual awareness of each other's existence and their common condition. Moreover activity in response to this condition can itself involve concrete communal organisation and a further strengthening of communal identity. This is well illustrated in key aspects of the nature and activity of the 'new social movements'.[36] Arguably, then, the designation by the all-affected principle of varying sets of persons widely spread and unconfined by state boundaries is compatible with those sets constituting communities. Hence a viable conception of varying 'peoples' is generated. Let us call this the 'international conception' of a people.

The second approach to identifying a wide spread of persons as a community takes up the old theme of the community of mankind.[37] This seeks to envisage the whole human race as 'the people', with a focus on 'the sovereignty of the embryonic world public' (Mulgan's remark quoted in Section 3 above), or at least the postulation of 'universal sovereignty' as the key democratic principle.[38] Such a universal community would of necessity comprehend all those affected. Let us call this the 'global conception' of the people.

The two conceptions of the people can overlap or merge as in some cases the spread of people conceived as affected becomes very general and the first approach merges into the second. Short of this, though, there remain two approaches with important differences between them. Some might argue that the first is untenable and that it is in the second that we find the only logical alternative to the territorial communities that are nation states. And from the point of view of the problem of responding to global warming it may be that the notion of a global people has the most significance. However – apart from the previous arguments concerning the all-affected principle – the view that non-state conceptions must necessarily be global can be powerfully challenged, as Hutchings shows in her critique of the view that there is a simple dichotomy between the local particularity of domestic citizenship and the universalism of global citizenship (see her chapter in this volume). Hutchings's critique, and the arguments of Camilleri and Falk already referred to, suggest that there are, indeed, types of community that can give us viable international but non-global conceptions of 'the people'. And such conceptions may well be more realistic than the idea of a global people, which seems 'a long way removed from the actualities of global political life' as Hutchings puts it. It may be, then, that whilst still transcending the states-system the international conception is of more practical significance than the global conception of the people.

Whatever their respective merits, however, it does seem that there are emerging supra-state conceptions of the people. It will not be our concern here to assess them so much as to note the significance of their existence and possible validity. But to do this we must complete the picture by following through to our third question suggested above: what modes of control are available for peoples so conceived? What mechanism(s), other than states, can there be for rule by an international or global people? These are large questions and here we can only briefly point to possible kinds of answers. There are two broad approaches complementing respectively the international and the global conceptions of the people, though again there is an overlap.

Modes of International and Global Popular Control
To discern potential modes of popular control one can focus on the (actual and potential) existence of a variety of supra-state mechanisms or organisations which aim to regulate international events and processes. At the moment these essentially involve and apply to states rather than to people; and this can raise an issue about the meaning of cosmopolitan democracy

which is taken up below in the discussion of the United Nations. Nonetheless we shall see that in some cases there is already a reference beyond states, and it is arguable that there is the potential for the development of connections directly with, and ultimately control by, the people affected by the regulatory efforts of these organisations. (Another, more radical, approach to instruments of international popular control is developed by Burnheim who gives us a vision of the non-governmental mechanisms that could exist after the dissolution of the states-system:[39] he builds on his non-state theory of 'demarchy'[40] and applies it explicitly to global dimensions. But here this somewhat utopian analysis will be to left on one side.)

The organisations roughly divide into those that have a general remit and which are global in scope, and those that have a particular remit and which involve only some states. The distinctiveness of the latter category, however, is blurred since it contains some organisations involving very many states and/or whose regulatory function has general application. The first category essentially includes one institution, the United Nations, to which we shall return below. Perhaps of most importance in the second category here are the various systems of supra-state international regulation which are referred to as international regimes.

An approach to possible modes popular control that focussed on international regimes is one which could complement the international conception of the people. The importance of regimes as regulatory systems has, of course, increasingly been stressed.[41] And regimes could have the potential to become instruments of control in the hands of international peoples. (It is also conceivable that as regimes become more important they could help to *constitute* international peoples: the shared situation of being affected by the actions of, and the desire to have some control over, a regime might help to integrate those affected into a people). At present regimes are typically controlled by, or accountable to, assemblies of affected states, so notions of 'democratic' control can get no further than control by an assembly in which *states* are equally represented – which raises the issue concerning the meaning of cosmopolitan democracy mentioned above. But there could develop the notion of control by, or at least accountability to, international *peoples*. Something of this kind is already developing, although since this is in respect of organisations whose categorisation is blurred the potential popular control overlaps from 'international' into 'global'.[42] At this point it is difficult to say what the processes of such control or accountability would amount to but it is worth noting some suggestions already made in a slightly different context, but which could be even better applied to international regimes. Held, for example, mentions 'the possibility of general referenda of groups cutting across nations and nation-states ... with constituencies defined according to the nature and scope of controversial transnational issues.'[43] And Brown, after invoking the principle that 'those whose behavior substantially affects the well-being of others are accountable to the affected', argues:

> At a minimum, the principle [applied in the international realm] would require that potentially victimized populations at least be consulted by those whose actions might cause them major harm. At a maximum, the substantially affected would be provided with a veto over actions they did not like. The international procedural and structural embodiments of such accountability obligations are potentially far-reaching, highly controversial, and will be extraordinarily difficult to negotiate in some fields, especially where the affected populations demand not merely a fair opportunity to express their view but also seats and voting power at the principal tables of decision.[44]

Besides possible formal or semi-formal systems of popular control and/or accountability one should not forget the importance of processes of popular influence. Just as within states pressure groups can be important influences on governmental action so in the international realm non-governmental organisations (NGOs) are becoming increasingly important influences on the actions of intergovernmental bodies. And just as intrastate pressure group activity can provide for popular participation and influence – and this is enshrined in pluralist democratic theory as a key feature of democracy – so interstate activities of NGOs can provide for popular participation and influence and can become a key feature of international democracy.[45] And there is an important linkage between NGOs and grass roots participation in much environmentalist thought and practice. Hurrell, for example, refers to the '"community approach" favoured by many NGOs [according to which] it is grass roots and peoples' organisations that need to play the predominant role in the transition towards a more sustainable society.'[46] Moreover, the role of NGOs is of increasing importance in environmental matters: 'perhaps the most noticeable change in the conduct of international relations visible in the environmental arena is the central role of NGOs.'[47]

Now, it might be argued that such an NGO process of influence would in fact be undemocratic. What interests and affected groups would or should be included as groups in the process, and what would or should be the extent of their influence? In relation to a global warming abatement regime would oil companies, for example, be included? If they were not, this could be seen as an undemocratic exclusion; and if they were their structural power may give them a disproportionate and undemocratic influence.[48] This type of argument raises large and difficult questions which will have to be left aside for another occasion. Three general points only can be made here. First it should be realised that the process of influence would ideally take place within, and be ultimately subordinate to, formal institutions of popular control, the function of which would include regulation of the process in order to mitigate these difficulties. Second there is a distinction between *the people* affected and bodies – such as oil companies – whose actions affect them; this distinction raises tricky issues, but is nonetheless crucial. Third whilst it is true this type of argument parallels an influential form of critique of orthodox pluralist democratic theory – where it is argued that the participation provided by the group process is crucially distorted and less than comprehensive[49] – that critique itself can be challenged.[50]

The NGO process, then, can be viewed and defended as democratic in the same sort of way as the pressure group process of orthodox pluralist democratic theory. However NGOs are often seen as being more than just pressure groups and to be actually constitutive – rather than simply representing sections – of an international people. Hurrell writes of the 'increased attention being given to the importance of environmental groups, not just because of their ability to influence state politics but also to create a transnational civil society and to define a new pattern of politics.'[51] And we have already referred to the linkage with 'new social movements' and the way they can be seen as constitutive of international peoples.

The second form of broad approach to our question of the mechanisms for popular control is comprehensively global and complements the global conception of the people. Here the focus is on a world-wide institution as the mechanism of control for use by a global people. The United Nations is the obvious candidate. And, indeed, the United Nations is already being seen as 'the most significant global institution embodying the democratic ideals and aspirations associated with the new world order.'[52] But this is primarily a statement about the United Nations and the global promotion of democracy – democracy within states – rather than the promotion of global democracy. And, of course, the existing United Nations can only be understood as an institution of a world constituted by states; the only way at present in which it could be considered an instrument of 'world democracy' is in the bogus sense of being the instrument of all the world's states, equally represented.[53] Cosmopolitan democracy, on the other hand, requires an organisation that is directly an instrument of the global *people* rather than one which represents the world's *states* – or at best represents the global people indirectly, and in a distorted way, via the world's states.[54] Whether the United Nations could evolve in this direction is, of course, highly problematic,[55] though it is possible to see in its commitment to human rights the germ of such a development.

As in the case of international conceptions, so too with the global conception, the importance of influence (as well as institutions of control) by the people should not be forgotten. It may be that developments here are both more fruitful and more likely. For example Rosenau[56] discerns developments involving a mobilisation of global citizenship with accompanying implications for world democracy which, because they involve 'governance' rather than 'government', require markedly less in the way of unlikely world governmental institutions. Moreover he sees worsening environmental conditions as spurring such developments.

5. Conclusion: Cosmopolitan Democracy and Global Warming

Let us now return to the first of the three questions that were posed earlier: why should popular control by the masses of trans-state events and processes be desirable? So far we have been concerned with the nature and possibilities of cosmopolitan democracy, but why might it be needed anyway?

This is, of course, a very large question and a full answer would involve consideration of traditional philosophical questions about the justification of democracy. But, although it cannot be divorced from the general issue of the justification of democracy, we are here especially concerned with a particular application of the question: in what ways might international or global popular control contribute to overcoming the difficulties in responding to the problem of global warming. A proper consideration of this issue is will have to await another occasion, but we shall conclude with some pointers to relevant lines of argument.

To begin with there is the basic difficulty of there being a need for *collective* global action to respond effectively to global warming when there are fundamental obstacles in the way of such action in a world of sovereign states. The general 'problem of collective action'[57] is greatly exacerbated by the states-system. This basic difficulty is helpfully surveyed by Hurrell and Kingsbury[58] and is well summarised by Dunn when he says that 'The problem of collective action permeates all politics' but is 'peculiarly intractable where there is little realistic prospect of creating an effective enforcement agency and where the rational appeal of seeking to free ride is often devastatingly apparent.'[59] Now it may be that we are stuck with the states-system, as Dunn and many others maintain. On the other hand it may well be that the current period of global change prefigures a significant modification to that system. And it has been the argument of this chapter that moves towards the development of cosmopolitan democracy are of great importance here. There could not, of course, be anything like a full development of cosmopolitan democracy within the time when action to combat global warming will still be possible, but moves towards it can still be helpful. Such moves themselves help to make integrated action more feasible by generating concepts and pointing towards mechanisms that transcend states, thereby increasing pressure for inter- or supra-state action. All such pressures help to overcome the obstacles to collective action created by the states-system. Such obstacles would, of course, be largely removed with the full development of cosmopolitan democracy, which would substantially transcend the states-system.

The obstacles to collective action created by the states-system are not confined to the 'problem of collective action'. There are also the large and important issues of international justice involved in responding to the global warming problem.[60] These are not only important in their own right but also present obstacles to the generation of successful responses to the global warming problem: the resolution of issues of international justice is, in effect, a necessary condition for effective action to combat global warming.[61] Cosmopolitan democracy can help here by modifying the issues and thereby rendering them less intractable (as before, short of its full development moves towards cosmopolitan democracy can still be helpful). It does this by helping to establish relevant communities. This is important for two reasons. First in the context of a community, with the associated moral links between members and the notion of a common good, issues of justice are clearly different from, and more manageable than, issues of 'international justice' in a world of discrete sovereign states.[62] Clearly here global democracy would be of most use, but international democracy too would break down moral barriers set by sovereign states and generate wider communities with larger horizons. The second reason why these wider communities would be important in resolving issues of justice lies in the very fact that they would constitute democratic peoples who could have the desire and ability to *demand* their resolution.

This brings us to a second main way in which cosmopolitan democracy can help in responding to global warming. Not only can it generate demands for the resolution of issues of international justice but also, and more generally, it can generate overall demands for effective action. Just as democracy traditionally involves effective popular pressure for action in the people's interest, so cosmopolitan democracy can involve effective pressure by the people of the world for action that is in their interest – the combating of global warming. 'If human beings are to re-establish control over the ecological dangers of which they are now becoming aware, they will certainly need to act together.'[63] Or, as Archibugi puts it, 'what the cosmopolitan democracy model proposes is, in the end, simply the creation of the appropriate institutions where the citizens of the planet may discuss the problems and take the decisions that shape their destiny.'[64] Again it is to global democracy that this argument most fully applies. And already the groundwork is there in the role of the United Nations, in the form of the United Nations Environment Programme. But international democracy is also very important here: the making of agreements between (increasingly 'less sovereign') states and the successful functioning of international regulatory regimes are made more possible and likely to the extent that international peoples press for agreements and control. As before, even if the focus on full cosmopolitan democracy is unrealistic, moves towards it can still be helpful. In the case of international democracy the making of agreements between states and the successful functioning of international regulatory regimes is made more possible and likely to the extent that international peoples press for agreements, or have influence on regimes. Something of this kind has already been manifested in the pressures that led to the Rio Conference and the Earth Summit Agreements.

The argument that just as democracy within a state ensures there will be action in the interests of the people of that state, so cosmopolitan democracy will ensure that there will be action to combat global warming involves, of course, two crucial contentions. The first is that global warming *is* a problem and that therefore action to combat it *is* in the interests of the people of the world; and the second is that the world's people will recognise what is in their interests here. The first contention is here assumed to be correct (see note 1 to this chapter). The second contention raises an important aspect of the issue posed at the beginning of the chapter is about the suitability of democracy for solving environmental problems. In doing so it poses again, in a specific form, some traditional general issues concerning the desirability of democracy, in particular the question of whether 'guardianship' rather than democracy is needed to secure action that is in the real interests of the people – interests that the people may well be incapable of recognising.[65] A discussion of these issues must await another occasion but two interlocking lines of argument will be involved. First there is the traditional general defence of democracy against arguments for guardianship, according to which the people are the best judges of their own interest.[66] Second there is a more particular argument to the effect that on the issue of global warming, where there is some dispute among the experts, final judgements and decisions are properly made by the mass of the people who would be affected.

Notes and References

*   I should like to thank Matthew Paterson and John Williams for their
        valuable comments on an earlier draft of this chapter. Improvements
        also resulted from discussion at a seminar at Royal Holloway and Bed-
        ford New College, University of London, at which an earlier version
        was presented as a paper.

1   It will be assumed here that there is, indeed, a problem. It is acknowl-
        edged that there is debate about the reality or extent of global warm-
        ing, but this is beyond the scope of this paper. It will be taken as
        sufficient evidence that there has for some time been a consensus
        among most of the world's climate scientists that there is a grave prob-
        lem. And now developments in Antarctica seem to be providing evi-
        dence of this. In 1994 scientists at the British Antarctic Survey were
        warning that a 'dangerous warming' is becoming evident in Antarctica
        (*Independent on Sunday*, 25 September 1994). Further confirmation
        was provided by dramatic disintegration of ice shelves observed in
        1995: the 'evidence so far shows that Antarctica has been warming up
        faster than anywhere else on Earth – which is precisely what the sci-
        entists who have been predicting global warming said would happen'
        (*Independent on Sunday*, 5 March 1995). The 1994 report of the Inter-
        governmental Panel on Climate Change concluded that the world's
        climate is seriously at risk and the chairman of the group that drafted
        the report said 'the rate of change is likely to be larger than the Earth
        has seen at any time during the past 10,000 years': J. T. Houghton,
        Global Warming: The Complete Briefing (Oxford: Lyon Publishing,
        1994), p. 88.

2   There is a burgeoning literature but a good overview is provided by A.
        Hurrell and B. Kingsbury, *The International Politics of the Environ-
        ment* (Oxford: Clarendon Press, 1992); I. H. Rowlands and M. Greene
        (eds), *Global Environmental Change and International Relations*
        (London: Macmillan, 1992) and C. Thomas, *The Environment and
        International Relations* (London: RIIA, 1992). For general back-
        ground see also T. Brenton, *The Greening of Machiavelli* (London:
        Earthscan/RIIA, 1994).

3   For example Saward's discussion of the tensions between democracy
        and 'the green imperative' in green political thought: M. Saward,
        'Green Democracy?', in A. Dobson and P. Lucardie (eds), *The Politics
        of Nature* (London and New York: Routledge, 1993).

4   See Saward, 'Green Democracy?' for the role of ideas of participatory and direct democracy in green political thought generally; but as Saward shows there are however tensions because there is a certain difficulty in getting away from the authoritarian implications of 'the green imperative' (see the previous footnote). On the issue of democracy in green political thought besides Saward, 'Green Democracy?' see for example A.Dobson, *Green Political Thought* (London: Unwin Hyman 1990) and R. Eckersley, *Environmentalism and Political Theory* (London: UCL Press, 1992).

5   M. Grubb, *et al.*, *The Earth Summit Agreements: A Guide and Assessment* (London: Earthscan/RIIA, 1993), p. xv.

6   F. Fukuyama, *The End of History and the Last Man* (London: Hamish Hamilton, 1992); B. Holden, *Understanding Liberal Democracy*, 2nd ed. (Hemel Hempstead: Harvester Wheatsheaf, 1993), Chapter 4. It is the idea of *liberal* democracy that has achieved this status: but one manifestation of this is the extent to which 'democracy' has now become synonymous with 'liberal democracy'.

7   As dramatically exemplified by action by outsiders to 'restore' democracy in Haiti: to argue that the Americans had other motives is beside the point – which is that in providing a rationale, a right to democratic government could trump state-sovereignty arguments against intervention.

8   C. Gershman, 'The United Nations and the New World Order', *Journal of Democracy*, 4 (1993), p.12 (quoting T. M. Franck, 'The Emerging Right to Democratic Governance', *American Journal of International Law*, 86 (1992) 46–91).

9   G. J. Mulgan, 'Democracy Beyond Sovereignty', in G. J. Mulgan *Politics in an Antipolitical Age* (Cambridge: Polity Press, 1994), p. 188.

10   D. Held, 'From City States to a Cosmopolitan Order?', in D. Held (ed.), *Prospects for Democracy* (Cambridge: Polity Press, 1993); D. Held, *Democracy and the New International Order* (London: Institute for Public Policy Research, 1993); Mulgan, 'Democracy Beyond Sovereignty'; D. Archibugi and D. Held (eds), *Cosmopolitan Democracy* (Cambridge: Polity Press, 1995); D. Held, *Foundations of Democracy: The Principle of Autonomy and the Global Order* (Cambridge: Polity Press, forthcoming, 1995).

11   The arguments here overlap with those against the 'myth of the self-governing community': see P. Hirst, *Associative Democracy* (Cambridge: Polity Press, 1994), p. 70 and B. Hindess, 'Imaginary Presuppositions of Democracy', *Economy and Society*, 20 (1991) 173–95.

12 Of course the tight connection between states and ruling is a characteristic only of the modern states-system. Previous to its emergence ruling was carried out by – and diffused amongst – a diversity of persons and institutions. (Indeed the contemporary developments upon which we are now focussing may be leading to a situation in some ways analogous to the 'pre-Westphalian' system.) Nonetheless democracy has up until now been tied to the state – since modern democracy only emerged after the consolidation of the modern states-system and the only other manifestation of democracy occurred in ancient Greece where the *polis*-system was in certain key respects similar to the modern states-system.

13 F. G. Whelan, 'Prologue: Democratic Theory and the Boundary Problem', in J. R. Pennock and J. W. Chapman (eds), *Liberal Democracy* (Nomos XXV) (New York: New York University Press, 1983), p.16. Interestingly in the present context, it might be argued that there is a cosmopolitan logic within the framework of democratic theory which provides solutions: 'as Archbishop Temple pointed out, "The abstract logic of democracy may tend towards cosmopolitanism", for "the people" have no theoretical interest in the boundaries of states which dynastic jealousies had caused to be so bloodily defended and extended over the centuries' (D. Heater, *Citizenship: The Civic Ideal in World History, Politics and Education* (London and New York: Longman, 1990), p.56). This general idea (aspects of which will be taken up below) has heretofore received little serious attention within democratic theory, but there has been some discussion of another idea which can be seen as having some cosmopolitan implications ('the all-affected principle') which is also taken up in the main text below.

14 Heater, *Citizenship*, p.56.

15 A. Ware, 'Liberal Democracy: One Form or Many', in D. Held (ed.), *Prospects for Democracy* (*Political Studies*, 40 (1992), special issue), p. 132.

16 Clearly the conception of 'a people' as a nation is historically very important; and there is nothing new in nations – and hence specifications of 'peoples' – being conceived as prior to, and possibly in conflict with the boundaries of, states. But, as indicated in the main text, the implications are different when such conflicts involve what are thought to be nation states. As suggested in the main text the norm of the nation state has bred a failure to distinguish between a people being conceived as a nation and being specified as the citizens of a state; and so thought about democracy has often simply assumed that 'the people' is specified by the state. Perhaps part of what is happening now, in 'the

crisis of the nation state', is that the concept of the nation state is being dissolved, thereby exposing the 'fraudulence' of the assumption of the state specification of the people. True, it might be argued that it is not the concept that is under threat of dissolution so much as existing alleged 'nation states' for failing to embody the concept (I. Hont, 'The Permanent Crisis of a Divided Mankind: "Contemporary Crisis of the Nation State" in Historical Perspective', in J. Dunn (ed.), *The Contemporary Crisis of the Nation State?* (*Political Studies*, 42 (1994), special issue, 166–231)). But this does not alter the essential point since, because the dominant perception of existing states is that they really are nation states, it is the nation state as such (and thereby the easy identification of the people with the state, via the nation) that is being questioned. It is worth drawing a contrast with the Versailles Settlement, where the very principle at work was – and was seen by all to be – the formation of nation states (the dissolution of the Habsburg empire was precisely not the dissolution of a nation state): that is to say the identification of nation, state and people was created or reinforced rather than called in question.

17 Whelan, 'Prologue: Democratic Theory and the Boundary Problem', p.16.

18 J. D. May, 'Defining Democracy: A Bid for Coherence and Consensus', *Political Studies*, 26 (1978) 1–14.

19 For example E. Spitz, 'Defining Democracy: A Nonecumenical Reply to May', *Political Studies*, 27 (1979) 127–8, and R. Kimber, 'On Democracy', Scandanavian Political Studies, 12 (1989) 199–219.

20 J. Burnheim, *Is Democracy Possible?* (Cambridge: Polity Press, 1985), especially pp. 5, 26–7, 29–30, 117, 120, 186.

21 In fact there are further important issues of democratic control here specifically connected with the foreign policies of states. The possible and desirable extent of influence or control of a state's foreign policy by the electorate of that state is a well-known issue; but of more interest here would be questions concerning influence on a state's foreign policy by those outside the state who are affected by it. There is, of course, a fundamental issue here since it would appear absurd to assert, for example, that where state A is in a situation of conflict (perhaps actually or imminently at war) with state B, the people in state B should have a right to influence or control the actions of the government of state A. This is, indeed, one of the criticisms of May's definition; and it might be maintained that this is precisely where the logic of the cosmopolitan democracy argument leads. But it only appears absurd to the extent that a crucial dimension of this logic is ignored. This is the

implied or explicit idea that the states system is to be transcended in some important sense. A proper discussion of the particular issues of foreign policy cannot be undertaken here and will be left on one side, except to the extent that they overlap with general issues concerning the relationships between (what are seen as) the domestic actions of a government and persons outside its state.

22 Another ingredient of the absurdity verdict derives from the tight conceptual relationships between established notions of 'the government', 'the state' and 'the people' such that *logically* a government of a state can have certain kinds of duties only to the people delimited by that state. But again this is to miss the crucial dimension of the cosmopolitan democracy argument concerning the logic of transcendence of the states-system and its established notions (see the previous note).

23 We are interested here in cases where the all-affected principle *extends* the range and number of people who are relevant by counting those beyond the confines of 'the people' as traditionally understood; but equally this principle can on occasion *limit* those who are relevant to only some amongst the 'traditional people'. In both cases, of course, the logic of the principle is in competition with the state specification of the people which clearly raises questions about its realisation (see also note 26). In the analysis below such questions are considered in relation to 'supra-state' conceptions of the people but these must overlap into questions about 'sub-state' conceptions of the people. The logic of the principle itself is that 'the people' are not identified as those persons who are members of a state but as those who are affected by actions of a government – whether this includes only those without, or all those within plus many without, or some within and some without, or only some of those within, (what now exists as) a state.

24 Of course within orthodox democratic theory (more accurately theories) there are varying accounts of the relationship between the people and the government, although all can be subsumed under the notion of the people, positively or negatively, making, and being 'entitled to make, the basic determining decisions on important matters of public policy' (Holden, *Understanding Liberal Democracy*, p.8). The term 'control' should here be understood in a wide sense to include the varying accounts that are captured within this notion.

25 Burnheim, *Is Democracy Possible?*; Hirst, *Associative Democracy*.

26 There are elements of Burnheim's theory which make it doubtful whether it is a theory of democracy at all; however he does in a sense espouse democratic values, and our concern here is with the fact that

he does this whilst dissolving traditional conceptions of rule by the people.

27 At this point the only supra-state element that is being referred to is the newly conceived people: but this 'people', although extending beyond a state, is nonetheless conceived as controlling and acting through the government of that state. There are, of course, conceptual difficulties with this idea, and hence practical difficulties in its realisation (see also note 22). However, as already suggested, this is only half the story and in the main text below we indicate how this idea may be supplemented with notions of supra-state agencies through which a supra-state people might be able to act.

28 There is a large literature, but see for example: D. Held, 'Sovereignty, National Politics and the Global System', in D. Held, *Political Theory and the Modern State* (Cambridge: Polity Press, 1989); R. J. B. Walker and S. H. Mendlovitz , 'Interrogating State Sovereignty', in R. J. B. Walker and S. H. Mendlovitz (eds), *Contending Sovereignties* (Boulder, Colo. and London: Lynne Rienner, 1990); J. A. Camilleri and J. Falk, *The End of Sovereignty?* (Aldershot: Edward Elgar, 1992); M. W. Zacher, 'The Decaying Pillars of the Westphalian Temple: Implications for International Order and Governance', in J. N. Rosenau and E-O. Czempiel (eds), *Governance Without Government: Order and Change in World Politics* (Cambridge: Cambridge University Press, 1992); M. Shaw, *Global Society and International Relations* (Cambridge: Polity Press, 1994); The Report of the Commission on Global Governance, *Our Global Neighbourhood* (Oxford: Oxford University Press, 1995).

29 For Burnheim and Hirst internal critiques are explicitly part of their critical analysis of the traditional idea of rule by the people. (In fact in both cases they do combine these with external critiques and some of the arguments invoked in the main text here and below are also deployed. For Burnheim besides *Is Democracy Possible?* see J. Burnheim, 'Democracy, Nation States and the World System', in D. Held and C. Pollitt (eds), *New Forms of Democracy* (London: Sage, 1986)). There is also of course the tradition of Marxist internal critiques – not now fashionable, but still powerful – but as our concern is with external critiques there is no direct need to consider these here (in any case the present author would exclude these because of their invalidity: Holden, *Understanding Liberal Democracy*, Chapter 3).

30 Of course this applies increasingly to domestic matters and not only to events and processes in the international realm. In fact there is an important overlap here: a key feature of the developments in question

is the extent to which they involve 'domestic' (most noticeably economic) matters becoming meshed into (sometimes global) processes extending beyond a state's boundaries in a way that prevents them being properly amenable to control by that state. Again the central point is the diminished extent to which states are effective agencies of control.

31 As Paterson points out in his chapter in this volume, interdependence is especially evident in the case of global warning, both in terms of how states are dependent on each other's actions for their welfare and in terms of how they are related to global warming. And, of course, 'globalisation' applies here with a vengeance! Global warming is a global problem which requires a global response.

32 J. Dunn, 'Introduction: Crisis of the Nation State?', in Dunn (ed.), *Contemporary Crisis of the Nation State?*, p.13. The collective action problem will be taken up again below.

33 There *is* a necessary and crucial element of individualism in traditional liberal democratic conceptions of the people (Holden, *Understanding Liberal Democracy*, p.172), but one of the functions of the conceptual linkage between such conceptions and the notion of the state is that the state supplies – or supplies a replacement for – this essential communal element. Communal identity may, of course, be seen as important for other reasons as well – the kinds of reasons central in communitarian political thought – but our concern here is merely with the necessary conditions for a democratic conception of 'the people'.

34 Burnheim, *Is Democracy Possible?*, p. 9.

35 For example J. A. Camilleri, 'Rethinking Sovereignty in a Shrinking, Fragmented World', in Walker and Mendlovitz (eds), *Contending Sovereignties* and Camilleri and Falk, *The End of Sovereignty?* See also Hutchings's chapter in this volume where she shows how the (necessarily community-oriented) category of 'citizen' – and hence sets of individuals communally linked *as* citizens – can transcend state boundaries and involve 'multiple political identities and agencies' rather than the 'inclusive communal' notion of global citizenship. The notion of international 'epistemic communities' – which are of (perhaps crucial) importance in the field of environmental regulation – is also instructive here: P. M. Haas, 'Obtaining International Environmental Protection through Epistemic Consensus', in Rowlands and Greene (eds), *Global Environmental Change and International Relations*.

36 For example Camilleri and Falk, *The End of Sovereignty?*, Chapter 8.

37 This is, of course, a large theme with a long history: see for example W. Schiffler, *The Legal Community of Mankind* (New York: Columbia

University Press, 1954). In the theoretical ferment associated with the current period of global change it is again being discussed: see for example A. Linklater, *Men and Citizens in the Theory of International Relations*, 2nd ed. (London: Macmillan 1990) and R. Falk, 'The World Order between Inter-State Law and the Law of Humanity: the Role of Civil Society Institutions', in Archibugi and Held (eds), *Cosmopolitan Democracy*.

38   B. Boutros-Ghali, 'Empowering the United Nations', *Foreign Affairs*, 71 (Winter 1992–3), p. 99.

39   Burnheim, 'Democracy, Nation States and the World System'.

40   Burnheim, *Is Democracy Possible?*

41   S. D. Krasner (ed.), *International Regimes* (Ithaca, NY: Cornell University Press, 1983). There is a large additional literature but for a recent survey, especially in relation to environmental issues, see M. List and V. Rittberger, 'Regime Theory and International Environmental Management', in Hurrell and Kingsbury, *The International Politics of the Environment*. For a recent assessment of the effectiveness of regimes see O. R. Young, 'The Effectiveness of International Institutions: Hard Cases and Critical Variables', in Rosenau and Czempiel, *Governance Without Government*. See also Section 8 of Barry Jones's chapter in this volume.

42   An example is provided by the way in which the International Sea-Bed Authority manages mineral resources on the floor of the deep ocean – resources which are conceived to be 'the common heritage of mankind' – for the benefit of the community of nations as a whole: see S. Brown, *New Forces, Old Forces, and the Future of World Politics* (Boston, Mass.: Little, Brown, 1988), pp. 270–71. The direct reference is still to nations rather than people – to the benefit of the community of nations rather than the community of mankind. However at least accountability to a body beyond the states of its governing assembly is invoked; moreover there is indirect reference to the community of mankind since the idea of 'the common heritage of mankind' is invoked. Significantly in the present context, in the most recent edition of *New Forces, Old Forces* Brown widens the argument to include management of 'international commons' generally and 'the new initiatives in international accountability launched' at the Rio 'Earth Summit' in particular: S. Brown, *New Forces, Old Forces, and the Future of World Politics: Post-Cold War Edition* (New York: Harper Collins, 1995), p. 264.

43   Held, *Democracy and the New International Order*, p.14.

44   Brown, *New Forces, Old Forces*, 1988 ed., p. 306. See also the analy-
     sis – including remarks on the 'political and legal arrangements for
     implementing the basic accountability principle' – on pp. 255–6 of the
     1995 edition of *New Forces, Old Forces*.

45   For example Brown, *New Forces, Old Forces*, 1995 ed., p. 257.

46   A. Hurrell, 'A Crisis of Ecological Viability? Global Environmental
     Change and the Nation State', in Dunn (ed.), *Contemporary Crisis of
     the Nation State?*, p. 157.

47   Thomas, *The Environment in International Relations*, p. 18.

48   I am indebted to Matthew Paterson for this particular example.

49   For what is still one of the best overviews see D. M. Ricci, *Community
     Power and Democratic Theory* (New York: Random House, 1971).

50   A. W. Kelso, *American Democratic Theory: Pluralism and its Critics*
     (Westport, Conn.: Greenwood Press, 1978).

51   Hurrell, 'A Crisis of Ecological Viability?', p. 163.

52   Gershman, 'The United Nations and the New World Order', p. 5.

53   In this sense the United Nations can already be judged as – or as the
     institution of – a world democracy. If it falls short of actually being
     a democracy in this bogus sense it is because of inequalities in the
     representation of states enshrined in the more salient role for the
     permanent members of the Security Council. But that we really are
     talking about a bogus sense in which the United Nations might be
     democratic is illustrated by the fact that the criterion of 'democracy' is
     met by the equal representation of all states, *including* those that are
     undemocratic!

54   There is, in a sense, a half-way house: the United Nations could
     become, or be supplemented by, an 'international democratic assembly'
     of all – and only – democratic states. This is advocated by Held, though
     he also dilutes the principle of state representation – by, for example,
     suggesting the representation of other 'democratic agencies' (for instance
     agencies comparable to the postulated democratised international
     regimes discussed above): Held, 'From City States to a Cosmopolitan
     Order?' and *Democracy and the New International Order*.

55   Any such development could only be connected with a general dilution
     of the states-system, although there could be reciprocal influences
     here: moves towards dilution of the states system could be spurred or
     encouraged by 'cosmopolitan developments' in the United Nations.
     For proposals of this kind see D. Archibugi, 'From the United Nations
     to Cosmopolitan Democracy', in Archibugi and Held, *Cosmopolitan
     Democracy*. See also *Our Global Neighbourhood*, Chapter 5.

58   J. N. Rosenau, 'Citizenship in a Changing Global Order' in Rosenau and Czempiel, *Governance Without Government.*

57   R. Hardin, *Collective Action* (Baltimore, Md.: Johns Hopkins University Press, 1982).

58   Chapter 1 in Hurrell and Kingsbury, *The International Politics of the Environment.*

59   Dunn, 'Introduction: Crisis of the Nation State?', p. 13.

60   See Paterson's chapter in this volume.

61   H. Shue, 'The Unavoidability of Justice', in Hurrell and Kingsbury, *The International Politics of the Environment.*

62   See Paterson's chapter for a discussion of international justice.

63   Dunn, 'Introduction: Crisis of the Nation State?', p. 14.

64   'From the United Nations to Cosmopolitan Democracy', p. 157.

65   See R. A. Dahl, *Democracy and Its Critics* (New Haven, Conn.: Yale University Press, 1989), Chapters 4 and 5 for an outline and assessment of 'guardianship'.

66   Besides Dahl, *Democracy and Its Critics,* Chapter 5 see for example Holden, *Understanding Liberal Democracy,* Chapter 4, Section 2.

PART 5

International Orders and the Environment

8

Ecological Change and Political Crisis

Ken Dark

1. Introduction: The Environment and International Relations

A decade ago environmental issues were only beginning to make an impression on scholars of international relations. It was in the 1980s that the famous reports prepared under the guidance of Willy Brandt and Gro Harlem Bruntland brought ecological issues to the fore, and subsequently these have attracted an increasingly great amount of attention from scholars and policy makers.[1] Notable in this flurry of attention have been the studies by individuals such as Daniel Deudney, Thomas Homer-Dixon, Michael Grubb, Andrew Hurrell, Mark Imber, Jessica Tuchman Matthews, Ian Rowlands, Jeremy Russell, Caroline Thomas, John Vogler and Arthur Westing and by a range of institutions.[2] Of the institutional programmes, perhaps the most significant for the field have been SIPRI's series of books on the ecological consequences of war, the World Resources Institute's assessment of the global resource-base, The Royal Institute of International Affairs' Energy and Environmental Programme, and the Global Security programme at the University of Cambridge. Any list of key studies in the development of environmental analysis in international relations must, of course, include the United Nations' environment programme.

Among the key issues to be identified as a result of these studies is the question of environmental security. This stresses the potential impact of environmental change on critical or strategic resources such as food supplies, and raises important practical and ethical questions. Among those related to the ethical dimension of global change are the issues of how one ought to respond to uncontrollable environmental change, the responsibility held by citizens of one state for the wellbeing of those of its neighbours and the moral aspects of international aid and human rights in environmental crisis situations. Ecological change can be seen as a challenge for liberal democracy and international cooperation in that it poses problems of individual freedom and collective responsibility. Such questions are examined by other contributors to this volume, not least that of the editor.

Here, however, it is the concept of environmental security as this has been defined by neo-realist scholars which will be examined. Neo-realist views of ecological change have concentrated on the potential for environmental crises to produce threats to state security and to undermine the stability of the interstate system.

These views which have been closely related to more wide-ranging neo-realist analyses of international security see ecological change as a potential source of 'threats without enemies'.[3] These threats are perceived in terms of damage to national interests or the interests of interstate alliances. While one need not be a neo-realist to envisage environmental change in these terms, this perception has been readily added to the neo-realist agenda, as has been discussed by Caroline Thomas.[4] Looking at global change in this way one can envisage primarily processes in the developing world – those centred in and principally directly affecting the South – as constituting a direct threat to the national interests of states in the North. For example differential population growth, which Homer-Dixon sees as likely to transform the human population of the planet from 5.3 billion in 1992 to over 8 billion by 2025, is likely to be a mainly developing world transformation.[5] Such changes, it has been supposed, combined with the environmental 'irresponsibility' of 'developing world' governments, would lead to extreme scarcity of basic resources.

Here I shall seek to demonstrate that ecological change is unlikely to constitute a direct threat either to the state or to the interstate system. That is, it does not lead to state-collapse or the collapse of international systems. Consequently the neo-realist concept of environmental security is flawed although, as we shall see, there may be one category of states for which this is not the case.

To demonstrate this historical sources will be used to show that there is no convincing evidence that the collapse of states or interstate systems has derived from environmental catastrophes. Ecological evidence and astrophysics enable us to show that, although ecological catastrophes could cause political crisis, this is extremely unlikely to happen in the near future. In short ecological change does not present a significant 'threat' to national interests nor to the stability of the interstate system.

2. Ecological Problems in the Contemporary World

Total global cropland amounts to approximately 1.5 billion hectares, although the total potential cropland may be as high as 3.4 billion hectares.[6] Most of this extra land is, however, of lower quality than that already exploited. In the developing world the amount of cropland per capita is declining, so that the present average of 0.28 hectares is likely to drop to 0.17 hectares by the year 2025.[7] This rate of decline is based only upon population growth and will, probably, be aggravated by other factors such as deforestation and hydrological changes.[8] If global warming increases this will severely aggravate this already alarming situation.[9] Such decline in the availability of agricultural resources will almost certainly impact upon the primarily agricultural populations of the South. Results expected by analysts from such changes include economic decline and large-scale famine and migration:[10] recent events in Rwanda form a graphic illustration of these processes.

If woodland is removed to increase the amount of agricultural land this is liable to produce further environmental disruption, notably by inducing hydrological changes and bringing about intensified erosion. The effects of erosion itself can be devastating to large areas of agricultural land: one need only recall the American 'dust bowl'.[11] Similarly the related problem of intensified farming as a response to restricted access to land will be liable to produce over-exploitation of soils, and their subsequent exhaustion. Again, climatic change would drastically aggravate this process. Perhaps the most graphic illustration of this is the deforestation of Easter Island in the Pacific, which led to the extinction of the local human population as agricultural systems collapsed following deforestation and soil-exhaustion.[12]

One can also draw attention to the potential impact of the scarcity of water resources in the developing world and in the Middle East.[13] Hydrological changes are likely to render the Nile Delta less suitable for human settlement in the near future and competition for water from the rivers Jordan, Indus and Euphrates is already increasing.[14]

Alternatively, desertification (the transformation of non-desert to desert) could form a major source of regional disruption. For example much of the circum-Mediterranean zone is experiencing this type of environmental degradation, although its effects are not uniform. The results can, however, be catastrophic, as in the mass migration from sub-Saharan Africa which resulted from the desertification of the Sahel.[15]

Each of these processes has the potential for major regional disruption and the stresses produced could easily result in interstate conflict and both international and civil war. Yet to characterise environmental security in terms of the interests of the North against those of the South not only raises crucial questions of morality and normative theory, but misrepresents the character of global environmental change. While these questions have to be considered when discussing regional security issues, even more potentially destructive processes are either entirely global, or centred on the developed industrial economies of the North.

The key example of this is, of course, global warming, discussed in this book by the editor and other contributors. The 'greenhouse effect' – the increase of global temperatures as a result of the build-up of carbon dioxide and other 'greenhouse gases' in the earth's atmosphere – is one of the most widely discussed aspects of global environmental change. Although the 'greenhouse effect' itself is generally agreed to exist, it is a subject of scientific controversy. The character of the subsidiary, 'side-' effects of this process is unclear. Some have envisaged changes in rainfall patterns or in ocean currents which might, in fact, render north-west Europe colder than at present, if the Gulf Stream were diverted. The most serious is also the most probable effect: the melting of ice caps in Greenland and Antarctica. This, combined with the expansion of newly-warm water, would intensify coastal erosion and drastically alter sea levels. The extent of the envisaged sea-level changes would pose a direct threat to many areas of high population including, in the developing world, the Nile Delta and Bangladesh (where a two-metre rise would displace approximately thirty million people if it occurred at present) and, in the North, cities including London.

While in Europe and the United States, for example, it may be possible to construct flood defences to protect major population centres, this is hardly a plausible solution for most areas at risk. To protect a major city against flooding produced by even a small rise in sea levels would be a huge project, expensive both in terms of finance and labour. It would, itself, be potentially extremely disruptive to local communications infrastructure such as road and rail.

As global warming derives primarily from the industrialised economies of the North, it serves as a useful example to warn us of the danger of characterising environmental degradation as an effect produced by the South to the detriment of the North. It also demonstrates the global scale of some forms of environmental change and their potentially catastrophic effects. For example, as the *Atlas of the Environment*[16] records, according to some scientific predictions of its impacts approximately 30 per cent of the agricultural production of the so-called 'corn-belt' of the North American Mid-West would be wiped out by small-scale temperature variations (under five degrees centigrade), a change which would result in a 70 per cent reduction in grain exports if the United States was to continue to feed itself at the present level (p. 96). Elsewhere, Greece and Italy would be severely affected, although the most extreme effects might be expected in north Africa, Latin America and south-east Asia (p. 96). Changes on this scale might, therefore, combine with the reduction of cropland and hydrological changes already discussed, to produce catastrophic food shortages. A related problem, also linked to the developed economies of the North, is the depletion of the ozone layer. Again this could have potentially devastating effects on agriculture: more than two-thirds of plant species have been shown, experimentally, to be damaged by the ultra-violet light admitted by ozone depletion (pp. 97–100). The most vulnerable are crops themselves. Of animals, sea plankton – which absorb over half the world's carbon-dioxide – are especially at risk, so that ozone-depletion is likely to feed back into both the marine eco-system and global warming (p. 97). Also deriving from the industrialised economies is pollution on a massive scale, whether the widespread poisoning of the sea through the deposition of toxic waste and oil slicks, or of the land through ill-advised use of agrochemicals (p. 97). Hazardous waste and agrochemicals have both been primarily produced in, and disposed of by, companies and governments in the developed economies of the northern hemisphere. Similarly air pollution and acid rain are principally products of the same areas, although in none of these cases is this exclusively so.

Ecological changes deriving from human environmental mismanagement are, therefore, not a characteristic specific to either the North or the South. Ecological catastrophe is not threatened by either Third World incompetence or the industrial system of the North in itself. Not all industries or companies have been characterised by irresponsibility or negligence in regard to the natural environment, nor are all major threats related to human action at all. The most potentially dramatic change, excepting perhaps global warming and ozone-depletion, are natural climate and sea-level fluctuations, astronomical events (such as meteorite collisions) and volcanic eruptions. The spread of highly contagious fatal and incurable disease could also have an impact on an equivalent scale.

3. Ecological Change and International Affairs

The key characteristic of changes taking place without human intervention is that no degree of international organisation or regulation could prevent them from occurring. Even in the case of meteorite- or comet-strike, it is debatable whether any form of SDI 'defence' system could work – could deflect or destroy a large meteorite or comet.[17] This does not mean that the development of such systems might not reasonably be a major priority in international cooperation between space agencies, but simply that it is questionable whether total protection from such events is possible using even the most advanced technology and resources available to a major interstate alliance such as NATO. It seems, therefore, that significant ecological change is almost inevitably going to take place, and probably will do so by 2050. If this is the case, and if any of the global-scale changes discussed so far happen, then for analysts of international affairs, a key question must be: what is their likely effect on both the international system and its actors?

This question relates closely both to the issue of environmental security and to the question of the role of ecological factors in the rise and fall of states and international systems. If global environmental change is near-inevitable and may be meliorated, but not averted, by international cooperation then it is distinct from most 'threats' examined in security studies for this reason alone. A partial analogy for this inevitability would be if one could state categorically that nuclear war was inevitable, merely its extent uncertain. The analogy is partial in part because – as Deudney has pointed out – environmental change (particularly that deriving from natural causes alone) cannot be considered the moral equivalent of war.[18] It is, as he has noted, misleading to talk of environmental processes using the language of security studies: 'threats' and 'enemies' are hardly terms applicable to climate change taking place over centuries, even if they may be used in relation to conscious or culpably irresponsible polluters.[19]

Nevertheless, it is probably unwise to underplay the danger of conflict rising from resource scarcity and migration in the face of ecological catastrophes.[20] Nor does the evidence so far rehearsed support his view that modern economic systems and technology are sufficiently flexible to overcome large-scale ecological change without major restructuring. However it is the matter of whether ecological change can be seen to constitute a danger to the continued existence of either the state or the international system that is central. That is to say it is central to the concept of ecological security, if we are to link this to general security studies rather than use it as a term for environmental diplomacy aimed at protecting resources employed by the state.[21]

4. Ecological Catastrophe and Political Collapse

The remainder of this chapter attempts to discover whether global environmental change constitutes a danger to the survival of states or international systems. To do so it will examine the historical and palaeoecological evidence for such changes having induced the collapse of the equivalent of states or interstate systems. Such an analysis does, of course, have its problems in that most of the 'states' and systems amenable to study in this way predate the Westphalian interstate system which has often been the focus of historical studies in our subject.

In this examination I shall mainly use examples from the previous two millennia, which provide us with a wide range of both 'states' and ecological changes, although where evidence permits I shall employ a longer-term perspective. The use of long time perspectives such as this is conventional in environmental studies and has come increasingly to the fore in international relations over the last decade.[22] By concentrating on the previous two thousand years one has the advantage of being able to draw evidence from societies which were, in many cases, themselves literate and which frequently included those interested in environmental changes. For instance throughout Europe medieval writers noted both astronomical events and ecological catastrophes in their annals and histories.[23]

Astronomical Impacts
Perhaps the most extreme form of environmental change of which there is historical record is impact on Earth by meteorites. As Walter Alvarez and Fran Asaro show in 'The Extinction of the Dinosaurs'[24] current palaeontological opinion favours the view that a major meteorite impact, in the region of one hundred million megatons, brought about the extinction of the dinosaurs. A meteorite of ten kilometres in diameter, the size required to have caused this event, has only to achieve a velocity of eleven kilometres per second for the Earth's atmosphere to pose no barrier (p. 42). It therefore enters the atmosphere intact and impacts upon the Earth, releasing energy equivalent to ten thousand times that of the simultaneous explosion of the world's complete nuclear arsenal (p. 43). The crater from this impact would be about 150 kilometres in diameter (p. 48). Plainly, such an event would be globally catastrophic, as would the resulting dust cloud which might be expected to darken the atmosphere for months. Ecological estimates of this effect suggest that this would collapse the global food chain (p. 44). Combined with this, water vapour trapped in the atmosphere would cause global warming, leading to unusually high temperatures following the dispersion of the dust cloud (p. 45). These might be sufficient to be lethal to surviving plants and animals on the Earth's surface (p. 45). Another resulting effect might well be global acid rain, which has been described by one scholar as 'truly serious' in comparison to the previous effects (p. 45)! Even in pre-prepared shelters it seems unlikely – even leaving aside the issue of a viable population – that the administrative structure of any state, would be able to survive an impact of this scale. The foregoing is unlikely to represent

an over estimate of the effect of a major meteorite impact: astronomers under estimated the effects of the recent impact of the Shoemaker-Levy comet on Jupiter. Nor do impacts occur only as isolated instances: there is some evidence – for example from Clearwater Lakes in Canada – that multiple impacts are possible (p. 49). Meteorite impacts are far from rare and Richard Grieve of the Geological Survey of Canada has compiled a list of more than a 120 craters, including several measuring 30 kilometres in diameter (p. 49). Impacts of this scale are, however, extremely unusual and no crater large enough to have been caused by a meteorite of the size imagined to have brought about the end of the dinosaurs is known (pp. 48–50).[25]

Alvarez and Asaro have observed that there are far more craters of thirty kilometres or more in diameter than there have been mass extinctions of animals. That is, global catastrophe on the scale referred to above rarely results from meteorite or comet strikes, even if meteorite impacts are more common than one might initially suppose. Early records of meteorite impacts, or what may be such impacts, seem to bear out this view. For example in the late Roman period a well-recorded comet sighting was followed by the first snow in the Mediterranean for six months during A.D. 442–3 and then a severe drought was recorded in Jerusalem.[26] This is exactly the pattern one would expect from a major impact, but it had no effect at all on the continued survival – or for that matter, macro-economics – of the Eastern Roman Empire. Likewise the comet recorded in A.D. 891 was followed by cold winters in A.D. 893–4 and a drought in the Middle East is recorded in the same decade.[27] This may indicate another impact and if so, again, it had no political or economic consequences for the states of its time so far as we can tell. This is merely to pick a couple of examples from a wealth of historical evidence which suggests that even major impacts, albeit of much smaller scale than the ten-kilometre meteorite supposed to have caused the extinction of the dinosaurs, were insufficient to collapse the political and economic structures of the first millennium A.D. In the nineteenth century a major meteorite impact in Siberia failed to have any political consequences.

Although, of course, if an impact centred on, or was close to, a major population or industrial centre the consequences for an individual state might be more severe, there is no evidence that this has in fact happened at any time in the historical past. Nor are major impacts common events on a time-scale of centuries. Very large impacts of the type which recently took place on Jupiter have been estimated to occur only once in millennia.[28]

Consequently, while a very large impact could undoubtedly collapse global political and economic systems (and even a lesser, if major, impact could severely damage an individual state), the chances of this happening in the near future are extremely low. There is no evidence that this has happened at any time in the past history of humanity.

Volcanic Eruptions
Volcanic eruptions are usually perceived to be local events, but this is a misperception as their ecological consequences are regional, or even global, in scale. Mike Baillie has demonstrated, on palaeoecological grounds, that a consistent pattern of environmental events seems to have occurred whenever a large-scale volcanic eruption has taken place.[29] First local damage caused by lava is followed by a dust cloud in the atmosphere. This results in a reduction of the sunlight reaching the Earth's surface and so in restricted plant growth. These characteristics have been recorded by correlating vol- canological, ice-core and dendrochronological records over the past four thousand years. There then usually follows famine resulting from crop failure and a weakening of the resistance of famine-affected populations to disease, causing plague. This pattern has been found in a wide range of historical sources for the same period, by employing both European and Chinese records building on the work of Kevin Pang and his colleagues.[30]

Associated work has included studies of the 1628 B.C. Thera eruption and the 1159 B.C. Hekla eruption, but the most intriguing case-study for a scholar of international relations is that of the major volcanic event in A.D. 536, which may indirectly have caused the global plague, today referred to as 'the Justinianic Plague' of the 540s.[31] This affected the entire Byzantine empire and also spread to China. In demographic terms it was catastrophic, but in political and economic terms its effects were negligible. Recent studies have shown that it was almost a century too early to have brought about the collapse of the Eastern Roman Empire. Nor did it coincide with the collapse of either the contemporary Persian or Chinese states.

This evidence leads to the conclusion that while ecological crisis can derive from volcanic eruptions – and this can include crisis in the demography of human populations – state-collapse and systemic change do not result from this. As volcanic activity occurs on a regular cycle, such patterns have almost inevitably been repeated throughout the last two millennia without once leading to the collapse of a major state or of an international system.

Volcanic activity does not, therefore, seem to pose a danger to the con- temporary international system. It is, however, not an easily controllable source of ecological change.

Plague
Ever since William H. McNeill's *Plagues and Peoples*,[32] which was first published in 1976, there has been a school of thought which stresses the role

of disease in human history. Although the impact of disease on urban populations and state societies is fiercely debated among both historians and biologists, in addition to others, the evidence that states and international systems can be irreparably damaged by widespread epidemics is extremely weak.

Even the Black Death and the Justinianic Plague did not wipe out contemporary populations in their entirety. Although dramatic demographic decline did occur in both the sixth and the thirteenth centuries as a result of these plagues, neither the Eastern Roman state nor medieval England suffered political or economic collapse as a result of them. Changes once thought by scholars to have resulted from them and to have led to economic re-organisation – such as increased social mobility in thirteenth-century England – have (in recent scholarly work)[33] been shown to have been part of longer-term processes of change.

Nor were phases of plague in the early Roman Empire and early modern Europe accompanied by phases of collapse. For example an epidemic struck Rome in A.D. 165, with another almost a century later in A.D. 251.[34] Neither of these can be shown to have brought about political collapse or economic ruin.

Plagues can be shown, therefore, to have caused demographic crises, rather than political or economic crises, in international systems and their component states. It may be held that their effect is analogous to that of volcanic events, with which – as we have seen – they can occasionally be linked. There is no evidence that they collapse states or international systems.

Climate and Sea-Level Variations

Evidence from ice-cores, geomorphology, and historical records enables us to reconstruct changes in climate and sea-levels over the past two thousand years. While cyclical patterning characterises both historical records of extremes of heat and cold, and also physical records of glacial advances and retreats, these cannot be consistently correlated with periods of state or systemic collapse.

For example although dramatic changes in sea-level and a global cooling took place during the late Roman period, these do not coincide with the end of the Roman Empire.[35] Likewise, the phase of global warming which brought the early modern 'little ice age' to an end did not have political or economic impacts on its contemporary interstate system.

Like volcanic and epidemiological impacts, natural climate and sea-level variations affect populations and require adjustment, but this is not of such a scale to bring about the collapse of states or systems.

Micro-States and Islands: An Exception to the Rule

In none of the above cases did ecological change cause irreparable damage to the state or to the international system. Micro-states, especially those on small islands, could, however, form an exception to this rule, as the example of Easter Island suggests. Their small size and limited local resources render them vulnerable to rapid ecological change. For example prehistoric occupation of Pacific islands has been shown by archaeologists occasionally to have been brought to an end following tidal waves which completely overwhelmed the island.[36] This could potentially happen to a micro-state in the modern Pacific, although meteorological and oceanographic monitoring might provide advance warning. Volcanic eruption could have a similar affect.

In the modern world the capacity to move populations and transfer resources out of the area at risk, combined with advance warning of such a catastrophe, probably makes this unlikely to cause the collapse of a state (unless accompanied by a permanent, or semi-permanent, rise in sea-level) and the effect of such a catastrophe on the international system would be limited. It is unlikely, therefore, that this is a valid exception to the general rule that ecological crises do not cause political collapse, although it might hypothetically result in state collapse.

It may be important to note that at the one place in the ancient world where this was formerly widely held by scholars to have occurred, on Santorini, this is no longer seen as the case.[37] There the Minoan state survived a major volcanic eruption in an island setting.

There is, therefore, no reason to suppose that ecological crises on islands have, in the past, collapsed states. Small islands have seldom been major actors in international systems and there is also no evidence that international systems have collapsed as a result of ecological catastrophes on them.

5. General Conclusions

There is no evidence on the basis of this study that natural ecological change is likely to bring about state or systemic collapse. A hypothetical exception could be the case of island micro-states, although this has not definitely occurred in the past. It is, therefore, strictly incorrect to see ecological change in terms of the security of either states or alliances. Such changes can, however, pose formidable problems and have widespread impacts upon the societies affected by them.

Most of these types of ecological change cannot be easily managed either by states or by international cooperation. Those forms of environmental degradation deriving from human ecological mismanagement are, however, amenable to political solutions if international cooperation can be achieved, as discussed in this volume by Barry Jones. Attempts at international environmental legislation and ecological management suggest that such cooperation may be possible, despite the difficulties. If so, the impacts of natural environmental crises can be lessened in all but the most extreme examples, particularly by cooperation between 'developed' and 'developing' nations.

Notes and References

1   Brandt Commission, *Common Crisis North–South: Cooperation for World Recovery* (London: Pan, 1983); World Commission on Environment and Development, *Our Common Future* (The Brundtland Report), (Oxford: Oxford University Press, 1987).

2   M. Grubb, *et al.*, *The Earth Summit Agreements: A Guide and Assessment* (London: Earthscan/RIIA, Earthscan, 1993); M. Grubb, 'The Greenhouse Effect: Negotiating Targets', *International Affairs*, 66 (1990), 67–89; D. Deudney, 'The Case Against Linking Environmental Degradation and National Security', *Millennium*, 19 (1990), 461–76; I. H. Rowlands and M. Greene (eds), *Global Environmental Change and International Relations* (London: Macmillan, 1992); A. H. Westing (ed.), *Global Resources and International Conflict* (Oxford: Oxford University Press, 1986) and *Cultural Norms, War and the Environment* (Oxford: Oxford University Press, 1988); M. F. Imber, *Environment, Security and UN Reform* (London: Macmillan, 1994); J. T. Mathews, 'The Environment and International Security' and T. Homer-Dixon, 'Environmental Scarcity and Intergroup Conflict', both in M. T. Klare and D. C. Thomas (eds), *World Security: Challenges for a New Century* (2nd ed., New York: St Martin's Press, 1994); J. T. Mathews, 'Redefining Security', *Foreign Affairs*, 68 (1989), 162–77; C. Thomas, *The Environment in International Relations* (London: RIIA, 1992); C. Thomas (ed.), *Rio, Unravelling the Consequences* (London: Cass, 1994); A. Hurrell and B. Kingsbury, *The International Politics of the Environment* (Oxford: Oxford University Press, 1992). For a recent review of the relationship between environmental issues and international relations theory see, A. Hurrell, 'International Political Theory and the Global Environment', in K. Booth and S. Smith (eds), *International Relations Theory Today* (Cambridge: Polity Press, 1995).

3   K. Knorr and F. N. Trager (eds), *Economic Issues and National Security* (Lawrence: Regents, 1977); B. Buzan, *People States and Fear,*

2nd ed. (Hemel Hempstead: Harvester, 1991), pp. 131–2; Imber, *Environment, Security and UN Reform*, pp. 8–12.

4   Thomas, *The Environment in International Relations*, Chapter 4.

5   Homer-Dixon, 'Environmental Scarcity', p. 290. For a graphic representation of trends in population growth see, M. Kidron and R. Segal, *The New State of the World Atlas* (4th Edn., London: Simon and Schuster, 1991), pp. 16–17.

6   Homer-Dixon, 'Environmental Scarcity and Intergroup Conflict', p. 294.

7   Homer-Dixon, 'Environmental Scarcity and Intergroup Conflict', p. 294.

8   Homer-Dixon, 'Environmental Scarcity and Intergroup Conflict', p. 294.

9   See S. Schneider, *Global Warming* (San Francisco: Sierra Club, 1989).

10   Homer-Dixon, 'Environmental Scarcity and Intergroup Conflict', pp. 295–8. On international migration see, S. Castles and M. J. Miller, *The Age of Migration* (London: Macmillan, 1993).

11   M. A. Jones, *The Limits of Liberty: American History 1607–1992* (Oxford: Oxford University Press, 1995), p. 467.

12   P. Bahn and J. Flenley, *Easter Island, Earth Island* (London: Thames and Hudson, 1992).

13   Imber, *Environment* pp. 2–3 and 9; P. H. Gleick, 'Water and Conflict: Fresh Water Resources and International Security', *International Security*, 18 (1993), 79–112; M. Lowi, 'Bridging the Divide: Transboundary Disputes and the Case of West Bank Water', *International Security*, 18 (1993), 113–38.

14   Imber, *Environment, Security and UN Reform*, p. 9.

15   Imber, *Environment, Security and UN Reform*, pp. 9 and 96. See also G. Loescher, *Refugee Movements and International Security*, Adelphi Paper No 268, International Institute of Strategic Studies (1991).

16   G. Lean and D. Hinrichsen (eds), *Atlas of the Environment* (Oxford: Helicon Publishing, 1992), pp. 93 and 95.

17   'The threat from space', *The Economist*, 7828 (11 September 1993) 15–16.

18   Deudney, 'The Case Against Linking Environmental Degradation and National Security'.

19   Deudney, 'The Case Against Linking Environmental Degradation and National Security'.

20   N. Myers, 'Environment and Security', *Foreign Policy*, 74 (1989), 23–41; D. Deudney, 'The Mirage of Eco-War', in I. H. Rowlands and M. Greene (eds), *Global Environmental Change and International Relations* (London; Macmillan, 1992); Homer-Dixon, 'Environmental Scarcity and Intergroup Conflict'; D. Pirages, 'Demographic Change and Ecological Insecurity', in M. T. Klare and D. C. Thomas (eds),

World Security. Challenges for a New Century, 2nd ed. (New York: St Martin's Press, 1994).

21 For a recent review of security studies see J. A. Tickner, 'Re-visioning Security', in Booth and Smith (eds), *International Relations Theory Today*, pp. 175–97. Note that security can be used to apply to the safe-guarding of the individual, social group, state or international system, as well as to the environment itself.

21 See Dark, 'Defining Global Change', in this volume.

23 D. J. Schove and A. Fletcher, *Chronology of Eclipses and Comets AD 1–1000* (Woodbridge: Boydell, 1984).

24 W. Alvarez and F. Asaro, 'The Extinction of the Dinosaurs', in J. Bourriau (ed.), *Understanding Catastrophe* (Cambridge: Cambridge University Press, 1992).

25 See also 'The Threat from Space'.

26 Schove and Fletcher, *Chronology of Eclipses and Comets AD 1–1000*, pp. 290 and 321.

27 Schove and Fletcher, *Chronology of Eclipses and Comets AD 1–1000*, pp. 297 and 325.

28 'The Threat from Space'.

29 M. G. L. Baillie, 'Dendrochronology and Past Environments', in A. M. Pollard (ed.), *New Developments in Archaeological Science* (Oxford: British Academy, 1992).

30 M. G. L. Baillie, 'Do Irish Bog Oaks date the Shang Dynasty?', *Current Archaeology*, 117 (1989), 310–13.

31 M. G. L. Baillie, 'Dendrochronology raises questions about the nature of the AD 536 dust-veil event', *Holocene*, 4 (1994), 212–7.

32 W. H. McNeill, *Plagues and Peoples* (Harmondsworth: Penguin, 1979).

33 C. Platt, *Medieval England: A Social History and Archaeology from the Conquest to 1600 AD* (London: Routledge, 1978), pp. 126–37.

34 McNeill, *Plagues and Peoples*, p. 113.

35 K. R. Dark, *Civitas to Kingdom* (London: Pinter, 1994), pp. 241–2.

36 I owe this point to discussions during 1993 with Dr Matthew Spriggs, the Australian National University, a specialist on the prehistory of the Pacific at that time a visiting fellow at Clare Hall, Cambridge.

37 M. G. L. Baillie and M. A. R. Munro, 'Irish Tree-Rings, Santorini and Volcano Dust Veils', *Nature* 332 (1988), 344–6.

9

International Justice and
Global Warming

Matthew Paterson*

1. Introduction

There is now a wide literature on global environmental problems, particularly global warming[1] which emphasises the need for the emerging regime to be based on the principle of equity or justice.[2] The predominant argument which emerges concerns claims for large scale transfers from North to South as a necessary part of such a regime. This is the implication of justice for most of the contributors to this literature and it is endemic in the global warming debate both among commentators and politicians. For example even Margaret Thatcher, when UK Prime Minister, expressed the sentiment that 'every country must contribute and industrialised countries must contribute more to help those who are not'.[3] The assumption is pervasive. On the one hand the Intergovernmental Panel on Climate Change has a group of authors writing a chapter on the subject for their next report,[4] and on the other hand one opponent of aggressive responses to global warming and to the UNCED project more generally asserted that the process was driven by 'Third world kleptocrats' trying to revive the agenda of the New International Economic Order.[5]

Oran Young would be representative of many of these writers when he asserts that 'the availability of arrangements that all participants can accept as equitable ... is necessary for institutional bargaining to succeed'.[6] But there are a number of viewpoints on what an equitable arrangement looks like.[7] This literature does not on the whole engage with the more general literature which emerged, in particular after the publication of Charles Beitz's *Political Theory and International Relations* in 1979, on international distributive justice. Rawls does get mentioned,[8] but he is not much more than mentioned. Most of the literature starts with already formed conceptions of justice or equity and proceeds with a technical discussion of how to implement it, reflecting the policy-oriented concern of most discussions of global warming.[9]

This chapter tries to fill this gap. It will concentrate on how the positions put forward regarding justice and global warming can find justifications in broader traditions of justice. Section 2 will outline the existing debate on equity and the global warming regime. Section 3 will reflect on what the more general debate on international justice might have to say about this question and the conclusion will relate the two sets of literature to each other. Some preliminary suggestions as to which is the most convincing position will also be presented throughout the paper, although this is not the primary focus.

2. The Equity/Justice Debate Regarding Global Warming

The general debate on global warming, as well as that on other global environmental problems, is replete with assertions that agreements need to be equitable in order to produce effective responses to those problems. The Oran Young quote given above is one example. However many others could be produced. For example:

> The key international challenge is therefore to find an approach to negotiations which is difficult for any of the major countries or groups to dismiss as unfair.[10]

> International co-operation on the scale required will not be achieved without addressing a series of potentially divisive equity issues.[11]

Virtually any general overview on the prospects for successful responses to global warming will have a paragraph on international equity. However the literature which discusses this in some detail is also considerable. This section will now review the arguments made by some of these works.

Henry Shue will be dealt with first, largely because he deals with the problem in a rather different fashion to the other writers and in a way which is logically prior.[12] His purpose in 'The Unavoidability of Justice' is to argue

that justice should be considered a legitimate focus in the climate negotiations, a purpose which is designed to counter suggestions, made by Susskind
and Ozawa and by Sebenius,[13] that they should be kept separate in what Shue
calls a 'two-track approach – climate now, justice later' (p. 375).

He argues convincingly against this latter position. Part of the argument
is to show that rational bargaining, while it may produce some North–South
transfers, would not meet the requirements of justice. His other arguments
show that the question of justice is not external to climate negotiations for
three reasons:

> first, ... if background injustices have produced the weak bargaining
> position of the poor nations, it is doubly unfair to exploit that bargaining
> weakness in order to insist that the poor nations sacrifice the interest
> in question;[14] and second, ... if the rich nations have caused, albeit unin-
> tentionally, the impending harms [of climate change] that co-operation
> would help to prevent, it is doubly unfair to leave poor nations that have
> pitched in on the prevention effort to cope on their own with what the
> effort fails to prevent. (p. 392)

His third argument is that the interests which 'poor nations' would be expected
to sacrifice are of a different order to those being sacrificed by rich nations:
they are 'vital interests – survival interests' (p. 394). Justice 'does not permit
that poor nations be told to sell *their* blankets in order that rich nations may
keep *their* jewellery' (p. 397).

Shue's final point is arguably slightly dated.[15] His implication is that
'poor nations' should not be forced to incur opportunity costs on their
development as a result of cooperating to respond to global warming. This
is slightly anachronistic as it quickly became recognised in the climate
negotiations that no obligations could be placed on developing countries
which were not dependent on finance and technology from the North – these
conditions are written into the Climate Convention.[16]

In later works Shue splits the question of justice up by suggesting it arises
at four points in relation to global warming.[17] These questions are:

1. What is a fair allocation of the costs of preventing the global warming
   that is still avoidable?;

2. What is a fair allocation of the costs of coping with the social consequences of the global warming that will not in fact be avoided?;

3. What background allocation of wealth would allow international bargaining (about issues, like 1 and 2) to be a fair process?;

4. What is a fair allocation of emissions of greenhouse gases (over the long-term and during the transition to the long-term allocation)?[18]

Shue gives arguments which are not purely egalitarian, but which regard existing inequalities as something which need to be challenged and greatly reduced if a response to global warming can be considered just. His goal is 'to allow every human being an equal minimum level of greenhouse-gas emissions'.[19]

The other discussions frame the debate rather differently to Shue. While they adopt largely similar positions their focus is different. The focus tends to be on just principles for distributing the burden of reducing global emissions, Shue's first question. Thus while briefly mentioning the point about coping with impacts of climate change as well as preventing it the focus is squarely on the latter, in part reflecting the policy oriented nature of the works, as well as the *post hoc* nature of many discussions of justice (righting a wrong which, by definition, has to have been done before it can be righted). The closest relationship these works have is with Shue's basic argument, simply that considerations of justice require that negotiations not be based purely on rational utility based bargaining.

H. P. Young puts the problem in terms of 'sharing the burden'. Young's argument focusses on criteria we might use in deciding the distribution of the entitlements to emit carbon which we might consider just. He gives three accounts, which he later conflates to two.[20] In *Sharing the Burden* the first is an egalitarian doctrine, that 'everyone is eligible for exactly the same number of permits' (p. 7). Permits would be distributed between countries on a per capita basis. The second is based on cumulative liability (p. 7). Responsibility for climate change is not allocated on the basis of present emissions, but on cumulative emissions over time. This is because warming to which society is currently committed (if the climatologists are correct) is the result of emissions over time, not purely those currently being emitted. At the same time inhabitants of a country can be said to benefit from past emissions, through infrastructure and so on. The cumulative emissions would be treated as a debt incurred by each country. The conceptual logic is therefore that permits to emit in the future should take into account this debt.[21] Young later in practice turns this into a variant of the first approach. The third approach is what he calls the 'status quo doctrine' (p. 8), which suggests that present levels of emissions by countries establish a common law right to those levels of emissions. In the hard form, no right to demand emissions reductions can legitimately be made, but in a weaker form it suggests merely that if reductions are to be made then these should be purely in proportion to countries' emissions, establishing an equal sacrifice for each country or person. The justice is seen to be not in the end state of the distribution of emissions but in the distribution of the burden of achieving the overall global reductions. Young's argument is for a mixture of the first and the last. He suggests the first is ultimately the fairest but if implemented immediately would place unjust burdens on the rich, so a phasing in of an egalitarian position over time, starting from the *status quo* position, would be the most just.

In 'Sharing the Burden' Grubb *et al.* give the most extensive list of positions.[22] These number six: 'polluter pays' rationales based either on current emissions or historically accumulated contributions to global warming; an equal entitlements approach under which all individuals have an equal right to use the atmospheric commons; a 'willingness-to-pay' justification derived from welfare economics; the argument that each participant should shoulder a 'comparable' burden based on their situation; the idea simply that the distributional implications of any agreement should be taken into account (a position drawing explicitly on Rawls); a conservative position that starts with the assumption that the *status quo* is legitimate in the sense that present emitters have established some common law right to use the atmosphere as they at present do; and a position which asserts that countries merely have a right to emit at a level which is 'reasonable' in terms of enabling them to meet (a fairly generous interpretation of) basic needs (the position adopted by Shue).

They then go on to elucidate some of the advantages and problems with these approaches. Their focus is, however, on technical and political feasibility. For example they discount the historical responsibility argument (while accepting its attractive ethical basis) on the grounds that past emissions and sinks cannot be calculated with sufficient accuracy. They also reject the 'comparable burdens' position on the basis that again it would be impossible to compare the various special pleas that it would enable countries to bring to negotiations to say why they should have a large CO_2 allowance: the negotiations would become a complex bargain based on problematic ethical criteria which are easily manipulated in practice and which would collapse into haggling.[23] And their objection to a pure form of an equal entitlements position is practical, that the major industrialised countries (they focus on the United States but it applies almost equally elsewhere) would not agree to the level of North–South transfers which would result from any allocation formula based on this position.[24]

Like Young, they come up with a formulation which mixes the equal entitlements position with the *status quo* position. The equal entitlements one is regarded as having the best ultimate ethical foundations, but is politically impossible in the short term. Also they give some ethical credence to a position which emphasises that any transition will impose costs on countries, and that it is unjust to place costs that are too great on particular countries – the *status quo* position. Therefore a formula for allocating emissions permits between countries would be based on a mix of equal per capita entitlements and current emissions (p. 321). The balance within the formula could change over time so that, gradually, equal entitlements would get more emphasis. This would reduce the annual North–South transfers to politically feasible amounts while retaining sufficient incentives to reduce emissions.

Bergesen likewise gives a list, but one which is organised around different notions of equality.[25] Her approach is firmly rights-based; the focus is on what level of emissions each country or person has a right to emit. The positions given are: objective equality; subjective equality; relative equality; rank order equality; and equal opportunity. Some equate to those given by Grubb *et al.* Objective equality corresponds to the equal entitlements position (with or without historical responsibility thrown in). Likewise, equal opportunity corresponds to the 'reasonable emissions' position – no one has the right to emit to such an extent that it compromises the rights of others to equal opportunity, a position Bergesen derives from Locke. And the 'subjective equality' position is very similar to the comparative burdens position, with Bergesen noting the similar objection that 'any system of priority can be easily contested'.[26] The other two, relative equality (which is ambiguous but looks most like a desert-based principle) and rank order equality (equality within ranks for example race, gender or income – but not between them), are disregarded by Bergesen as politically impossible and self-evidently unfair.

In addition to these specific works there are sets of literature which invoke the language of justice or equity and presume one or other of these positions. The first assumes that justice means that those who have caused global warming should rectify the damage caused. This is the predominant approach in much technical work on allocating responsibility.[27] It is also the basis of the work on indices of greenhouse gas emissions for each country, a debate which is highly politicised. The focus is on the most appropriate methodology for calculating the (net) emissions[28] of countries and therefore their contributions to greenhouse warming. The debates on how to do this have been highly politically charged, particularly through the well publicised dispute between the World Resources Institute in Washington DC and analysts at the Centre for Science and Environment in New Delhi, which focussed on WRI's methodology.[29]

Two points are useful here about this debate. One is that most of those accepting Agarwal and Narain's critique of WRI accept a method of calculating responsibility based on cumulative historical emissions, as outlined by Young above.[30] Secondly an important distinction between WRI and Agarwal and Narain concerns the difference between calculating emissions purely by country and taking into account per capita emissions. For example WRI simply refers to six countries – the United States, the Soviet Union (as was), Brazil, China, India and Japan – as the leading (net) emitters of greenhouse gases, and then concludes that developing countries are as much causes of global warming as are industrialised countries.[31] However if taken on a per capita basis, the contributions of individual Chinese, Indian or Brazilian people to global warming pales into insignificance compared to those of individuals in industrialised countries. This of course relates to distinctions between communitarian and cosmopolitan ethics which would place ethical focus on the state (or community) or the individual respectively, which will be followed up below.

The second set of literature assumes the equal entitlements position. The most prominent works advocating this position unequivocally are those by Agarwal and Narain and by Krause, Koomey and Bach.[32] Both put these arguments in a similar manner to those outlined above, and thus need no repetition here.

2. International Justice

International distributive justice is commonly asserted to be something which only became thinkable in recent decades.[33] This was made possible by three developments: the increasing disparities in wealth across the globe, the increasing awareness of those disparities and the increasing capacity to redistribute wealth, income and resources across the globe.

The main reasons why considerations of distributive justice are still not often extended beyond societal boundaries originate in the terms of political discourse which we inherit from before the occurrence of these developments. Considerations of justice beyond boundaries (beyond the considerations of justice of and in war, and duties of hospitality to strangers) were not considered important for the reasons mentioned above: in practice inequalities across countries were relatively small until the twentieth century (and certainly smaller than inequalities within countries); the awareness of those beyond boundaries was small and therefore cosmopolitan culture and ethics was not widespread – the focus of ethical claims remained within countries; and in practice little could be done about any inequalities which did exist.

However the developments indicated above undermine the claims of communitarians. In Onora O'Neill's words, 'It is not a world of closed communities with mutually impenetrable ways of thought, self-sufficient economies and ideally sovereign states'; therefore, 'if complex, reasoned communication and association breach boundaries, why should not principles of justice do so too?'[34] With respect to global warming this argument is of course even more compelling. The interdependence between countries in this case is undeniable, both in terms of the degree of interdependence (how dependent each country is on the actions of others for its welfare) and of the meaning of that interdependence (how this constitutes each country's relationship to global warming).

3. Principles of Justice

Communitarians suggest that since ethical ideas are rooted in specific communities, arguments which suggest justice can transcend community boundaries are unconvincing. As suggested above this is implausible regarding global warming. What principles of justice are therefore thrown up in the debate on international justice? This section will outline six, and consider their relevance for the global warming debate. The first is a rights-based approach. The other five are derived from Chris Brown's review essay on the subject, largely for the sake of simplicity.[35]

Rights are still a prevalent way to think about justice. Perhaps surprisingly then the global warming debate does not invoke the language of rights to a great extent, with the exception of Bergesen.[36] However there are good reasons why rights would give a very poor grounding for action on global warming. Two important reasons for this can be drawn from O'Neill's discussion. Firstly rights often fail to specify those who hold correlative obligations. Thus rights may not be realised, 'not merely because obligation-holders may flout their obligation, but for the deeper reason that no obligation-holders have been specified'.[37] This is especially true of welfare rights (as opposed to liberty rights[38]), which would have to be invoked to justify international transfers in relation to global warming. It would involve invoking rights to a stable climate on which agriculture and so on depend, which require positive action by others (as opposed merely to non-intervention by others). Secondly rights are notoriously hard to ground.[39] If this has been true of those rights conventionally associated with human rights (liberty, freedom from want and so on) it would be particularly difficult to ground essentially new rights, such as those which global warming may threaten.

The first notion discussed by Brown is one based on causality or responsibility. Justice is in this sense righting a wrong – those responsible for harming others have a moral responsibility to put the situation right.[40] Brown's discussion focusses on the general question of inequality between societies, and makes the argument in unproblematic terms:

> If it is the case that the poverty of poor countries/peoples is the result of actions by rich countries/peoples, then there would seem to be quite a strong *prima facie* case for saying that the latter have a clear responsibility to act in such a way as to make reparations.[41]

This argument has immediate resonances (perhaps more than any of the others given below) with the global warming debate – as shown above, many base their considerations of justice on the historical responsibility of industrialised countries for causing global warming.

An immediate objection would be a communitarian one, that such obligations can only operate within a society which has shared norms and political institutions. Brown makes the claim that responsibility creates an obligation, but this is inconsistent with his general defence of communitarianism in his book. His version of communitarianism leads to principles of international justice which only cover the conventional principles of international law (just war, rules of coexistence) adopted by mainstream international relations theory. These would not normally include a principle of righting all wrongs caused to other states.[42] However we have seen the limitations of the communitarian position above, which apply equally here.

However a stronger objection is posed by O'Neill.[43] Discussing the general argument in relation to the West's historical responsibility for colonialism she shows that while in principle causing a problem does bestow obligations to rectify the situation, it is often virtually impossible to trace the lines of causality with any clarity. A particular problem is to place obligations on people in order to repay damages caused by their ancestors. The lines of causality are perhaps clearer in relation to global warming than for imperialism, but the problem remains. As soon as we try to identify in any detail those who have caused global warming historically, this problem looms large.

The second position given by Brown is a utilitarian one, exemplified by Peter Singer.[44] Singer's argument is straightforwardly act-utilitarian, that 'if it is in our power to prevent something bad from happening, without thereby sacrificing anything of comparable moral importance, we ought, morally, to do it'.[45] His concerns, like Brown's, are with the extremes of poverty and affluence, particularly concerning famines.

One basic difficulty is the ethical problems traditionally associated with utilitarianism. For example it is commonly argued tthat utilitarianism ignores the distinction between persons – that each person has a life-project which we may not reasonably expect them to subordinate to generalised utility.

However the position offered by Singer has specific problems here. One is that its focus is on individual action. Obviously the location of utility is always in individuals. However Singer's version places the location of obligation also at the level of the individual, rather than at the level of social and political institutions. Therefore while this might be a guide to action for individuals (for example, at the crude level, 'stop using your car to help those in small island states'), it is not clear how political institutions should respond. In simple terms, they could follow the same prescription, but this would in practice be more difficult to do, since they would have more problems than individuals in identifying the actions they could in practice carry out which would have the most beneficial effect. Should they, for example, enact policies to reduce car use or on the other hand increase the energy efficiency of cars? Should they reforest substantially or insulate homes? Obviously these are not necessarily either/or decisions but will often in fact be so in terms of allocation of state resources. But here the relationship between the intention of the action and its result is much less clear than in the case of individuals. States will also arguably be much more compromised by competing obligations in this case than will individuals.

A second problem is that in practice Singer's position may well be impossible to apply at the global level. The complexities involved in global warming lead to it being impossible to ascertain what might improve the general level of welfare. To the extent that we can interpret Singer to develop prescriptions for political institutions, this might move us in the direction of welfare economics, which is ethically based on utilitarian considerations. However environmental economists, whose work is generally based on welfare economics, have great difficulties in identifying what actions would improve overall welfare.[46] The problems are numerous. Firstly the uncertainties involved in global warming are such that even in pure monetary terms the 'zone of uncertainty', required to be small to undertake cost-benefit analysis, is too great.[47] Secondly the sorts of prescriptions coming out of cost-benefit analysis are often diametrically opposed to those given by Singer. Thirdly, and I think most importantly, global warming throws up great questions concerning the *meaning* of human welfare. Do we value material goods and economic growth over risks to do with climate change impacts and so on?

Brown's third position, which also tends to be outlined in individual terms, is the Kantian position as given by Onora O'Neill.[48] O'Neill rejects both utilitarian and rights-based approaches in favour of Kant. Obligations in this system derive partly from the categorical imperative itself, of acting only on universalisable principles. But she also argues that a precondition of human beings acting as moral and rational agents is threatened by poverty, famine and so on, so we are obliged in a Kantian system to act in order that all humans may become moral and rational agents.[49]

In the climate change context it is perhaps hard to see how to put this into practice. It would be possible to generate universalisable principles, but less easy to define the actions to which these principles would apply. What universalisable principles could we invoke to justify particular policies? For example O'Neill writes that 'beings who ... find that their individual abilities are not adequate to achieve their ends must be committed to relying ... on others' help; hence, if they reject non-universalisable principles, they must be committed to a principle of offering (at least some) help to others'.[50] Presumably an analogous story could be written regarding a principle that no one should consciously make the environment in which others live deteriorate. This could provide the basis within the literature on international justice for arguing that states which have polluted disproportionately should reduce their emissions and that unequal efforts by different states can be justified. This particular argument could also justify North–South transfers, by making them fulfil the obligations to enable others to become moral and rational agents regarding global warming.

At a more general level we could say that we are obliged not to act in such a way as to knowingly undermine the capacity for others to act as moral agents. We could derive obligations from this, such as not knowingly to cause others to lack the basic means of subsistence (for example through causing a sea-level rise). However, especially given scientific uncertainties, this would be underspecific as far as actions are concerned. To generate specific obligations from this principle we would have to have detailed knowledge of the effects of our actions on others, which is not possible given the uncertainties involved in global warming.

The fourth position given by Brown is a Rawlsian one.[51] Brown outlines Rawls's well known difference principle (that 'social and economic inequalities are to be arranged so that they are ... to the greatest benefit of the least advantaged'[52]) and then moves on to a discussion of whether this should be applied globally. Rawls maintains that a precondition for participation in the original position is membership in a particular society – he is a communitarian in this sense. A society for Rawls is a 'cooperative venture for mutual advantage',[53] which forms the basis of Charles Beitz's original critique of Rawls.[54] For Beitz the increased interdependence in the world as a consequence of the expansion of trade and so on, which means that the world as a whole should be treated as such a 'cooperative venture'.[55] Beitz later retreated from this position, largely on empirical grounds, but maintained an argument that the difference principle should be applied globally on the more ethically plausible grounds that, like intelligence and so on, membership of a particular society is morally arbitrary.[56] Global warming could be used to illustrate this; it makes it more obvious that it is morally arbitrary where one lives – one's vulnerability to climate change is entirely a matter of chance.

The Rawls/Beitz position, of all those given here, generates probably the most straightforward way to ground practical arguments as to the justice or otherwise of responses to climate change. They are just to the extent that they improve the position of the worst off. However this does not mean it is the most acceptable principle of distributive justice. Two problems are perhaps worth emphasising here. First is Shue's comment that Rawls provides no basic conditions below which people should not be allowed to fall: 'The Rawlsian difference principle can be fulfilled while people continue to drown but with less and less water over their heads'.[57]

Secondly Brown notes that Beitz's revised position is unstable – Rawls defines his principle of justice as being about distributing the products of cooperation (from his definition of society), while Beitz has abandoned the notion of society as a criterion for participation in the original position.[58] More broadly, what this illustrates is that at a basic level Rawls's position is ultimately utilitarian – justice is about the fairest distribution of goods, but only for those engaged in the society in question (those cooperating for mutual advantage).[59] As Barry suggests, this is to 'systematise self-interest'.[60] Rawls's position thus has some similar limitations to that of utilitarianism.

Brown's fifth position is that of Brian Barry.[61] Barry starts from a critique of Rawls's notion of 'justice as fairness' – as about the distribution of the products of cooperation – which Barry terms 'justice as reciprocity'.[62] For Barry, the main problem with justice as reciprocity is that it fails to provide reasons for applying considerations of justice in situations where justice may be most needed – where the weakest have no leverage. He cites the relationship between the United States and Bangladesh as illustrative of this. 'The probability, in the lifetime of anyone now alive, that the USA will be asking Bangladesh for aid is so low that aid from the USA simply cannot be construed as mutual aid'.[63]

Barry argues then for a notion of 'justice as impartiality'. In place of Rawls's veil of ignorance, where individuals presume self-interest but do not know their own identity, Barry constructs a situation where individuals are presumed to have interests, some of which conflict, but 'are motivated by the desire to reach agreement on terms that nobody could reasonably reject'.[64]

In other words 'the role of moral philosophy is not to systematise self-interest but to promote a willingness to submit to reasoned judgement'.[65] From this Barry constructs a set of principles for international justice not unlike those given by Beitz (although not as explicitly cosmopolitan), although the reasoning is very different. As Brown points out Barry's position has the advantage of not denying the pain which acting on these principles could cause in the rich countries, but proceeds from the proposition that if they submitted themselves to reasoned judgement they could not justify the level of existing inequality across the world.

In relation to global warming, one preliminary point is to repeat the point made above. While justice as reciprocity might get further in relation to justifying North–South transfers for global warming than in international relations in general, it would only help large developing countries or rapidly industrialising ones, and leave out the smallest, poorest, and often most vulnerable, who may be most deserving of considerations of justice.

The focus on communication in Barry's position as the route through which ethics are realised could be applied in this context by suggesting that justice requires that countries should not act on self-interest (even broadly conceived) but should start by asking what it is reasonable to expect of each other. For example is it reasonable to continue emitting CO_2 at several times the global average, knowing the possible/probable consequences of this on other countries? Is it reasonable to deny the transfers which would enable developing countries to reduce their rate of emissions, when they do not have the technological or financial resources to enable them to do this autonomously? This seems to me the most fruitful way to begin discussions of justice in this context. And against the charge that state policy-makers in practice will not submit themselves to these judgements, the response can simply be given that if this is the case, then no considerations of justice can be usefully discussed.[66] This at least has the advantage of involving those policy-makers themselves in constructing the considerations of what may be considered just. However were policy-makers to start with this question it is difficult to see how they could come to radically different positions on tangible matters to that offered by Henry Shue. In the light of this discussion of Barry, Shue's arguments clearly come within this framework, of starting by asking 'what is reasonable?' Shue's argument, already quoted, that justice 'does not permit that poor nations be told to sell *their* blankets in order that rich nations may keep *their* jewellery',[67] is consistent with this approach.

4. Conclusion: The Relationship Between the Two Sets of Literature

The discussion above of the international justice literature has given some indications as to how it might ground different positions within the global warming debate. There is clearly not a one to one fit between the two, except perhaps in the cases of the causal responsibility argument, and the Rawlsian position. The figure below shows some of the ways in which different positions in the global warming debate can be grounded.

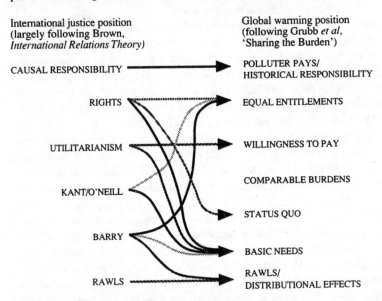

International justice position
(largely following Brown,
International Relations Theory)

Global warming position
(following Grubb *et al*,
'Sharing the Burden')

CAUSAL RESPONSIBILITY → POLLUTER PAYS/ HISTORICAL RESPONSIBILITY

RIGHTS → EQUAL ENTITLEMENTS

UTILITARIANISM → WILLINGNESS TO PAY

KANT/O'NEILL → COMPARABLE BURDENS

→ STATUS QUO

BARRY → BASIC NEEDS

RAWLS → RAWLS/ DISTRIBUTIONAL EFFECTS

The international justice literature fairly unambiguously indicates that it is difficult to justify existing levels of international inequality.[68] The global warming literature also, although more ambiguously, suggests that equity requires differential obligations between industrialised and developing countries, and transfers from the former to the latter. The mixing of the equal entitlements with the comparable burdens position by Grubb *et al.* or Young is primarily a result of questions of short term practical politics rather than justice.[69] It is perhaps not surprising therefore that neither the comparable burdens position nor the status quo position can easily be justified by reference to the broader traditions of international justice.

This reflects a broader weakness within the global warming literature, that the discussion of justice is often derived from the need for an 'effective' climate regime. Deriving the need for justice this way, rather than independently, has three problems. Firstly it is closely related to an argument about whether climate change alters the balance of power between North and South. However what is clear from this debate is that only some developing countries gain leverage, and it will be those countries most in need of justice which will not gain leverage.[70] Secondly this is arguably not a discussion of justice at all, which should need no justification from elsewhere; it is rather a discussion about practical politics. Thirdly if the basic empirical assumption, that agreements need to be just to be effective, is incorrect then the whole argument collapses.

Regarding the other positions, the figure suggests that most of the positions could be justified by a number of routes. What is perhaps interesting is that each global warming position can be justified by a number of routes, and each broader position does not unambiguously lead to a single position in the global warming debate. Hopefully, however, what this chapter has done is to illustrate how participants in the debate concerning global warming could defend their positions in broader terms of international justice and also, in a preliminary way, how this makes some positions held in the global warming debate untenable.

On this reading, the basic needs position would be the most plausible of those given. It was suggested that Brian Barry's argument concerning justice was the most convincing. According to the figure his argument could have three interpretations regarding global warming. Besides the basic needs position, it could justify an equal entitlements position or a Rawlsian difference principle. But either of these could probably be objected to within Barry's framework. Equal entitlements could be objected to on the grounds that entitlements to emit CO_2 bear little relation to meaningful indicators of human welfare or other values. The difference principle could be objected to using the argument given by Shue above. But it appears difficult to find grounds for arguing that meeting basic needs is unreasonable. Basic needs also seem able to be justified through more routes than any of the other global warming positions, including utilitarian, Kantian and rights-based approaches, which makes it even more persuasive.

Notes and References

*   I am grateful to the participants at the Reading University Workshop on 'The Ethical Dimensions of Global Change' for helpful comments. I am also grateful to John Barry, Richard Devetak, Andy Dobson, Andrew Linklater, John MacMillan, Peter Newell, Richard Shapcott and Hidemi Suganami for helpful comments on an earlier draft of this paper.

1   Three terms have been used in relation to this environmental problem: 'climate change', 'the greenhouse effect' and 'global warming'. I will use the latter for largely arbitrary reasons, and for practical purposes there is no significant difference. However the politics over the nuances of each term and which was to be used was itself interesting. For details see M. Paterson, 'Explaining the Climate Convention: International Relations Theory and Global Warming', unpublished Ph.D. Thesis, University of Essex, 1994, p. 2.

2   While in technical terms equity is different from distributive justice, they are used in this debate (Henry Shue apart) largely synonymously. There are also a number of ethical questions relevant to these discussions, which I am not considering here. These include intergenerational equity, the ethics of action under uncertainty; and the broader environmental ethics debate about anthropocentric or ecocentric bases of ethics. On intergenerational equity see for example E. B. Weiss, 'Climate Change, Intergenerational Equity and International Law: An Introductory Note', *Climatic Change*, 15 (1989) 327–35; B. Barry, 'The Ethics of Resource Depletion', in *Democracy, Power and Justice* (Oxford: Oxford University Press, 1989), or R. Malnes, *The Environment and Duties to Future Generations. An Elaboration of 'Sustainable Development'* (Oslo: Fridtjof Nansen Institute, 1990). On the precautionary principle, see A. Jordan and T. O'Riordan, *The Precautionary Principle in UK Environmental Policy and Law*, CSERGE Working Paper GEC 94–11 (Norwich: University of East Anglia, 1994). The third of these questions has not entered the field of international relations but has a wide literature in political theory and philosophy. The exception to this is H. Dyer, 'Environmental Ethics and International Relations', *Paradigms: Kent Journal of International Relations*, 8 (1994) 59–72. For an overview see R. Eckersley, *Environmentalism and Political Theory* (London: UCL Press, 1992).

3   As quoted in the *Guardian*, 9 November 1989.

4   T. Banuri *et al.*, *Equity and Social Considerations*, Intergovernmental Panel on Climate Change, Working Group III Report, Chapter 3, Draft 7.1, 1995. The IPCC was set up originally in 1988 to investigate the science, impacts and responses to climate change and produced three first reports in 1990, which precipitated (along with other events) negotiations towards the climate convention which was signed in 1992.

5   S. F. Singer, 'Earth Summit Will Shackle the Planet, Not Save It', *The Wall Street Journal*, 19 February 1992.

6   O. Young, 'The Politics of International Regime Formation: Managing Natural Resources and the Environment', *International Organization*,

43 (1989), p. 368.

7   M. Grubb, J. K. Sebenius, A. Magalhaes and S. Subak, 'Sharing the Burden', in I. Mintzer (ed.), *Confronting Climate Change: Risks, Implications and Responses* (Cambridge: Cambridge University Press, 1992).

8   For example in Grubb *et al.*, 'Sharing the Burden' and in H. P. Young, *Sharing the Burden of Global Warming* (College Park: University of Maryland 1991). Young, however, completely misrepresents Rawls's position, suggesting that the difference principle which he summarises as suggesting that 'resources should be distributed so that the worst-off group is as well-off as possible' is an egalitarian principle. He correctly notes that the wording he gives could imply that 'the industrialised countries should do everything they can to help developing countries achieve a *standard of living comparable to their own*' (emphasis added). However this is based on his erroneous interpretation of Rawls as an egalitarian. See Young, *Sharing the Burden*, p. 4.

9   For example many chapters in Hayes and Smith's edited volume give the impression of being concerned with justice, but concentrate on statistics and indices, presuming a particular conception of justice. See P. Hayes and K. Smith (eds), *The Global Greenhouse Regime: Who Pays?* (London: Earthscan, 1993).

10   M. J. Grubb, *Energy Policies and the Greenhouse Effect: Volume One* (London: Dartmouth/RIIA, 1990), p.279.

11   W. Nitze, *The Greenhouse Effect: Formulating a Convention* (London: RIIA, 1990), p. 14.

12   H. Shue, 'The Unavoidability of Justice', in A. Hurrell and B. Kingsbury (eds), *The International Politics of the Environment* (Oxford: Oxford University Press, 1992).

13   L. Susskind and C. Ozawa, 'Environmental Diplomacy: Strategies for Negotiating More Effective International Agreements', Harvard Disputes Program, MIT, Cambridge, MA., 1990; J. K. Sebenius, 'Designing Negotiations Towards a New Regime: The Case Of Global Warming', *International Security*, 15 (1991) 110–148.

14   This case could be made without the contentious first clause of the phrase – it could be considered unjust to exploit bargaining weaknesses wherever their origin.

15   The chapter which ended up being published in 1992 originated in a paper to a seminar in Oxford, although no date for the seminar is given in the book.

16   United Nations, *Framework Convention on Climate Change* (New York: United Nations, 1992), Articles 4.3 and 4.5.

17   H. Shue, 'Subsistence Emissions and Luxury Emissions', *Law and Policy* 15 (1993), p. 51; H. Shue, 'Environmental Change and the Varieties of Justice: An Agenda for Normative and Political Analysis', paper for conference on *Global Environmental Change and Social Justice*, Cornell University, Ithaca, NY, September 1993, p. 19; H. Shue, 'After You: May Action by the Rich be Contingent on Action by the Poor?', *Indiana Journal of Global Legal Studies*, 1 (1994), p.344.

18   Shue, 'After You', p. 344.

19   Shue, 'Environmental Change and the Varieties of Justice', p. 30.

20   Young, *Sharing the Burden*. Earlier on (p. 4), he discounts an Aristotelian account focussing on desert/responsibility and a Rawlsian one which he suggests (wrongly, as already noted) is egalitarian. I am not qualified to say whether his account of Aristotle is accurate. However these look surprisingly like the first and second of the three formulations he later offers.

21   There are obvious technical problems with this, not least uncertainty about the atmospheric lifetimes of each gas (which change over time with their concentrations), as well as with the fact that data about emissions get more problematic the further back we go. However Hayes and Smith's *The Global Greenhouse Regime*, which is based extensively on this approach, argues persuasively that these problems do not make the approach inapplicable. This of course does not make it necessarily desirable.

22   Grubb *et al.*, 'Sharing the Burden', pp. 312–14.

23   They give the following examples to illustrate the problem:
Cold countries require energy for heating; hot countries use it for air conditioning; and those in between may use it for both, according to season. Large, sparsely populated countries may require more energy for travel (more densely populated countries might seek an allowance for the resulting congestion!), but they are also more likely to have relatively more non-fossil energy sources ... Corrections might be attempted for the availability of non-fossil energy source, but it is impossible to quantify these to any degree of accuracy ... (p. 315).

24   They suggest that with the tradeable permits system, to create a situation which would generate sufficient financial incentives to meet abatement targets the annual transfers would involve the US giving 0.42 per cent of GNP, and European countries 0.16 per cent of GNP, to Southern countries, approximately equal to current ODA (p. 319).

25   H. O. Bergesen, 'A Legitimate Social Order in a "Greenhouse" World: Some Basic Requirements', *International Challenges*, 11 (1991), pp. 23–25.

26 Bergesen, 'A Legitimate Social Order in a "Greenhouse" World', p. 24.

27 For example Hayes and Smith, *The Global Greenhouse Regime*.

28 'Net emissions' refers to the emissions of a country minus its sinks. Overall contributions to global warming can in theory be reduced either by reducing emissions or by increasing sinks (for example reforestation). Net emissions are, however, not always used in these assessments, hence the parentheses.

29 World Resources Institute, *World Resources 1990–91* (Washington DC: World Resources Institute, 1991); A. Agarwal, and S. Narain, *Global Warming in an Unequal World – a Case of Environmental Colonialism* (New Delhi: Centre for Science and Environment, 1990); Global Environmental Change, 'Greenhouse Equity', Special Issue of *Global Environmental Change*, 2 (June 1992).

30 Young, *Sharing the Burden*. For example Hayes and Smith, *The Global Greenhouse Regime*.

31 *World Resources 1990–91*, pp. 15–17; M. Redclift, 'Throwing Stones in the Greenhouse', *Global Environmental Change*, 2 (1993), p. 90.

32 Agarwal and Narain, *Global Warming in an Unequal World*; F. Krause, J. Koomey and B. Bach, *Energy Policy in the Greenhouse: From Warming Fate to Warming Limit* (El Cerrito: International Project for Sustainable Energy Paths, 1990).

33 C. Brown, *International Relations Theory: New Normative Approaches* (Hemel Hempstead: Harvester Wheatsheaf, 1992), p. 156; O. O'Neill, 'Transnational Justice', in D. Held (ed.), *Political Theory Today* (Cambridge: Polity Press, 1991), p. 176.

34 O'Neill, 'Transnational Justice', p. 282.

35 Brown, *International Relations Theory*, Chapter 7.

36 Bergesen, 'A Legitimate Social Order in a "Greenhouse World"'. Even Henry Shue, whose well known contribution to the international justice debate, *Basic Rights* (Princeton, NJ: Princeton University Press, 1979) uses rights-based reasoning, does not use it here.

37 O'Neill, 'Transnational Justice', p. 287.

38 O'Neill, 'Transnational Justice', pp. 295–6. Bringing in entitlement theories such as those of Robert Nozick would of course complicate matters further. These focus on individuals' rights to non-interference from the state, and entitlement to their wealth (see R. Nozick, *Anarchy, State and Utopia* (New York: Basic Books 1974)). There is clearly a substantial potential clash between rights to wealth and to a stable climate.

39 O'Neill, 'Transnational Justice', p. 288.

40 Technically of course this is corrective rather than distributive justice.

(I am grateful to John Barry for pointing this out.) However it has clear distributional implications regarding global warming and is therefore relevant here.

41   Brown, *International Relations Theory*, p. 159.
42   Of course international law, especially international environmental law, does include a principle approximating to this. The infamous Trail Smelter Case established this precedent, where Canada was required by a tribunal to pay reparations to the United States for allowing air pollution to damage property in the United States. For a discussion of this see A. L. Springer, 'United States Environmental Policy and International Law: Stockholm Principle 21 Revisited', in J. E. Carroll (ed.), *International Environmental Diplomacy* (Cambridge: Cambridge University Press, 1988). The Stockholm Conference of 1972 incorporated this into its sovereignty principle. However it is by no means clear that this principle is taken as a *general* principle of international law. On sovereignty at the Stockholm Conference see M. Pallemaerts, 'From Stockholm to Rio: Back to the Future?', in P. Sands (ed.), *Greening International Law* (London: Earthscan, 1993).
43   O'Neill, 'Transnational Justice', pp. 291–3.
44   Brown, *International Relations Theory*, pp. 165–9.
45   P. Singer, 'Famine, affluence and morality', *Philosophy and Public Affairs*, 1 (1972) 229–43; quoted in Brown, *International Relations Theory*, p. 166.
46   D. Pearce, 'The Global Commons', in D. Pearce (ed.), *Blueprint 2: Greening the World Economy* (London: Earthscan, 1991), pp. 13–22.
47   Pearce, 'The Global Commons'.
48   O'Neill, *Faces of Hunger* (London: Allen and Unwin, 1986); O'Neill, 'Transnational Justice'.
49   See the summary in Brown, *International Relations Theory*, pp. 169–70.
50   O'Neill, 'Transnational Justice', p. 299.
51   Brown, *International Relations Theory*, pp. 170–177.
52   J. Rawls, *A Theory of Justice* (Oxford: Oxford University Press, 1973), p. 302.
53   Brown, *International Relations Theory*, p. 173.
54   C. Beitz, *Political Theory and International Relations* (Princeton, NJ: Princeton University Press 1979).
55   Note that this is different from O'Neill's resolution of the liberal/communitarian debate given earlier – there her claim is simply that communities are not neatly bounded. Here the claim is much stronger, that interdependence has extended so far as to make claims that a global

society (in Rawls's sense) has emerged.

56 C. Beitz, 'Cosmopolitan Ideals and National Sentiment', *Journal of Philosophy*, 80 (1983) 591–600.
57 H. Shue, *Basic Rights*, p. 128. I am grateful to John Barry for reminding me of this useful quote.
58 Brown, *International Relations Theory*, p. 177.
59 This is of course ironic since Rawls explicitly attacks utilitarianism. However it is difficult to see how defining society as a system of cooperation for mutual advantage is not utilitarian at a fundamental level. See B. Barry, *A Treatise on Social Justice*, Volume 1, *Theories of Justice* (Hemel Hempstead: Harvester Wheatsheaf, 1989).
60 As paraphrased by Brown, *International Relations Theory*, p. 181; Barry, *Theories of Justice*, Chapter 10.
61 Brown, *International Relations Theory*, pp. 179–82.
62 B. Barry, 'Justice as Reciprocity', in *Democracy, Power and Justice* (Oxford: Oxford University Press 1989).
63 Barry, 'Justice as Reciprocity', p. 483.
64 Brown, *International Relations Theory*, p. 180.
65 Brown, *International Relations Theory*, p. 181.
66 Brown, *International Relations Theory*, p. 182.
67 Shue, 'The Unavoidability of Justice', p. 397.
68 The exception would be an entitlement theory which follows Nozick. This has not been discussed here, except in passing. It would fit in the diagram as the link between rights theories and the status quo position. However in the extreme case that rights to property conflict with rights to subsistence, which is clearly implicated in the case of global warming, it seems difficult to justify arguing for the priority of entitlements to property.
69 Grubb *et al.*, 'Sharing the Burden'; Young, *Sharing the Burden*.
70 M. Paterson, 'Global Warming: The Great Equaliser?', *Journal für Entwicklungspolitik*, 8 (1992), pp. 221–222; also Shue, 'The Unavoidability of Justice', pp. 379–381. This reinforces the point made by Brian Barry, that the notion of justice as reciprocity fails in situations like these (see Barry, 'Justice as Reciprocity'; also Brown, *International Relations Theory*, pp. 179–180). Haiti (for example) cannot be considered in an meaningful reciprocal relationship with (for example) the United States on climate change – it is a relationship of almost pure dependence. The way in which the North–South balance of power in global warming is related to a discussion of justice can only be through some implicit notion of justice-as-reciprocity.

PART 6

Perceptions of War in a Changing World

10

The New World Order and the Ethics of War

Anthony Coates

In the aftermath of the Gulf War talk of a 'New World Order' filled many with a feeling both of apprehension and of déjà vu. For those of a realist persuasion a sense of foreboding, rather than the intended sense of moral expectancy, was dominant. Once again the old moralistic illusions, which had wrought such havoc in times past, threatened to take control of foreign policy and, thereby, to undermine the fragile construct of international order. Realists like Kissinger warned that idealism had led America astray in the past and was likely to do so again.[1]

The talk was activated by two principal events: the end of the Cold War (and superpower rivalry) and the 'success' of the Gulf War itself. Even those who entertained considerable moral doubts about the latter event recognised its novelty and moral potential so far as the conduct or management of international relations was concerned. The Gulf War may not have been the most propitious beginning but it was *a* beginning. The international community seemed to many to be acquiring a new capacity and will to act denied it during the period of the Cold War. For idealists what these events revealed was an historic opportunity to bring about the qualitative transformation of international relations, the opportunity to leave behind the discredited world of power politics and rival interests and to promote in its place the common good of the international community and the rights of its members.[2]

Realists were more sceptical: behind all the high moral rhetoric lay the old realities and constraints of power. The post-Cold War world was filled with dangers and uncertainties rather than moral opportunities. Moral rhetoric was tolerable as long as it was not taken seriously. Traditional concerns and traditional instrumentalities were still seen to apply. In the midst of post-Gulf War euphoria Kissinger counselled caution and reminded his readers of traditional verities like the dependence of international order on a balance of power to the preservation of which foreign policy should remain dedicated. In the interests of peace the old and dangerous illusion that a radical moral reordering of international relations was close at hand must be resisted.

The conception of a new and more moral international order included a new moral role for war. This was a radical departure. Throughout the period of the Cold War and the rivalry of nuclear superpowers the moral instrumentality of war was either played down or simply rejected. Even in circles traditionally inclined to defend that instrumentality a deep scepticism, of the kind more usually associated with pacifism, became apparent in the wake of World War Two. Papal pronouncements, for example, expressed strong dissatisfaction with the continued application of just war thinking to the case of modern war. 'The theory of war as an adequate and fitting method of solving international conflicts is now superseded', declared Pius XII. 'Defence against injustice of any kind is not justification for the use of violence which is war. Even when the damage it causes is not comparable with that caused by injustice which is tolerated, we are under an obligation to suffer that injustice'.[3] The threat of a nuclear holocaust, as well as the recent experience of total war, engendered a widespread anti-war mentality according to which the idea of a just recourse to war seemed not only futile but dangerous.

With the threat of a nuclear Armageddon receding as East and West appeared to approach some kind of moral and political consensus, nuclear war no longer monopolised the moral debate about war. In the past the dangers of a conventional war escalating into a nuclear exchange had led to the same moral prohibitions being applied to conventional as were applied to nuclear war. Moreover it had seemed to many that the differences between nuclear war and conventional warfare in its modern and strategic form were often exaggerated. In an era of total war those differences had seemed morally insignificant. The political and military success of the Gulf War, in which limited goals were achieved efficiently, discriminately and (more arguably perhaps) proportionately, weakened the conviction that in the modern age all major wars, whether nuclear or conventional, were unavoidably total wars fought in a wholly indiscriminate and quite disproportionate way.

These developments appear to have led to the partial restoration of the moral instrumentality of war. The vision of a reordering of international relations in accordance with considerations of human rights and international justice found room for the instrumental role of armed force. In the new moral order military force would play a key role, no longer as the instrument of power and national interest but as the instrument of justice and the international common good. Wars in the new order would be just wars, fought with the express intention of bringing about an end to all war.[4]

Realists have regarded this changing conception of war with deep suspicion. It is not of course a novel view of war. Throughout military history war has often been resorted to out of pure motives and to fulfil higher moral purposes, with dire consequences. 'He who plays the angel,' wrote Aron, 'plays the beast.'[5] Experience teaches that the greater the 'moral' investment in war or the more 'morality' is allowed to define the end of war the more destructive war becomes. In the Western world the fiercest and most destructive wars by far have been those 'missionary wars' which were fought for a redemptive purpose, whether religiously or ideologically conceived. In modern times secular and ideological purposes have embraced the cause of democracy and freedom as well as racial or class hegemony, and even (perhaps especially) those whose declared interest has been the cause of world peace have succumbed to this 'moral' generation and intensification of anarchy and conflict.[6] More often than not, therefore, it is the fear of the consequences of applying morality to the unwelcoming domain of war and international relations that has lain behind the general moral scepticism of the realist. Inevitably that fear resurfaces amidst the talk of a radical reconstruction of international affairs and of a new and more 'moral' war agenda.

From a traditional 'just war' perspective the fears of realism seem more than justified (though the realist conclusion that any attempt at the moral determination of war is out of place needs to be resisted).[7] The just war tradition has learned, partly from its own bitter experience, the dangers of investing war with too great a moral purpose.[8] The moral elevation of war does threaten to undermine the moral as well as the pragmatic limitation of war, and the first lesson for those who seek to apply morality to the case of war is that its moral instrumentality is real but severely limited. The second lesson is that the moral structure of war as of international relations is inherently complex. Though the idea of a 'new world order' is not in itself alien to the just war tradition (as it perhaps is to the realist tradition), from *both* a realist and a just war perspective much of the present talk about it smacks of the old moralistic illusion that war and international relations are more purely moral or more amenable to a certain kind of moral determination than in fact they are, or even perhaps ought to be.[9]

The assumption which lies behind the realist's critique of the attempted moral determination of international relations is that the moral approach is always and necessarily 'moralistic' and indifferent to 'reality'. Though the

assumption is false, the concern is both legitimate and not without foundation. Many attempts at the moral determination of war and international
relations show scant regard for moral instrumentalities and an extravagant
regard for moral ends or purposes. Those who, often in legitimate opposition to realism, advance the claims of morality in the relatively infertile realm
of international relations may betray the cause of morality by exaggerating
the moral potentialities of war and international relations and by eschewing
the very means which empower morality in the first place.

At the heart of this moralistic approach a certain moral perfectionism or
moral puritanism is discernible which seems out of place even in the domain
of personal morality let alone in the less morally determinable domain of
international relations. However the failure to recognise important differences between the private and the public domains of morality is a large part
of the problem. Moralism leads to the oversimplification of political and
international ethics and either overlooks or deliberately discounts their
distinctive requirements.[10]

In the first place the moralist tends not only to apply the same moral standards to the political sphere as are applied to the personal or private sphere
but to entertain the same moral expectations of both spheres, disregarding
the limited nature and limited purposes of political morality in comparison
with the morality of personal life. Hegel's discussion of the relation between
religion and politics is instructive in this regard.[11] The moral perfectionism
which is rightly applied to the religious life is out of place in the domain of
politics Hegel argues. The attempt to apply too high a standard ('the wish to
have the whole in every particular') is fraught with danger. It must lead to
what Hegel calls 'the fanaticism of destruction', a fanaticism which cannot
tolerate the concrete and seemingly less than perfect world of politics, which
cannot find room for the particular in its universalist and hypermoralistic
vision of the state. In moralism matters of personal morality are allowed to
dictate and to submerge matters of political morality.

Secondly the moralist disregards the relative simplicity of personal
morality in comparison with the hugely complex nature of political morality.
It is this inherent complexity which accounts for the more artistic and technical nature of 'political' ethics. Moral judgement in the political domain
calls for the deployment of skills and forms of understanding which are
redundant in the less complex personal domain. It demands an attention
to, and understanding of, the means or instrumentalities of power, and an
awareness of the limits as well as of the possibilities of moral action.[12]

Thirdly moralism discounts both the element of moral uncertainty which
clings to all moral action in the political sphere as well as the moral nerve
which acting with this uncertainty requires. This uncertainty is no doubt a

feature of all moral action but it is greatly magnified in the complex world of politics where moral reasoning is so dependent upon technical judgements of the likely consequences of a course of action and where the control of subsequent events is necessarily limited. Decision-making, particularly in the field of international relations, is of necessity a risky business.

Fourthly moralism disregards the more morally conflictual, and hence more ambiguous, nature of political decision-making. Again the difference is not an absolute one but more one of degree: the conflict of values, which dictates a hierarchical ordering of values and which seems so inescapable a part of the moral life as a whole, is a *predominant* feature of political life, where the promotion of one value is rarely without damage to another value. It is this which accounts for the negative form which so many moral characterisations of politics take. Choosing the lesser evil rather than the greater good is the morally less satisfying but none the less typical form which moral choice takes in the political sphere.

Fifthly moralism resists the largely (though by no means exclusively) consequential form which moral reasoning as it applies to the political domain suitably takes, in favour of an ethics or 'morality of intention', according to which 'what matters is not what you do but why you do it ... an act is moral only when its motive is altruistic ... If any element of self-interest creeps in, the act is corrupt and sinful.'[13] Here as elsewhere 'the direct transference of personal values into social life' without regard to the distinctive needs and relative autonomy of politics leads to 'the wreckage not only of public policy but also of morality itself'.[14]

As the above quotation implies it is not just the one-sided preoccupation with intentions that characterises the moralistic approach. Just as damaging so far as the moral determination of war is concerned is the restricted understanding of moral intentionality which moralism displays, an understanding which manifests itself in a puritanical insistence on the systematic divorce of duty and inclination, or of justice and interest, a divorce effected most famously perhaps by Kant but which continues to play an influential role in moral theory and practice.

In Kant's ascetic ethic *disinterestedness* is seen to be inherent in morality, authentically conceived: 'pleasure, self-interest, happiness ... can never be the motives of the moral act itself and as such, even conjoint and secondary motives of the weakest order. Insofar as they intervene in the intention, they taint it and cause it to cease to be moral. They cannot act as motives for the autonomous will, the pure moral will'.[15] Kant argues that the moral act 'does not subserve my inclination, but overpowers it, or at least in case of choice excludes it from its calculation'.[16] The presence of inclination or interest, at least in the order of motivation, is seen to be destructive in its moral effects:

'the springs [incentives] it provides for morality are such as rather undermine it and destroy its sublimity'.[17]

Kant's ethic is essentially an ethic of self-sacrifice according to which the 'highest moral worth of all' is assigned to the character who 'is beneficent, not from inclination, but from duty'.[18] The war between duty and inclination, to the peaceful resolution of which philosophers like Rousseau and Hegel dedicated their best efforts, served as the fundamental principle of Kantian morality. 'In this inquiry', Rousseau writes at the beginning of *The Social Contract* , 'I shall try always to bring together what right permits with what interest prescribes so that justice and utility are in no way divided'.[19] Kant's project is the very antithesis of Rousseau's (and of Hegel's). 'Reason issues its commands unyieldingly', he writes, 'without promising anything to the inclinations, and, as it were, with disregard and contempt for these claims'.[20]

This assumption that morality requires the performance of duty for its own sake, and therefore the deliberate exclusion of considerations of interest and power, appears to underlie many contemporary assessments of international relations and war, where it gives rise to distorted judgements about the moral value and instrumentality of war. It is an assumption which idealism (or moralism) shares with realism where its impact is very different but equally distorting. It is the assumption that the moral point of view necessarily, or at least typically, excludes the standpoint of interest or utility which largely accounts for the moral scepticism of the realist. Out of the false antithesis between morality and interest emerge the two contrasting traditions of realism and idealism, one sacrificing morality to interest, the other sacrificing interest to morality.

In the case of moralism the assumption leads to the rejection of war's moral instrumentality in those cases where the warring powers appear to be acting from 'mixed' or 'impure' motives. Much of the opposition to military intervention in response to the Iraqi invasion of Kuwait took this form. The war in the Gulf was characterised by many of its moral critics as 'a war over oil' and *therefore* as a morally suspect or even indefensible war.[21] The presence of an American or Western interest served to devalue the moral case for war, namely, the restoration of Kuwaiti sovereignty and the defence of the rule of law. 'Why are we at war?' asked one US church leader, whose own answer was quite unequivocal: 'Because human greed, lust for power and national self-interest are alive and well. Ask yourself, if the primary export of Kuwait were broccoli and not oil, would we be joining this war?'[22] The moral case was seen to be further undermined by the alleged double-dealing or moral duplicity of the US and its allies and the highly selective and self-serving way in which the right or duty of intervention was being exercised. In other words the moral criticism took the form of an unmasking of US or

Western interests, the defence of which constituted the real motive for military intervention.[23]

From the moral purist's standpoint the recourse to war must be judged by a very different yardstick. Just as the presence of an interest encourages the moralist to renounce war so the perceived absence of an interest leads to the enthusiastic and often quite uninhibited support for a war untainted by impure motives. In cases such as Bosnia and Rwanda the moral nobility of the cause may seem so overpowering as to be sufficient in itself to justify recourse to war. By way of criticism moralists are quick to point out that it is precisely this kind of war, in which no clear self-interest is discernible, that states are most reluctant to fight. While the US and Britain hastened to the aid of an oil-rich Kuwait, both have dragged their feet over a more active military intervention in Bosnia, the prime motivation of which would be humanitarian. These 'moral' or 'disinterested' wars are the very wars which ought to be fought but which are not fought because they are seen to be interest-free. It is the perceived 'purity' of humanitarian wars of intervention (or, similarly, of revolutionary wars which have as their aim the reconstitution of society and the consequent elimination of all war), which enables some of the fiercest critics of more conventional interstate war to embrace these 'holy' wars with such unbridled enthusiasm.[24]

A concern with intentions is not of course out of place in moral theorising about war. The just war tradition recognises this by giving *right intention* a key place in the moral apparatus which it employs in its analysis of war. The danger, however, is twofold: firstly that 'right intention' may be too narrowly and too puritanically defined; and, secondly, that intentionality, in this attenuated form, may be allowed to monopolise the moral debate about war to the neglect of other essential moral considerations, such as the consideration of consequences.[25]

What is the proper moral interest in right intention? In the first place it is the perception that the moral appeal in war *may* serve a purely ideological end, masking baser motives. Behind the moral rhetoric and the appeal to just cause may lie a hidden and unwarranted agenda. The Argentinian invasion of the Falklands in 1982, for example, is thought to have owed at least as much to considerations of domestic politics and the securing of the junta's usurpation of power as it did to those of national sovereignty, the ostensible and presumed 'just cause'.[26] Less plausibly, the British response to the invasion has been seen as unduly influenced by the Conservative government's wish to improve its electoral prospects. The normal moral assessment of war does depend on a healthy scepticism regarding the declared and altruistic aims of the warring parties, all of whom are likely to have additional and sometimes hidden motives. The issue, so far as the debate about moralism is concerned, is whether this additional motivation, secret or declared, nullifies just cause and undermines just recourse to war.

For the moralist the answer is affirmative. The just war is a pure war, an altruistic war fought for high moral ideals. The intrusion of self-interest is necessarily corrupting and devaluing to such an extent that the war itself may have to be renounced. In just war theory, on the other hand, the criterion of right intention does not rule out diversity of intention or the presence of secondary motives. There is nothing puritanical about the just war assessment.

The moral issue is not whether an interest is present but whether that interest is *legitimate and relevant* to the case of war. If it is, its mere presence does not invalidate just recourse. On the contrary, it may strengthen the moral credentials of the war in question. The presence of an interest only becomes morally problematic when the interest itself is illegitimate (or legitimate but out of place), or when a legitimate and relevant interest is advanced disproportionately to the detriment of other, perhaps superior, moral claims (as seems to be the case in those forms of realism which, judged from a just war position, are seen to exaggerate the claims of state sovereignty and the national interest and to neglect those of the international community).

In fact, from a just war perspective, the positive as well as the negative moral potential of *interest* requires equal emphasis. In general terms its morally beneficial effects are evident in the way that considerations of interest often serve to make moral ideals more concrete and to anchor the moral debate about war, ensuring that moral enthusiasm for war does not get out of hand and prove prejudicial to other essential concerns. Moreover the articulation of ideals in a form that is not exclusive of interests makes those ideals more practicable, providing key incentives to action which, as far as the moral determination of politics and of war is concerned, cannot afford to be ignored. More specifically *interest* can be seen to play a decisive role in the operation of several key just war principles.

The first criterion of just recourse, *legitimate authority*, appears to entail the adoption of the standpoint of interest. Rulers are authorised to use force by the community which they represent. The decisions which they take relating to war are taken in a public capacity not in a private or personal capacity. They must not regard public office as if it were their own moral preserve where decisions are taken purely in accordance with personal ideals or on the strength of personal moral convictions. Promoting or safeguarding the particular interests of the community which they serve is *a* good and one the deliberate setting-aside of which would constitute a major dereliction of duty and a violation of one of the basic criteria of just recourse. Such setting-aside of both public interest as well as public opinion is common in the 'all too moral' war. As far as the criterion of legitimate authority is concerned those who are enthralled by the justice of their cause need little further sanction or authorisation in order to resort to war. They share the conviction attributed to the Jacobin wing in the French Revolution that 'the truth of its vision [is] sufficient guarantee of its authority to act'.[27]

Secondly interest has a part to play in the definition and articulation of *just cause* . In the first place the interest itself may be important enough to constitute just cause for war, as in the case of self-defence. But even where this is not the case and where the primary cause of war is not one of interest, interest may play a contributory and supporting role. Moreover advancing the standpoint of interest may help with the articulation of just cause and with the specification of the aims of war. Making the calculation of interest part of the moral assessment encourages a more prudential approach[28] and requires decision-makers to reflect on the instrumentalities and likely outcomes of their actions and not just on broadly and loosely conceived moral ends or purposes, no matter how noble or exalted those ends might appear to be.

The need for such specification can often be acute. The hypermoral and interest-free approach to war may lead to such a generalised and unspecific definition of just cause as to make recourse to war justifiable regardless of circumstances. The failure of a government or state to comply with religious or ideological principle can be deemed sufficient cause for war irrespective of the circumstances of the case or of the concrete needs and possibilities of the society in question. As Burke argued in respect of the French Revolution, such prudential and circumstantial reasoning is alien to this way of thinking: a government which fails to comply with a preferred form stands condemned however benevolent or lenient its rule or however dim the prospects of improving on its record.

The standpoint of interest also encourages the adoption of a more bilateral and morally sceptical view of just cause, both of which seem fundamental to the just conduct of war. The morally 'impure' war discourages belligerents from making exaggerated moral claims and from regarding the conflict in absolute moral terms as a contest between the forces of Darkness and Light. Some moral blurring of the contours of war is essential to a proper moral understanding of war. Blurring is often noticeably absent. Many of the calls for increased military intervention in Bosnia, for example, seem to rest on a moral oversimplification of the conflict according to which the Serbs are seen straightforwardly and unilaterally as the unjust aggressors and the prime source of conflict. This is to ignore not only historical but contemporary realities and the great suffering which the different ethnic communities have inflicted on each other. Realistically, of course, taking sides may be a necessary condition of effective military action but whether such intervention would be just is another matter. Demonisation of a potential adversary is never a sound basis of just recourse. Both (or all) sides have interests which form the basis of moral claims. Without recognition of the potential validity of some or part of an adversary's claims a just war seems impossible. The purer the moral perception of war the more likely it is that war will be seen in the absolute and morally oversimplified form of a contest between Good and Evil, and a war fought on such terms is more rather than less likely to breach the moral defences of war.

The concept of interest can be seen to play a key role in the argument about a war's *proportionality* , that is, whether the good to be sought in war outweighs the harm which it seems likely to inflict. When a British foreign secretary responds to a humanitarian plea for greater military intervention in Bosnia by raising the question of its impact on British interests he is not thereby eschewing or disavowing morality. On the contrary the question is fundamental to the issue of just recourse. Just as it would be wrong to allow the argument to be driven entirely by considerations of interest so it would be wrong to exclude such considerations from the moral calculus of war. The problem with a war too grandly conceived ('the war to end all wars') is that no price can seem too high to pay for its prosecution. In short, a 'moral' war is never disproportionate.

The positive and structural influence of *interest* on the moral assessment of war does not end there. The *prospects of success,* regarded traditionally as one of the key determinants of just recourse, may well dictate its presence. To have recourse to war with little thought being given to the likelihood of its successful outcome seems more self-indulgent than just and conflicts with the requirements of proportionality. Gauging the prospects of success involves, among other things, a calculation of interest, for without the popularly perceived presence of an interest it seems unlikely that a government, particularly a democratic government, could sustain a prolonged and costly war. The point has been made forcibly by democratic politicians in the case of Bosnia. Many have expressed scepticism about the possibility of retaining public support for a war of humanitarian intervention once the death toll begins to mount. This was a matter of prime concern even in the Gulf War where motives were clearly mixed and interests present. Indeed the assumption that the US would not be able to fight a war of attrition in the face of fierce domestic opposition was an essential part of Saddam Hussein's strategy. The willingness to sustain losses, and thereby the prospects of success, may be greatly increased if the public can be convinced that in the war in question right and interest coincide. Without that public conviction the prospects of success may become so slim as to rule out just recourse to war.

From the standpoint of the moral purist success is measured by a very different calculus so that even a war which seems doomed to military and political failure can still be thought worth fighting. Indeed from this heightened moral standpoint the prospects of defeat may even increase the moral allure of a war conceived in the heroic and noble mould. Likewise, the expressive and more than instrumental moral value attached to this form of war serves to undermine the criterion of *last resort*. The moral opportunities afforded only in war (for example to die a martyr's or a hero's death with all its perceived rewards) may establish a moral preference for war over peace. A real lust for war may be the result of its moral glorification. In this way the 'moral' war is readily transformed into the war of first rather than of last resort.

The above criteria determine the issue of just recourse but in just war theory the conduct of war (*ius in bello*) is of as much concern as the recourse to war (*ius ad bellum*). However just the cause for which a war is being fought it must remain within moral boundaries. The frequently voiced and influential view that in the pursuit of a just cause all means become permissible is firmly resisted. Taken to extremes such a view collapses into incoherence since a war which is tolerant of *all* means must become indistinguishable from the evil which it fights. The assumption that the employment of evil means leaves a good end intact is not well founded.

The primary and specific requirements of just conduct are proportionality or economy in the use of force and discrimination or recognition of non-combatant immunity. On balance both seem more attainable in a war in which considerations of interest inform (without dictating) policy than in one in which such considerations are deliberately set aside for the sake of moral purity.

The immunity of prisoners of war, for example, or of other non-combatants, is more likely to be respected when justice is seen to be allied to utility: killing prisoners of war and other non-combatants is not only an unjust but a more costly method of warfare since it encourages an adversary to do the same and makes his surrender less likely. Similarly in counterinsurgency warfare, where the strategic objective is retaining or winning the hearts and minds of the civilian population, conducting the war in a disproportionate and indiscriminate way can be seen to be neither moral nor effective. Such utilitarian or pragmatic considerations, which may lend support to the more moral conduct of war, tend to be lost sight of in the greater the moral or ideological intensification of war.

As in respect of just recourse so in respect of just conduct, the moral or historical immensity of the aims of 'holy' war override considerations of *proportionality*. The 'proportionality of means' suffers the same fate as the 'proportionality of ends': no price can be too high to pay in the pursuit of such a cause. Profligacy rather than economy in the use of force is the predictable result. Judged by this moral calculus the deaths of millions pale into insignificance alongside the prospect of a world without war or of some universal hegemony on which human destiny or historical progress is seen to depend. 'With the rest of my generation,' wrote Kopelev, a party activist who helped to execute the policy of 'terror by hunger' in the Ukraine, 'I firmly believed that the ends justified the means. Our great goal was the universal triumph of Communism, and for the sake of that goal everything was permissible – to lie, to steal, to destroy hundreds of thousands and even millions of people, all those who were hindering our work or could hinder it, everyone who stood in the way.'[29]

The 'disinterested' war is a war which is not only conceived but fought with reckless intensity. Those whose motives in fighting a war are 'mixed' or 'impure' are likely to have more reason to live than those who see themselves as engaged in a 'holy' war. Their conduct of war may, therefore, be more inhibited, and less destructive, than the conduct of those who fight from 'purer' motives. The latter often have a vested 'moral' interest in dying that scorns the calculation of risk and which seems incomprehensible to a combatant with a more interest-led understanding of war. As an American soldier who took part in the battle of Okinawa put it: 'Our infantrymen landed on Pacific islands knowing they might die but hoping they wouldn't. Kamikaze men knew the outcome in advance.'[30] For the latter death had acquired an intrinsic value: 'The impossible odds at Okinawa enhanced rather than diminished the lure of an exquisite death, for the more obvious the futility, the greater the glory and seductiveness of the sacrificial feat.'[31]

It would be comforting but mistaken to see this attitude to war as uniquely 'fascist'. It can be, and has been, engendered in any war given sufficient moral, religious or ideological investment in war. In this aspect, as in others, the key lies not in the *specific* ideology but in the ideological form of war-making itself. The moral or historic grandeur and importance of the cause for which the war is fought gives such a war an intrinsic and not just instru-mental value. Those who die in a war fought for such glorious ends find a satisfaction in death denied to those who die in defence of less grandiose and more 'impure' ends.

The reckless conduct of the 'moral' war is often matched by its ruthlessness, a trait which results from the absolute moral terms in which such wars tend to be defined and in accordance with which the enemy becomes an enemy in his entirety, an 'existential foe'. Such total enmity must engender total war. 'A noble is not of my species,' claimed one of the French revolutionaries, 'he is a wolf and I shoot.'[32] The moral recognition of an adversary, the acceptance and constant upholding of his common humanity, on which the just conduct of war ultimately depends, is here suppressed.[33] In contrast, when moral perceptions are informed by considerations of interest the adversarial status of the enemy is more clearly and more restrictively defined. The enemy is less likely to appear as an enemy in his totality or as the embodiment of evil the less 'pure' the moral perception of war itself. In the 'interested' war enmity remains a matter of specific actions, injuries or threats which justify specific responses and which are remediable through specific concessions or restitutions. The war of annihilation, in which conversion or death is the stark choice with which an adversary is confronted, and to which, historically, more purely moral wars have been prone, is out of place here.[34]

A just war is one which is fought in such a way as to facilitate its peaceful conclusion. A war which is at least in part interest-led is more likely to remain a war which is fought for specific and limited goals. The standpoint of interest itself encourages the adoption of an instrumental view of war which, in turn, promotes the more limited conduct of war. If this view can continue to inform the conduct of war (something which is difficult to secure given the tendency of modern warfare to become total), then a negotiated and earlier peace appears the more probable outcome. The less 'moral' and therefore less vindictive nature of such a war will enable those who have achieved a military ascendancy to settle for something less than total victory or unconditional surrender, recognising that even a defeated enemy has certain interests and rights. In short a moral climate or culture which embraces interests is more favourable to a negotiated peace (the kind of peace which has moral primacy in just war thinking) than a more morally intense and exalted climate of war, one which is deliberately neglectful of interests and in which the search for a perfect or utopian (and perhaps one-sided) peace leads to the unnecessary prolongation and intensification of war.[35]

It appears, therefore, that, far from being morally destructive, the assessment of war from the standpoint of interest promotes its greater moral limitation, by helping to bring essential moral considerations to the fore and by providing powerful incentives to the moral conduct of war (incentives which seem indispensable given the collective and non-heroic nature of the morality proper to war and politics). Conversely, the exclusion of interest or the moral purification of war threatens to undermine the moral limits of war. The alluring prospect of a war to end all wars or of a new order free of all previous imperfections releases all moral inhibitions and generates an enthusiasm for war which imperils both just recourse and just conduct. A disinterested war is, paradoxically, a less morally determinable war than one fought for more mundane and less exalted purposes.

The just war tradition's opposition to such a hypermoralistic under-standing of war stems in part from its own experience and its consequent awareness of the great risks which attend all attempts to subject war to moral regulation. The realist's distrust of morality is not without foundation. Though the realist is wrong to regard every moral intervention as an unjus-tified and dangerous intrusion, it remains true that there *is* a fine line to be drawn between the subjection of war to moral limits and the dismantling of those same limits in the name of morality. Though morality has a place in the business of war the moral limitation of war depends on keeping the moral impulse itself under control.

The idea of a 'new world order' is not alien to a tradition like the just war tradition in which 'realist' *and* 'utopian' concerns vie for attention. The latter ensure that within the tradition war is everywhere subject to the moral primacy of peace, and that the peace which is upheld is a dynamic and cre-ative peace, one which seeks to treat the causes and not just the symptoms of conflict. Though the 'realism' of the tradition allows it to recognise the practical and moral utility of such instruments as the 'balance of power' there is here no danger, as there is perhaps in the case of realism itself, of confus-ing means with ends. There is more to a 'just' peace than the maintenance of the balance of power. The moral transformation of the international order is an end to which just war theorists as well as others aspire. The aspiration itself, however, is not without certain dangers and in the search for its fulfilment that 'bastard' morality, 'patched up from limbs of various derivation', on which Kant poured such scorn[36] appears a safer guide than some more exalted moral approaches.

The cause of morality, particularly of international morality, is ill served by moral puritanism. The more disinterested attempts at the moral transfor-mation of international politics become the less likely they are to succeed. The moral strategy in the international domain should be the same as the moral strategy in the domestic domain of the state: to find ways of promoting and advancing the marriage of duty and inclination rather than their divorce. That duty and inclination, or justice and utility, are distinct and that they often conflict are not denied: there are times when the performance of duty is as painful for states as it sometimes is for individuals. But to construct a moral principle out of the fact of conflict appears misguided: those who seek a moral transformation of international politics cannot afford to hold interest in con-tempt.

Notes and References

1   H. A. Kissinger, 'America cannot police the world forever', *The Times*, 12 March 1991.
2   Even such a seasoned and detached observer as the military historian John Keegan detected 'a profound change in civilisation's attitude to war' and 'the emerging outline of a world without war'. To Keegan the evidence suggested 'that mankind, wherever it has the option, is distancing itself from the institution of warfare.' J. Keegan, *A History of Warfare* (London: Hutchinson, 1993), pp. 58–9.
3   Quoted in P. Régamey, *Non-violence and the Christian Conscience* (London: Darton Longman and Todd, 1966), p. 249.
4   Keegan, for example, argued that 'the elements of a new world resolution to suppress the cruelties of disorder are ... clearly visible.' According to Keegan: 'The effort at peacemaking is motivated not by calculation of political interest but by repulsion from the spectacle of what war does. The impulse is humanitarian, and though humanitarians are old opponents of warmaking, humanitarianism has not before been declared a chief principle of a great power's foreign policy, as it has now by the United States, nor has it found an effective supranational body to give it force, as it has recently in the United Nations, nor has it found tangible support from a wide body of *disinterested* states, willing to show their commitment to the principle by the despatch of peace-keeping, and potentially peace-making forces to the seat of conflict.' (Keegan, *A History of Warfare* p. 58, own emphasis). The factual basis of such optimism seems shaky. This is *not* the first time that the United States has declared humanitarianism the chief principle of its foreign policy. (Has the United States ever fought a war in this century without a humanitarian purpose?) More importantly, so far as the general argument is concerned, Keegan's central assumption that 'humanitarians are old opponents of warmaking' flies in the face of the evidence. Humanitarianism has been the driving force of some of the bloodiest wars of modern times.
5   R. Aron, *Peace and War* (London: Weidenfeld and Nicholson, 1966), p. 609.
6   Once he had resolved upon war there was no more ruthless advocate of war than the pacifically and democratically inclined Woodrow Wilson: 'There is ... but one response possible from us', he declared, 'Force, Force to the utmost, Force without stint or limit, the righteous and triumphant Force which shall make Right the law of the world.'

Cited in D. Rees, *Korea: The Limited War* (London: Macmillan, 1964), p. x.

7   It is a just war perspective rather than a realist one which informs the present argument. While accepting some important affinities between the two traditions, differences of principle need to be kept firmly in mind. In the first place, though recognising the pitfalls and dangers which accompany any attempt at the moral determination of war, just war theory nevertheless insists on its moral and not just on its political and strategic limitation. This already marks it out from some (amoral) forms of realism. Secondly just war theory rejects the narrowing of the moral horizons which takes place in those more moral forms of realism where the moral debate is conducted entirely in terms of state sovereignty and the national interest. While recognising the legitimate and *enduring* claims of particular political communities, just war reasoning remains a form of moral universalism and not a form of moral particularism. Its concept of the international community may be one of a plurality but a plurality is still a unity. (On the subject of realism the attention of the reader is drawn to the discussion by Mason and Wheeler in Chapter 5 which bears upon the argument of this chapter at several points.)

8   One of the earliest examples of war getting out of control in the course, and in no small measure because, of its moral elevation is the First Crusade initiated by Urban II. While in its official conception preserving the idea of a limited war (the declared aims of the war were the defence of the eastern churches and the recovery of Christian possessions), by the moral energy and boundless enthusiasm for war which its spiritual characterisation inevitably generated the Crusade opened the way to a form of religious fanaticism in accordance with which war was fought in a triumphal and merciless fashion. The pope may not have seen the Crusade as a war of religion as such but that is how it was understood by many of the crusaders. As the crusading army passed through the Rhineland en route to Jerusalem it turned with unbridled savagery on the Jewish communities of the Rhineland towns. In the minds of those who saw the Crusade as a war against the infidel, waged on account of infidelity and not on account of any specific injury done to Christians or Christendom, it was inconceivable that the war should be carried to the infidel in the East while ignoring the greater infidel in the midst of Christendom itself: the Jew or Christ-killer. The Jerusalem massacre, for the perpetration of which the First Crusade has become notorious, was the culmination of a series of similar atrocities. All were the predictable result of a war which was, in the words of a contemporary

manuscript, 'not a carnal but a spiritual war'. The record of the crusades suggests that the holier or more exalted war becomes in its conception the more likely it is to breach those moral defences with which the just war tradition has sought to confine it. This judgement appears to be amply confirmed by the subsequent history of 'holy war' both in its religious and in its, now more common, secular or ideological forms.

9   The problem with moralism is not simply that it is too demanding. It also makes the wrong demands by failing to do justice to the particular and by failing to recognise its moral worth. It is this denial which accounts for the frequent espousal of a one-sided cosmopolitan conception of the international order which rests on the assumption that the interests of states and those of the international community are necessarily antagonistic and that the only way of advancing the latter is at the expense of the former (the readiness to do so being regarded as the test of virtue). On this subject Rousseau's advice seems well taken: 'Distrust those cosmopolitans who comb their books for duties they disdain to fulfil around them. Such a philosopher loves the Tartars in order to be excused loving his neighbours': J.-J. Rousseau, *Émile* (Paris: Garnier Frères, 1964), p. 9.

10   The following points are applied not just to the conduct of international relations, in peace and in war, but also to the conduct of domestic politics. However they can be seen to apply with much greater force to international relations, particularly in time of war, than they do to the internal politics of the state.

11   Cf. G. W. F. Hegel, *Philosophy of Right,* trans. T. M. Knox (Oxford: Oxford University Press, 1952), para. 270, addition.

12   The admiration which Rousseau expresses for the natural man who 'hurries without reflection to the relief of others' is more convincing as a counsel of personal rather than political ethics. Political responses are, and ought to be, more artful. Cf. J. Maritain, 'The End of Machiavellianism', in J. R. Evans and L. R. Ward (eds), *The Social and Political Philosophy of Jacques Maritain* (London: Geoffrey Bles, 1956).

13   John Courtney Murray, cited in G. Weigel, *Tranquillitas Ordinis* (Oxford: Oxford University Press, 1987), p. 123. In the moral reasoning traditionally associated with just war theory a consideration of consequences informs the assessment of war without monopolising it. In this respect the tradition attempts to steer a middle course between the extremes of deontology and consequentialism.

14   Weigel, *Tranquillitas Ordinis,* p. 124.

15   J. Maritain, *Moral Philosophy* (London: Geoffrey Bles, 1964) p. 98.
16   I. Kant, *Fundamental Principles of the Metaphysic of Ethics* , trans. T. K. Abbott (London: Longman, 1962), p. 19.
17   Kant. *Fundamental Principles,* p. 73.
18   Kant, *Fundamental Principles,* p. 17.
19   J-J. Rousseau, *The Social Contract*, ed. M. Cranston (Harmondsworth: Penguin, 1968), p. 49.
20   Kant, *Fundamental Principles,* p. 25.
21   See the chapter by P. Jones in the present volume.
22   Rev. Linda Kimmelman, quoted in C. Bremner, 'Bush launches crusade to counter church doubts', *The Times* , 8 February 1991, p. 4. In similar vein James Gaffney wrote: 'faced with a threat of much more costly oil, we are ready to kill, we are ready to die, but we are eternally unready to curb our environmental prodigality or attempt a practical reorganisation of our economic priorities' ('The Moral Equivalent of War in the Middle East', *America* , 163:6, 8 September 1990, p. 126).
23   Unmasking was an essential part of Kant's moral enterprise. Mere conformity with what duty prescribes is not sufficient. The act must be performed for the sake of duty. Kant contrasts 'the actions we see ... with those inward principles of them which we do not see'. Even the moral agent himself cannot be sure that 'it was not really some secret impulse of self-love, under the false appearance of duty, that was the actual determining cause of the will' so that 'a cool observer ... may sometimes doubt whether true virtue is actually found anywhere in the world.' (Kant, *Fundamental Principles,* p. 28).
24   Two points seem worth making at this stage in order to avoid possible misunderstanding, one general and the other specific.

Firstly the argument being advanced is intended, in part, to underline the moral dangers associated with wars of humanitarian intervention not to rule such wars out. Far from ruling intervention out the just war tradition has always emphasised the duty which members of the international community have to render each other assistance in certain circumstances. War is not understood merely, or even primarily, as an instrument of *self*-defence. On the contrary, even when states employ force in defence of their particular interests they are justified in so doing only to the extent that, at the same time, their actions can be convincingly construed as a defence of the international order and a securing of the international common good. The *principle* of humanitarian intervention is wholly in accord with this way of thinking.

Secondly and more specifically, the criticism of a certain 'moral' characterisation of the Bosnian conflict is not intended to foreclose the argument about the desirability or otherwise of increased intervention. It may be that those who argue for such intervention on purely human-itarian grounds are in fact suppressing important considerations of utility or interest. It has been argued by some (albeit a minority) of those of a more realist disposition and frame of mind that the grounds for greater military intervention in Bosnia are less humanitarian than strategic. On the assumption (which is of course arguable) that more active intervention would ensure containment and even perhaps resolution of the conflict in the Balkans, it can be seen to be in the long-term interests of the West as well as of the peoples of the region to act accordingly and, therefore, to be not only right but prudent to do so. In other words the case for intervention can be made to rest on the coming together rather than the separation of justice and utility. Even if it cannot, however, intervention may still be justified. The argument being advanced here does not start from the principle that justice and utility are the same thing.

25 Kant's own neglect of the consequences was deliberate and systematic. In the *Fundamental Principles* he is at pains to establish the noncon-sequentialist basis of morality. His attack on moral consequentialism is part of his distrust of inclination and interest: a morality based on consequences *is* a morality based on inclination and interest. He con-cludes: 'The moral worth of an action does not lie in the effect expected from it, nor in any principle of action which requires to borrow its motive from this expected effect.' (Kant, *Fundamental Principles*, p. 20). From a just war perspective Kant's exclusion of a consideration of consequences is unwarranted and must lead to a distorted and unsound moral judgement. At the same time the calculation of conse-quences must not be allowed to dictate the terms of the moral argu-ment. To say that the consequences play a part in moral reasoning is very different from saying that they constitute the whole of moral reasoning, as moral consequentialists maintain. A consideration of consequences must inform moral reasoning about war without mono-polising it.

26 Three days before the invasion of the islands, 'the streets of Buenos Aires erupted not to the exultant cries of war fever but to anti-govern-ment demonstrations and mob violence of a ferocity not seen in Argentina since the military coup of 1976. It made the junta's decision final. As *La Prensa* had prophetically remarked a month earlier, "The only thing which can save this government is a war"': M. Hastings

and S. Jenkins, *The Battle for the Falklands* (London: Michael Joseph, 1983), p.65.

27 R. Scruton, *A Dictionary of Political Thought* (London: Pan Books, 1983), p. 237.

28 From a Kantian moral perspective prudence is not the virtue which just war theory considers it to be: 'For to deviate from the principle of duty is beyond all doubt wicked; but to be unfaithful to my maxim of prudence may often be very advantageous to me.' (Kant, *Fundamental Principles*, p. 22).

29 From *The Education of a True Believer,* quoted in R. Conquest, *The Harvest of Sorrow: Soviet Collectivization and the Terror-Famine* (London: Hutchinson, 1986), p. 233.

30 Quoted in G. Feifer, *Tennozan* (New York: Ticknor and Fields, 1992), p. 207.

31 Feifer, *Tennozan,* p. 210.

32 Cited in N. O'Sullivan, *Fascism* (London: Dent, 1983), p. 49.

33 The nature, and the effects, of this suppression are also discussed in Levy's chapter in this volume.

34 In some cases even that choice may appear too generous and accommodating. The racial and anti-Semitic basis of Nazi ideology made it more exclusive and more destructive in its implications. In earlier massacres, as in the case of the 'First Holocaust' which accompanied the First Crusade (see note 7), Jews could avoid death by accepting baptism. For the National Socialist, however, the Jew was completely beyond redemption or assimilation into the community of the elect, even beyond preservation in the form of enslavement (the fate assigned to the Slavs). The Final Solution was also the *only* solution to the Jewish problem as defined by Nazi ideology.

35 Lord Owen, the ex-European Union peace negotiator for former Yugoslavia, criticised 'the moralists in Washington or Sarajevo [who] wait for this perfect peace ... while Serb towns like Bijeljina and Banja Luka, which had a Muslim population when the Vance–Owen strategy began, were ethnically cleansed ... they find it easier not to grapple with the moral dilemma, easier to espouse the perfect peace.' (*The Times* , 9 June 1995, p. 14).

36 Kant wrote: 'We cannot too much or too often repeat our warning against this lax and even mean habit of thought which seeks for its principle amongst empirical motives and laws; for human reason in its weariness is glad to rest on this pillow, and in a dream of sweet illusions (in which, instead of Juno, it embraces a cloud) it substitutes for morality a bastard patched up from limbs of various derivation,

which looks like anything one chooses to see in it; only not like virtue to one who has once beheld her in her true form.' In a footnote Kant added: 'To behold virtue in her proper form is nothing else but to contemplate morality stripped of all admixture of sensible things and of every spurious ornament of reward or self-love.' (Kant, *Fundamental Principles*, pp. 52–3).

11

Ethics in the Conduct of War

Sheldon G. Levy*

1. Introduction

Most social science examinations of war are concerned with its occurrence, the admirable goal being to eliminate or at least reduce its frequency. However the destructiveness of wars and other incidents of mass killing are primarily a function of their size rather than their occasion. This chapter is most concerned with the psychological bases for the lack of restraint in inter-group conflict as expressed in event magnitude. It reports on the views of 'bystanders' to history, that is, individuals who were not directly involved in the events, as obtained from standardised questionnaires. The discussion, which is based on results from several large groups of college students in a number of locations, examines their beliefs about both the general principles that should be applied to armed conflict as well as the degree to which specific historical events were viewed as exceeding acceptable standards of behaviour.

The extent of the destruction of both soldiers and civilians in war is obvious but probably underestimated by most. Rummel,[1] after examining all available sources and weighting for the quality of the information, concluded that the best estimate of the number of deaths from 'democide' (that is, politicide, genocide, ethnocide) in the twentieth century during the period 1900–1987 is 200 million in addition to the 40 million battle deaths. This human devastation poses two questions: why does conflict engender such large loss of life, and how might this be reduced? One rationale of this research project is that reducing the levels of hostility rather than the number

226

of incidents themselves may be a more tractable approach to limiting the human suffering.

Some preliminary attempt at addressing these questions has been undertaken in the research reported in this chapter. However it is important to embed the investigations within a broader context of the relevance and rationale of the approach.

The focus is on ethics in the conduct of war rather than the justice of war itself (*ius in bello* rather than *ius ad bellum*) and some justification should be provided for the relevance of ethics to both general behaviour as well as that associated with aggressive conflicts.[2] Secondly global changes – political, economic, technological and environmental – should be evaluated for their implications for both the ethics and tactics in war as well as for their potential effects on basic psychological processes that may underlie inter-group conflict. The introductory sections will proceed to outline the fundamental assumptions of the research endeavour and provide a broad preface to the nature of the investigations.

The replicable generalisations that have emerged from the data will then be discussed. Concluding sections will examine both the additional questions that future research should address (with some investigations already in progress) as well as the implications of the current findings for reducing the human toll.

2. The Relevance of the Moral Code

A large proportion of the deaths in battle and almost all in democide resulted from violations of a moral code which, in the abstract, all parties might endorse. It is evident that the great proportion of actions violate international agreements among nations (or domestic law) governing the treatment of soldiers and civilians during conflict. Some of these provisions antedate the twentieth century although a large number were concretised after the world wars. Of course general principles are redefined for specific instances so that the conduct may not be viewed as a violation of ethical principles. Therefore any attempt to determine current support for restraint in war must examine, in addition to principles, actual events.

3. The Effects of Change

It is not likely that the fundamental cognitive and emotional bases of human behaviour have been modified over the past few thousand years. However there have been technological, environmental and political changes and these also alter social environments. They would therefore be expected to affect human interactions through social definition of what is ethical, through psychological salience thus affecting the awareness of what is moral, and through tactics utilised in resolving conflict.

There are predictable effects of technology on both the nature and the psychology of war. The inventions of dynamite up through chemical and biological weaponry and then on to nuclear possibilities influence military strategy as well as the immediacy of the target.

First changes in weapon lethality should increase the number of deaths from any particular attack. Although there is no substantial statistical demonstration of an increase in battle deaths during the past two centuries, over a longer period of time changes do occur.[3] For example with the development of dynamite symbolic war becomes less likely since the weaponry leads to tactics in which armies are arrayed against each other.[4] Of course symbolic war is still possible but, historically, the technology has been associated with a change in strategy.

Secondly and less debatably weaponry alters the psychology of battle by increasing the distance between attacker and target, a relationship that was forcefully illustrated in Milgram's experiments.[5] The consequences are to increase the likelihood of pre-humanisation[6] so that moral restraints against killing are irrelevant and to reduce the target's ability to induce gestures of appeasement.[7] The destructiveness of the Gulf hostilities of 1990–1 were partly a consequence of both the lethal weaponry and the distance between attacker and target.[8] Thus technology appears to reduce the need for hate or other emotional bases for engaging in mass destruction. The Nazi's Final Solution combined technology with immediacy and demonstrated the ultimate ability of the human mind to minimise any innate tendencies towards restraint when an accommodating hierarchical social organisation is coupled with an 'appropriate' definition of the target.

The effects of non-military technology on the environment also impact on human conflict.[9] Exhaustion of resources such as potable water and breathable air increases the competition for them. This may result in a reduction in other sources of inter-group friction so that overall levels of hostility remain the same, although the wish fathering that thought may be illusory. The limited resources do increase the likely dominance of the privileged over the deprived since the former strive to maintain their standard of living and have the technology to enforce their wishes. The proposal that the whole world should be raised to the level of the most advanced meets a brick wall of reality. There are insufficient resources for this to be accomplished. (Brammer has identified some emerging consequences of the demand on oil.)[10] For example the per capita energy usage in China is one-eleventh that of the average citizen in the United States (and the ratio for India is 1:31). Since China's population is four times that of the United States, oil supplies would be depleted almost overnight were China to achieve energy consumption levels anywhere close to those of the United States.[11] And then there are the other three to four billion people in underdeveloped nations. It is thinkable but unrealistic to suppose that the industrialised democracies will reduce their levels of consumption so that greater international equality can be reached. Of course there may be new developments of alternate sources of energy, for example wind, solar and hydrogen, which would alter the above assumptions.

Further increases in world consumption based on currently dominant technologies will increase damage to the environment. Destruction of forests and of clean water, ozone depletion, soil erosion and other environmental degradations will create crises in which competition is likely to induce war if dominance of a few over the many cannot be achieved in any other way.

Even in the industrialised democracies the vast amount of wealth is held by the upper one-fifth of the population, and this is extrapolated across countries, that is the wealth of nations resides in those with one-fifth of the world population. The vast majority of people therefore (approximately 90–95 per cent of the three to four billion in non-developed countries) are living in poverty, abject or otherwise.[12] The vast majority of world resources are consumed by the upper five to ten per cent of the world's population. All of this encourages dominance or war (military, economic or otherwise) to maintain the quality of life. Pre-humanisation is the likely psychological process by which this will be achieved, aided by the lethal weaponry that can be delivered at a distance. (One might also raise the question of whether the trend toward multinational corporations will exacerbate the problem of dominance over resources with economic power, utilised to also obtain political power, being a major force. Lack of interest in the welfare of Third World countries might be evidenced by the increasing arms transfer from manufacturing societies to contesting groups in less developed countries.)

4. Fundamental Assumptions of the Research and its General Design

Amidst this pessimism the question arises whether it is possible to decrease the number of humans who are destroyed. The fundamental assumption of this chapter is that norms of restraint against the squandering of human life might be strengthened.[13] However it is first necessary to evaluate current support for the principles, uncover the psychological bases for them and assess the factors that appear to be associated with greater or lesser restraint. Were this to be accomplished, implications for increasing constraints should be apparent. (A distinction is made in this discussion between norms – the general view of a population – and principles, such as those embodied in a set of laws. Thus a law is not necessarily a norm. See Barry Jones's chapter, this volume, for further discussion of norms.)

As with any crime, violations of laws, even when believed legitimate, may derive from many sources. First there may be lack of knowledge that the action in question constitutes an infraction. In most instances, though, there is a recognition that the behaviour represents an offence. One clue is the attempt to prevent information about the event from becoming public. A second source is a belief that the prohibition does not apply in the current circumstances. A third is a large emotional outburst that reduces behavioural restraints that would otherwise be in effect, that is, disinhibits the individual.[14]

One cannot assume that an international agreement or law is generally known. Even if recognised, the effectiveness of the code depends on wide-spread support of the norm. Therefore the levels of endorsement of the current restraints must be ascertained. Of course many of these are philosophical positions that are seemingly accepted by the large majority, for example opposition to wanton killing of innocent civilians or mass rape by armies. Nevertheless, within the context of a specific event, such actions may not be perceived as a violation of a legitimate prohibition, for example the atomic bombing of Japan or the firebombing of Dresden. Further, many of the rules of war that concern the treatment of soldiers are not generally understood, and even cursory knowledge of the actual conduct of war leads one to conclude that they are not uniformly accepted by either the public or large portions of the military.

The research presented here relies on one important social axiom: *norms influence behaviour*. In this instance those of warfare are assumed to be related to the behaviour of those conducting war. Of course the question is whose norms are relevant. Certainly those of the attackers themselves are important. However these are not the focus of this study; rather it is the values of the broader community. The hypothesis is that these norms affect the likelihood and intensity of gross violations of restraint in war as exhibited through massive and unnecessary killing.[15]

It is difficult to discover examples in which this is not true. German standards about raping Eastern European women were different from those governing Western Europeans during World War Two. Danes sent Jewish citizens to Sweden (thus exhibiting a rather different norm than those of the Germans). The Germans, capitalising on historic anti-semitism in central and eastern Europe, placed concentration camps in those regions. Nevertheless they realised that the violation of generally acceptable behaviour was so great that camouflaging the machinery of death was required. The same recognition led to the attempted secrecy of the Gulags. Massive Allied bombing of civilian centres during World War Two was cloaked in the language of military targets. Members of a Canadian peace-keeping force in Somalia in March 1993 brutally beat to death a Somali youth who had invaded the compound. The incident, along with some rather juvenile and offensive abusive treatment (hazing) in the unit, so offended the Canadian public that the corps, even though elite, was dissolved.[16]

The massacre at My Lai was supported at various levels, although not uniformly. First there was the US public whose historical denigration of orientals provided socialisation for some who became soldiers. Then there was the dehumanisation of the Vietnamese through euphemisms such as securing zones and labels such as 'gooks'. There was further disinhibition of restraints through generalisation: all Vietnamese were Viet Cong. This was aided in part by the nature of the war in which civilians sometimes did carry with them body bombs. Of course beliefs vary from person to person. They do not apply to every individual, in many instances not even to a majority. However, within some subset perceived as relevant by the actor, the disinhibition of restraint through norms that provide justification for the actions almost always precedes the actual event. True unprepared spontaneous mass killing by social groups is extremely rare, if in fact it ever occurs.[17]

Although it is the norms of the wider public which are central to the present research, the assumption, treated as a demonstrated historical certainty, is that such norms also affect behaviour of the portion of that group engaged in direct attack.

The reasoning for this indirect influence is supported logically by massive experimental social psychological research on aggression. One of the primary factors in whether or not aggression will be elicited is the reward structure. One of the most important rewards that a person can receive is social approval.[18] To the extent that the group with which the individual identifies places value on restraint, that behaviour is more likely to be exhibited by the distal actor. The effect of social approval for killing is comparably deducible.

It is true that the psychological distance of the reference group from the actor should decrease its influence, but it is nevertheless assumed that the general values are relevant because the actors are selected from the larger group. That group, therefore, still maintains, in the mind of the actor, the ability to sanction the behaviour or withhold social approval even in circumstances in which the primary social reward structure is provided by one's immediate associates.

In addition to obtaining information about the degree of normative support for principles that pertain to the conduct of war, two additional basic questions should be included among the data gathering goals. The first concerns the basis for the values. Are public beliefs about the various prohibitions against excessive killing accounted for by a single psychological foundation or is there more than one? Equally important is the question of what accounts for variations in levels of support. Here a first approach would be to examine the relationship of individual demographic characteristics to the amount of support.

Adherence to general principles is not necessarily predictive to the specific case.[19] Murder may be opposed in principle, but the circumstances, motives and relationship of appraiser to victim or offender alter the interpretation of the instance at hand. This is also true, even more so, in views about the conduct of war.

The research, therefore, included a series of studies in which brief descriptions of actual historical incidents were presented. The first question addressed was the extent to which the respondent felt that greater restraint should have been demonstrated. This was obtained by asking for an evaluation of the appropriate penalty for the attackers. Since almost all of the previous research that even indirectly relates to this topic centers around the obedience to orders syndrome,[20] the penalty assessments were requested for three levels of command: those directly involved (for example soldiers), those who supervised (officers generally) and those who had overall responsibility for the operations or planning (such as generals).

Perceived attributes of the attackers and victims were then obtained from the research participants to determine which were most associated with the endorsement of either small or large penalties. This was accomplished through a set of statements with which level of agreement was expressed, for example 'The attackers simply went out of control under the conditions', or 'Those who directly engaged in the conduct had a responsibility to obey orders'. Other items dealt with victims, for example, 'The value of life among those attacked was not as important as for others', or 'It was the behaviour of those who were attacked that was responsible for what happened. They brought it upon themselves'. A fundamental question is again whether these evaluations are driven by one, or more, basic psychological properties or traits.

As with the general protocol-based prohibitions the question of predictability arises. What accounts for variations in the evaluated seriousness (as measured by penalty levels) of the incidents? Is it demography? Do positions on general principles predict to perceived seriousness of specific events? What is the relationship of the evaluations of attacker and victim attributes to the gravity with which an incident is viewed?

In summary a basic axiom of the research is that norms affect behaviour even when the members of the ingroup are no longer in close proximity to the majority of the members (for example soldiers in battle). The primary mechanism occurs through social reward in the form of social approval, either imagined or explicit. A second assumption is that the questionnaire format is a reasonable initial methodology for assessing those norms. The investigations must proceed, however, on two planes. One is that of the general principles, for example those expressed in the agreements already extant among nations. The second is the evaluation of specific historical incidents. For each level there are two important questions. First are the expressions of the population reducible to some more limited number of psychological traits or dimensions which account for the full range of the evaluations? The second concerns the predictability of levels of restraint from both the demographic characteristics of the respondents as well as any discovered psychological foundations. Should this endeavour be even minimally successful, intervention strategies for altering the public value system to increase restraint – that is, lessen the likelihood of mass killing – should be directly implied by the findings.

5. The Evaluation of Norms

Examination of the international agreements among nations since St Petersburg, 1868, identifies a number of restraints in the conduct of war.[21] These may be translated into assertions that epitomise the relevant principles, such as 'Leaders who are responsible for starting wars should be held guilty of war crimes' or 'A soldier who kills innocent civilians under orders from a superior should be considered to have committed a war crime'. Twenty-seven such statements were developed and respondents identified the extent to which they agreed with them. Occasionally the language was not a direct translation of a protocol principle although the international agreements might provide some incorporation of the standard. For example the principle of proportionality might be stated as: 'In a war, the amount of damage a nation may inflict upon an enemy country should be limited by the degree to which the enemy has inflicted or can inflict damage on one's own country.'

Results from the first study[22] did not identify strong support for restraint. Rather than specify a clear position of agreement or disagreement with items such as the above, there was a tendency to either slightly agree or slightly

disagree with them. The analyses suggested that the study should be repli-
cated with some alteration in the design.

General statements, such as those illustrated, are ambiguous. They allow
for individual definition and changing frames of reference from one person
to another. To increase the precision as well as to examine ingroup–outgroup
differences, a second study was conducted in which some subjects received
the general statements but others evaluated a version in which the United
States was the actor and still others a version with an enemy of the United
States specified. For example: 'A United States leader who is responsible for
starting a war should be held guilty of war crimes' or 'A leader of a nation
who is responsible for starting a war with the United States should be held
guilty of war crimes'; or: 'A leader of a nation who is responsible for starting
a war with the United States should be held guilty of war crimes'. Results
from both the Wayne State University and the University of Michigan
samples were consistent with prediction. Less restraint was required of the
United States than of an enemy. Even though the absolute differences were
not large, they were frequently sufficient to place the United States as actor
on the 'disagreement with restraint' side of the scale and the enemy in the
'agreement' region.

Although the subjects as a group provided differences in overall levels
of restraint for the various items and the different versions, there was
consistency in rank order; that is, those behaviours for which the greatest
restrictions were demanded, and those for which the least were required,
were similar across versions.

Each separate item is unlikely to elicit a response based on a unique
psychological process. This reasoning is no different from that for a set of
intellectual-ability items. One suspects (and empirical support can be provided) that a general quantitative aptitude underlies performance on different
mathematical problems. For opinion responses (or any other set of overt
behaviours) the assessment of underlying psychological processes proceeds
in much the same way. Answers that are an expression of a unifying
psychological source would be expected to cluster together, that is, show
similar profiles.[23]

Analyses of the results from over a thousand subjects suggested that there
are three underlying psychological bases upon which the protocol-derived
items were evaluated. The interpretation is not as clear as has been demonstrated for quantitative, verbal, or musical abilities. Nevertheless, there is a
demonstrated stability in these clusters from one analysis to another.

An important question is whether there are variables that differentiate
those who endorsed high restraint from those who did not. Predictions from
demographic attributes were not substantial but two were consistent. The

first was gender with females favouring greater restraint. The second was opinion about the death penalty in criminal cases. Those who favoured the death penalty consistently supported *less* restraint than those who opposed it. In order to avoid a questionnaire bias, the death penalty item was presented after both the attitude and major portion of the demographic sections.

The general results that have been discussed were obtained from a number of samples, identified in footnote 21 as samples 1, 2, 5, 6, 7 and 8. Although samples 7 and 8 were too small to replicate the cluster analysis, they do provide important additional information about norms.

The ROTC unit mirrored closely the general student body at the University of Michigan, although they did shift somewhat in the direction of less restraint in the conduct of war. However the New Zealand students demonstrated noticeably more restraint and, perhaps more importantly, provided small differences between New Zealand and an enemy.[24]

6. The Evaluation of Historical Events

Event Selection
Examining variations among real events is, from a methodological point of view, a practical impossibility for two reasons. First the number of variables is very large. Cases differ in the following ways, among others: size, nature of target groups, level of hostility, religion, economics, language, culture, historical period, prior conflict history and the relative military capabilities of the two sides. Over a thousand incidents would be required to simply exhaust the combinations of the above variables even if each were divided into only two categories. Moreover, were this problem solved, another cannot be. An event, for example My Lai or the Pearl Harbor attack or the Dresden firebombing, is judged within the context of the whole war and may, in fact, be symbolic of the individual's overall evaluation of the wider historical context. If one selects incidents that are not within the person's knowledge, then they are not 'real', that is, they may be considered primarily on the basis of abstract (and ambiguous) principles.

The solution to this problem was to sample from the domain of events a representative set that provided differences on a number of key variables. Among those included were the following: role of one's own country, size of the event, nature of the violence (for example rape, killing, property destruction), historical distance (the earliest event was the sack of Jerusalem by the crusaders in 1099), provocation (retaliatory or not) and nature of the target (for example civilian or military). The goal was to obtain sufficient data from which regularities could be identified. These patterns might then become the basis for hypotheses that would be tested through future data collections.

The Structure of the Questionnaire

After a specific historical event was described, the subject was asked the following question: 'Based on the description just provided, what penalty, if any, should the [actors in the event] have received if there had been some way to bring them before an independent group of judges?' The penalties ranged from 'none' to 'a death sentence'. The three middle categories were: a reprimand but no prison, a short prison term and a long prison term. This question was applied to three levels of command: the attackers (usually soldiers) who were the immediate actors in the event, those who were the immediate supervisors (usually officers) and those who had overall responsibility (such as generals). (These were not always soldiers, officers, and generals because some events, for example the crusades, required descriptions that utilised different terms but identified similar levels of responsibility).

Each subject was provided with only a single historical incident so that overall reaction might be obtained without the moderating influence that might occur if the subject attempted to maintain self-consistency in evaluating a second.

The respondent was then asked to specify the level of agreement or disagreement with a number of statements that described the characteristics commonly ascribed to parties engaged in mass conflict, for example: the victims brought it upon themselves, the victims were not very civilised (inferior culture), the soldiers were required to obey orders, revenge justified the actions, the soldiers simply went out of control. The statements that were selected conform well to descriptions from historical analyses.[25] Altogether there were 24 such items. Finally demographic information was requested, including previous exposure to war, length of residence in the country and self-assessed familiarity with the incident prior to reading the description.

Results

Three important findings emerged from these investigations. First the following US actions resulted in the ascription of very low penalties: the atomic bombing of Hiroshima–Nagasaki, the Dresden fire-bombing (Allied), the invasions of Grenada and Panama and the bombing of Iraq, 1991–92. Somewhat higher penalties were evident in the responses to two events dealing with the Vietnam war, the massacre at My Lai and the rape by US forces of Vietnamese women; and two additional incidents during the Gulf hostilities, the bull-dozing in the field of Iraqi troops and the attack upon the Iraqis along the Highway of Death.[26] However, although these were the most negatively evaluated of the US actions, the specified penalty levels were below those of the most nearly comparable incidents of other nations.

When the United States was not the initiator, larger penalties (around the level of a long prison term) were designated. The size of the event did not appear to be of great consequence. Thus the German shooting of 190 men in Lidice, Czechoslovakia during World War Two was as strongly condemned as a Holocaust event in which hundreds of thousands were killed, or the Khmer Rouge massacre. Further, the ingroup–outgroup distinction was not evident for earlier historical events. All of the following were highly negatively evaluated: the sack of Jerusalem by the crusaders in 1099, the Spanish destruction of the Maya civilisation, the planned massacre of Indians at Sand Creek, Colorado by the Colorado Volunteers under the direction of Colonel Chivington, and the massacre of surrendered black soldiers at Fort Pillow, Tennessee by Confederate soldiers during the US Civil War.

Other events which were not as strongly condemned as these, but were viewed as more serious than those in which the United States engaged, included the Soviet invasion of Afghanistan, the Japanese attack on Pearl Harbor and the German Blitzkrieg of World War Two. These were evaluated at the higher penalty end of the middle group.

The seriousness (indexed by judged penalties) of the events was highly replicable from one sample to the next.

Another important observation emerged consistently in all samples. Officers were uniformly assessed, on average, as deserving greater penalties than were the soldiers who directly engaged in the actions even when these included massacres of civilians. There was, however, a very important and consistent exception – mass rape. Four incidents were included: the Japanese impressment of Korean women as prostitutes for their soldiers during World War Two, the Germans' rape of Eastern Europeans during World War Two, the Serbians' rape of Bosnians, and the Americans' rape of Vietnamese. In all of these soldiers were assigned penalties equal to or greater than those assigned to the officers.

Although the uniform assignment of greater penalties to officers than to soldiers is consistent with the dominant obedience paradigm – soldiers do what they are ordered – this interpretation has both logical difficulties, and now, empirical exceptions. First the hierarchical organisation may be a context within which an event may occur but it is not necessarily the sole determinant. Secondly there are those who dispense the orders but the reasons for initiating them must be explained. Finally the empirical results identify that respondents do not always relieve the direct attackers of responsibility even though their actions occur within the hierarchical context of the military, as evidenced by the results for mass rape by soldiers. (The rape of

Bosnians was specifically described as 'official policy' although one might argue that there is psychological differentiation between officers who order actions and those who fail to restrain offences. This point deserves further empirical investigation).

A major reason for including the victim and attacker attributes was to determine whether the judgements of either or both of these factions were related to the judged penalties. However, prior to addressing that question, the first problem was to determine whether there are clusters that identify a limited number of psychological bases upon which the victims and attackers were evaluated.

Extensive analyses identified three important clusters and these emerged in each sample from which sufficient data were collected to provide statistically meaningful information. The primary cluster represents, for the most part, the extent to which the circumstances were believed to justify the action that was described. This justification is complex and includes characteristics of the victim, such as perceived threat, dehumanisation (they value life less, they are not as civilised), defence capability (the defenders were sufficiently armed) and victim blame (the victims brought it upon themselves, they could have avoided the consequences if they wished).

The second, and smaller, cluster, basically represents respondent views of the inherent nature of war in which the hierarchical structure of the military (obedience to orders) is embedded. The third cluster deals with the extent to which the observer believed that the actions were excessive. Included here is individual responsibility. These clusters are independent of each other, a score on one is not predictive of the score on the others (but scores on an item in a cluster are predictive to others in the same cluster).

The foundations are now in place to examine the variables that predict to the evaluation of the events. Since sufficient time was allotted in three data collections to assess both the general protocol-based principles as well as an historical event (samples 5, 7 and 8 in note 21), it was possible to relate three categories of variables to judged seriousness: position on general principles, demography and scores on the victim–attacker clusters. Event seriousness was measured by the penalties assigned. The brief summary of these results is that the victim–attacker characteristics accounted for almost all of the variation in seriousness of the events. Not only were relationships of demography and even general principles quite small, they disappeared once the victim–attacker relationships were taken into account. This held even for gender among the incidents of mass rape.

It does not appear, from the point of view of non-participants, that tolerance rather than abhorrence of mass killing is based purely, or even centrally, upon obedience to orders. Of course the bases upon which the participants themselves initially acted is another question. Existing research provides no clue that their actions were compelled by psychological foundations other than those identified in the observers who responded in this research but of course the question can only be answered, ultimately, by data. Such data are not, however, easy to obtain. Interviews with direct participants would not necessarily provide veridical insights since they may offer far more self-serving reasons for their behaviour. For example from the historical record it would be reasonable to expect that obedience to orders might well emerge dominant in self-explanations.[27]

One of the profound observations from this research (if the author may be permitted the liberty of so describing his own efforts) is the consistency of the results for the historical events. Analyses of the samples separately yielded comparable rank orders of seriousness, the same relationship between officer and soldier responsibility, almost identical clusters for the victim–attacker dimensions and similar levels of predictability to event seriousness from among the three major variable categories.

Finally it should be noted that results have been obtained across incidents that differ greatly in gravity, from those in which respondents concluded that virtually no penalty was appropriate to others in which large penalties were assigned. However analyses across a wide range of situations may not be supported by results within a single occurrence or event type because the former differ greatly from each other. (An analogy might be an attempt to explain the driving behaviours that result in violations of the law. Results obtained from drivers across all types of vehicles, from motorcycles through automobiles and buses, may not be the same as those obtained when only a particular segment is considered, for example sports cars.) Unfortunately the large number of subjects upon which the overall research has been conducted still yields only a small set for each event, since each subject received only a single historical description.

To partially overcome this difficulty events were evaluated for similarities of their profile ratings to each other (based on the driving analogy, types of vehicles would be examined to determine if there were sets of vehicles with similar driver patterns). Three clusters of events emerged and analyses within these clusters yielded results comparable to those obtained earlier.

7. Directions for Future Research

The information gathered, even at this stage of the research programme, is extensive. This, in addition to the regularities that have been found across samples, leads to two types of questions. One is the direction in which further research should proceed to expand the understanding and the second is the social engineering (alterations in socialisation) implied by the current findings.

The directions for further research may be divided into four major categories, analytic, samples, experimentation and theory. Each will be briefly discussed.

The analytic questions relate to the chain of command, assessments of inter-group symmetry and the boundary problem.

Chain of Command

Although the average perceptions concerning levels of responsibility suggested for all but instances of mass rape that officers (or those who commanded) should receive larger penalties than the soldiers (or those who engaged in the direct attacks), there were variations among individual subjects. It is important to assess the differences between those who emphasised individual responsibility and those who appeared to be obedience oriented. This problem is of consequence because reduction in the number of people killed is most likely to occur if both the order-givers and the order-takers develop greater acceptance of norms of restraint.[28] (It is again assumed that regularities that differentiate among subjects in the research will provide clues about those who are active participants. At least this seems to provide a reasonable preliminary approach to understanding the bases for the behaviour.)

Inter-Group Distances and Symmetry

One of the additional opportunities for understanding inter-group conflict and the psychological basis for the intensity of such events is through examining the views of both sides of historical incidents and/or of current conflicts. Two reasonable questions may be investigated. One relates to distances between the groups and the second to symmetry. For example, what are the corresponding views of Germans and English about (a) the blitzkrieg warfare of the Germans and (b) the allied firebombing of German cities such as Dresden? (Both of these are in the current event materials.) To the extent that representative samples agree on the evaluation of the events, the distance between the two would be considered small and the prediction would be that there has been a corresponding reduction in mutual hostility. (A small distance would not necessarily imply a 'correct' or 'moral' point of view.) If the samples disagree about either (a) or (b) or both, the distance between them is larger. (It is possible that size of the difference is unrelated to importance but data thus far do not support this possibility and a control variable on the importance of the incident is included among the victim–attacker set.)

One reason for including events in which each side is a protagonist is to examine the question of symmetry. Do the two sides perceive a similar distance between them? Research objectives would require expansion to Ireland (England), Germany (United States, England, Russia) and Southeast Asia (Japan) to further examine this issue.

The Psychological-Boundary Problem

Finally one may cite the problem of the boundaries of the psychological foundations. Is the basis upon which events are evaluated broad enough to include some general concept of justice that extends beyond inter-group violence? For example are the three consistently obtained dimensions applicable to acts of individual crime, corporate fraud, governmental corruption and other social issues? The first data collection on this issue has been obtained and analyses should be substantially completed by the time this chapter is published.

Sampling Issues

Results thus far suggest that random samples of a large population may not be the most fruitful approach to further these investigations. Given the substantial inter-sample reliability obtained it is necessary to determine if similar results will appear under the most unfavourable circumstances. Thus the possibility of generational differences might be considered. A second source of difference may be military experience or service. The University of Michigan ROTC unit provided important information but this sample should be supplemented. In addition it would be worthwhile to secure samples from actual military personnel, particularly those at lower ranks. Selecting a working class sample would be valuable since it is important to not only investigate the nature, but also the number, of the psychological dimensions. Although college students, particularly in the United States, are not an elite segment of the overall population, they nevertheless do engage in greater symbolic activity than may be the case for those employed as labourers.

Finally cross-national and cross-regional samples are very important. Both would allow greater generalisation of the results and such samples are also required to assess inter-group differences already discussed. Again the need is less for a broad sample across the whole population than for a focussed sampling of those who are members of a relevant category. Simple random samples might incorporate so few members of some components of the population that the results would obfuscate actual differences.

Experimental Contributions

Understanding the normative restraints would also be improved by some experimental work. For example do changes in verbal descriptions alter the ratings? Some preliminary studies have been conducted which thus far reveal no discernible differences. Part of the problem is that prior knowledge may substantially outweigh any short verbal input. A sample has been collected in which the variation in two wordings of the same event was increased substantially and analyses are currently in progress.

Video documentaries of contemporary events should be far more power-ful – both in visual impact and because of length – than short verbal descrip-tions. In a carefully controlled experiment, students in actual classes in social psychology were exposed to filmed materials that were a regular part of the course presentation. These included aspects of World War Two (*Triumph of the Will* and *The Wansee Conference*) the US invasion of Panama (*Panama Deception*) and the consequences of the Gulf hostilities of 1990–1 upon the Iraqi civilian population (*Report from Iraq*).[29] Presented with the original questionnaires and descriptions of these events that were the basis of data collections in the other samples, little change was noted as a consequence of exposure to the documentaries. However a second questionnaire that specif-ically focussed on the documentaries and included questions similar to those on the standard instrument provided evidence of a large impact of the films. The explanation appears to be one of context. If the information (visual presentation in this case) is not recognised as part of the foreground, it may not be perceived as relevant. But filmed documentaries do appear to have a substantial impact on observer judgment of culpability if appropriate data gathering techniques are employed.[30]

Finally it might be possible to develop two versions of a conflict that emphasise the extremes of the repeatedly obtained dimensions. That is, one might select events that diminish justification (humanise the target), min-imise the nature of war component (emphasise control over events) and emphasise its excessiveness while others would stress the opposite. The descriptions would require greater length than has been utilised thus far to reduce the impact of prior knowledge. Very large samples would be valuable so that separate analyses might be legitimately conducted among those who identified themselves as having little prior knowledge.

8. Theoretical Implications

To the extent that the research results relate to participants as well as to observers, they suggest that there may have been an over-reliance on the obedience paradigm in earlier attempts to explain mass death resulting from inter-group conflict. Although the context within which the violence occurs is generally hierarchical, the hierarchy may not be determinative. Even hate is not necessary, although it obviously helps and historically it has been an important factor. The responses of subjects as outsiders suggests that whether or not anyone should be held culpable depends on a combination of factors. These include the circumstances (for example, a revenge-retribution-no choice context), as well as a fatalistic orientation (such occurrences are expected to follow a highly destructive path) and a judgement as to whether the loss of life should be considered excessive given the individual's full understanding of the incident. This mechanism appears to be influenced substantially, at least among the US subjects, by the ingroup–outgroup distinction. However even when this is reduced, for example among the New Zealand sample, the same basis for evaluating the events emerged. The perception and the actuality may be that mass killing does not occur because of obedience to orders, although the hierarchical context may exacerbate the outcome, but rather that it is a consequence of the perception of the event as 'natural', in some perverse sense, given the total social environment.

9. Applications

Based on the assumption that the findings also have implications for the participants, the analyses thus far provide some clues about the efforts that are required if there is to be greater adherence to the ethical standards that have been internationally agreed upon in the conduct of war.

Since the ingroup–outgroup distinction is an important one, efforts to minimise the boundaries between groups are fundamental. Boundaries are sometimes created by dehumanisation. Attitudes toward the Gulf hostilities, although characterised by dehumanisation of the populace through their identification as appendages of the leader (generalisation of the dehumanisation of Saddam Hussein), also included a great deal of pre-humanisation – a failure to ever accord the Iraqis, particularly the Iraqi soldiers, status as human beings. As a result they were objects, not people, to be destroyed.[31] This is different, for the most part, from a genocide such as the Holocaust. The Jews were dehumanised, partially through demonisation, as a means of justifying their elimination.

Pre-humanisation has great advantages over dehumanisation. First it allows destruction without hate. Secondly, it reduces the mental conflict between ethical beliefs and overt actions (or dissonance).[32] Reducing group boundaries will, at a minimum, reduce pre-humanisation and also increase the difficulty of subsequent dehumanisation.

The recent political changes in the world present a mixture of directions on the issue of group boundaries. The former Soviet Union and associated Eastern Bloc countries appear to have increased ingroup–outgroup distinctions that were partially masked by the previously authoritarian systems which controlled the general population and were able to identify superordinate goals.[33] However it is possible that the European Union will result in a diminution of group boundaries in much of the remainder of the continent. A great deal depends on economic equality. If economic discrepancies develop within the Union, then antagonisms are likely to increase.

If the clusters of victim–attacker attributes become more firmly established, they imply the directions in which socialisation strategies should proceed to achieve a reduction in the intensity of conflict. These would include a cultural priority that reduces the justificatory basis for mass killing with a specific emphasis that mass deprivation, humiliation and death are not intrinsic components of the nature of war. Reducing the intensity of conflict would also be furthered by greater education about the principle of proportionality with an important extension being the tenet that offensive actions should not exceed the minimum effort required to reach the stated objectives. Of course there must also be greater definition and restriction of what constitutes legitimate objectives.

The data suggest that the ingroup–outgroup distinctions are not as critical when the events are more distant historically. Increasing information about the history of the ingroup presents a possibility that citizens might realise that the same principles apply to contemporary conflict behaviour.

The underlying foundation of all applications is the utilisation of information transmission. For example it would be worthwhile to increase awareness of the existing international agreements so that the sanction of international law has some opportunity to exert an influence. Ultimately it is necessary to alter, through education and mass communication, socialisation about principles – to whom they apply and the circumstances under which they are relevant – and to emphasise the responsibility of the individual for the violent actions in which each might engage. The issue of individual responsibility is addressed next.

10. General Theoretical Formulation

Although the research identifies components associated with lack of restraint that reach beyond the obedience paradigm, there is little doubt that increasing individual responsibility in organisational settings would be a restraint against mass killing, given prior socialisation to the appropriate standards. Further, the evaluations of victims and attackers that have been observed in the studies reported in this chapter may be significantly influenced by authority. The understanding of authority is, therefore, of substantial importance even should it be the case, as argued from the results presented here, that the proximate causes of mass killing are not as crucially dependent on obedience as has been previously theorised.

The explorations in social psychology, beginning with Stagner's 1936 article,[34] identify the psychology of those that rely upon or follow authority. *The Authoritarian Personality* developed further the psychological attributes and Rokeach then extended these foundations.[35] In addition specific research on obedience to an authority figure was demonstrated by Milgram in one of the most important series of experiments in social psychology.[36] An interpretation of behaviour in war within the obedience paradigm has been presented by Kelman and Hamilton.[37]

An article by the present author, based on both original research and a review of the earlier literature on authoritarianism, proposed a Theory of Reduced Alternatives that integrated and extended the psychological process. The elements of the reasoning follow.[38]

A major effect of stress is to reduce cognitive and behavioural alternatives.[39] Stress also increases reliance upon leadership. The Theory of Reduced Alternatives argues that dogmatism develops as a result of anxiety generated by the reduced alternatives. The sequence, therefore, is from systemic punishment – defined as relatively low payoffs in institutional environments, for example in education, income or housing, and which functionally operate as external stress and induces biological stress – to a restriction in cognitive and behavioural alternatives.[40] The complexity of social relationships creates anxiety because of the inability of the systemically punished, and thus cognitively restricted, individual to cope with the environment. This anxiety is resolved by relying upon and then identifying with authority.[41]

This reliance upon authority also has consequences. It increases group cohesion with a subsequent increase in antagonism toward outgroup members. It also increases the likelihood of scapegoating which enhances ingroup cohesion and strengthens ties to the leader.[42]

As a result the individual is likely to be so identified with authority that leaders will be supported even when they act oppressively against that person.

Perhaps the most important implication of the theory is that it is not those who are most oppressed that will undertake action against the government, but those who are systemically rewarded. Since the rewarded have a wider range of cognitive and behavioural alternatives there is less need to rely on the government for achieving goals in the social environment. This independence of mind allows for opposition when the authorities engage in oppressive actions.[43]

There are several important additional refinements that are necessary. First the theory is not all inclusive. That is, it does not argue that the psychological processes defined above are the only relevant ones. It hypothesises a psychological tendency to react in a particular direction. There may also be counter-tendencies.

For example the educational system may be specifically oriented towards adherence to authority. Religious institutions in which the clergy are hierarchically organised may inculcate the importance of obedience to church authority. In Germany, prior to the outbreak of World War Two, there was an emphasis on the importance of obedience to authority in general. These tendencies run counter to the direction of the relationships specified in the theory. Nevertheless, even in Germany, the attempt to assassinate Hitler did not arise from those who were most punished under the dictatorship.[44] It was planned by the systemically rewarded, including highly placed military personnel. Of course the assassination of a leader requires access and those who are systemically punished are less likely to have such opportunity.

However even the planning is less likely to occur among those that are without resources. In fact the theory argues that they may be the most supportive of the government.

There are two issues in addition to that of socialisation for obedience to authority, that require further examination; these concern two major subgroups.

First there are those who are so excluded from the society that there is no basis for identification. African–Americans during slavery might be considered one such example. They were defined to be outside of the system and could not enter it. It would not be expected that systemic punishment would lead to identification with authority in the extreme case. Nevertheless this is not quite as simple as it appears. Blacks accepted the religion of the masters, adopted the names and other symbols and views of the masters, and in some cases fought in the Civil War for the masters. Although a great deal was forced upon them, it is difficult to argue threat and force as the sole bases for the behaviour. (Bettleheim provides evidence of identification with authority even in Nazi concentration camps.)[45]

The extremely wealthy are another exception. Although systemically rewarded, they frequently support oppressive government. However it can be argued that they require the force of governmental authority to protect their assets.

Finally it is worthwhile to examine the concept of oppression. The theory is that those who are systemically punished will identify with oppressive authority except under the circumstances discussed in the immediately preceding paragraphs. Opposition will derive, most likely, from a portion of the systemically rewarded. This does not mean that revolts are conducted solely by them. Prior alienation of the systemically punished frequently leads many to be apathetic but predisposed to follow authority in opposition. It is from among these that the main body of the revolution is formed. Nevertheless the leadership is unlikely to arise from this element.

Several occurrences of opposition to government among those that are systemically punished may appear to be a contradiction of the theory. For example the civil war riots in 1863 in New York (the anti-draft riots in which as many as 1300 were killed) were in opposition to government conduct of the Civil War. As many as 50 000 people participated in the mobs, most of them poor Irish immigrants. They attacked and killed a number of blacks (13 identified and 70 missing). Although there were a number of reasons for the riot, including opposition to conscription which was instituted two days earlier and the fact that the rich were allowed to exempt themselves from the draft by payment of $300 for a substitute, the attack on the blacks suggests a hostility toward an element of the population that was competing economically at the lower end of the ladder. In a less violent series of contemporary events the South Boston riots in 1974, in which school buses were burned because of opposition to school integration, may be cited.[46]

There is a major difference, however, between these examples and opposition to oppressive government. Democratic government is defined primarily by an emphasis on individual liberties which increase complexity by distributing rights to the many and away from the few. These changes also reduce ingroup–outgroup distinctions. Those who are least able to tolerate the greater complexity are the systemically punished. The attempt to resolve the anxiety would be expected to follow one or both of the forms that have been discussed – identification with authority in opposition to democratic government and/or aggression, both of which are simple solutions. Thus the systemically punished are more likely to be involved in opposition to democratic government than are the rewarded.

Oppressive government does the opposite: it concentrates power, increases ingroup–outgroup distinctions and simplifies the social world. It would be expected to reduce the anxiety of the systemically punished. Since a reduction in anxiety is almost always rewarding, there is an instrumental effect that favours support of the government. This does not occur to the same extent among the systemically rewarded since no comparable level of anxiety existed. As discussed earlier, this independence from authority is a pre-condition for opposition.

Roger Brown identified two fundamental dimensions of social organisation among a wide range of animal species. One is dominance (hierarchy) and the other is solidarity. The following brief discussion will not deny a multiplicity of social motives among humans but is based on an assumption that underlying a great deal of social behaviour, and particularly that relating to ethics in the conduct of war, is the desire for control.[47]

If control is posited as a fundamental social motive a great deal of human activity can be incorporated, from status and hierarchy (controlling others), to both science (understanding that reduces anxiety over the uncontrolled unknown) and religion (which operates similarly but increases control through supernatural vehicles). Aspects of solidarity would also be included since solidarity increases control through identification with a more powerful group, thus reducing risk from danger and from the unknown and adding understanding through common social definition. Unfortunately it appears that the existence of groups that are different threatens the perception of control, either because the awareness of the differences (in race, religion, creed, custom and many other variations) reduces the feeling of the power of one's own group, or because it reduces the unanimity of social definition or introduces other elements of uncertainty. Control may be reasserted by converting the other group to one's own point of view, or enslaving them as a direct expression of control, or through their elimination physically which increases social homogeneity and returns the individual to the security of the group. Coupled with the Theory of Reduced Alternatives it would seem reasonable to argue that the need for dominance is greatest among those that have the least, and identification with authority is a major vehicle through which imagined but reality-distorting mastery is regained. Leaders implicitly comprehend this and their understanding provides them with great flexibility in manipulating large numbers of people by providing them with the illusion of control through adherence to the group and through the combination of ingroup cohesion, reliance on leadership, and increased distance from out-group members.[48]

All of this implies that norms that constrain actions that incur mass death require individuals who have been socialised to not rely on authority for their perception of control. This increases the ability to resist obedience to authority and increases the ability of the individual to adhere to personal standards of morality, assuming that appropriate standards have been developed. However the Theory of Reduced Alternatives argues that such mental independence is more likely among the systemically rewarded. It follows rather directly that social justice is likely to remove an important basis upon which mass killing relies.

Notes and References

* I would like to thank Barry Holden for his valuable suggestions and Professors Mark Lumley at Wayne State, Tom Collier and Michael Riordan at the University of Michigan, Pat Regan at the University of Canterbury, New Zealand and Joyce Francis at American University for their gracious cooperation in data collection.

1 R. Rummel, 'Power, Genocide and Mass Murder', *Journal of Peace Research,* 31 (1994) 1–10.

2 Einstein implied a relationship: '…we do not feel at all that it is meaningless to ask such questions as: "Why should we not lie?"' (A. Einstein, 'The Laws of Science and the Laws of Ethics', in H. Feigl and M. Brodbeck (eds), *Readings in the Philosophy of Science* (New York: Appleton-Century Crofts, 1950), pp. 779–80. One would expect that the relationship of ethics to behaviour in general would also apply to the conduct of war specifically (see for example B. Donagan, 'Atrocity, War Crime, and Treason in the English Civil War', *The American Historical Review*, 99 (1994) 1137–66.) However Coates, in his chapter in this volume, presents a thoughtful argument to the effect that 'moralistic' war frequently results in great loss of life. The discussion in the present chapter differentiates between 'moral', attempting to achieve a just and peaceful social order, and 'moralistic', the attempt to impose one's own political, religious or other philosophical views upon others. (Coates also makes a distinction between 'moral' and 'moralistic' but with a somewhat different meaning attached to the latter term.)

3 Quantitative data sets developed for example by Richardson and by Singer and Small have not yielded evidence for changes in battle deaths over the past two centuries: L. F. Richardson, *Statistics of Deadly Quarrels* (Chicago: Quadrangle Books, 1960); J. D. Singer and M. Small, *The Wages of War* (New York: Wiley, 1972).

4 I am indebted for this insight to Paul Forage, University of Michigan History Department. Symbolic war, in which representatives from each side meet in either symbolic or actual battle to determine a victor, was engaged in by both the Samurai in the middle ages as well as among the Chinese.

5   S. Milgram, *Obedience to Authority* (New York: Harper and Row, 1974).

6   Dehumanisation is the more common term. It usually denotes the divesting of human beings of their essential human characteristics. A separate term, 'pre-humanisation', is suggested that would specifically refer to the failure to ever provide human attributes to the target. A more common label for this phenomenon is pseudo-speciation. Those who are different are frequently not accorded the full qualities generally assigned to humans. However the distinction may still be worthwhile since pseudo-speciation is frequently applied to circumstances in which there is also hatred toward the target. That seems an uncommon emotion in actions against sub-humans. Pre-humanisation does not carry with it this encumbrance.

7   R. Brown and R. J. Herrnstein, *Psychology* (Boston: Little, Brown, 1975) pp. 205–8.

8   P. Jones in his analysis of the Gulf hostilities in his chapter in this volume, argues that the New World Order may have been a euphemism for 'Old Power Politics', and, if that is the case, no new moral imperatives operated in that conflict.

9   Dark's Chapter 8 in this volume presents an extensive analysis of the effect of the environment on international structure. The brief analysis presented here is an attempt to provide some conjectures about the possible effects on the relationships between states. See also the chapters by Holden and by Paterson in this volume that deal specifically with the issue of global warming.

10   R. Brammer, 'Up and Down Wall Street: Oil Change', *Barron's*, 6 March 1995, pp. 3–4.

11   Even were the large amounts of frozen methane and of energy from Canada (shale oil) to be tapped, the handwriting is on the wall (and in the sea, and under the rocks): *The World Almanac and Book of Facts, 1994* (Mahwan, NJ: Funk and Wagnalls, 1993), p. 151.

12   Per capita GDP–GNP in the United States is in the neighbourhood of 60 times that in China and India, which combine for around one-third of the world population (the economists can quibble about the exact GDP numbers), *The World Almanac*, pp. 752, 772, 822). A recent report in the United States identified the upper one per cent of the US population as retaining 40 per cent of the total wealth. The upper one per cent in England, in spite of its history of nobility and subsequent accumulation of wealth, currently possesses about 20 per cent, a decrease from the almost 60 percent in the 1920s. (The figures require some additional interpretation: see *Newsweek*, 1 May 1995, p. 62.)

13 Although one might argue that such norms would apply to both the outbreak as well as the conduct of war, the concept of war is more abstract. One may engage in war with limited recourse to human sacrifice. The outbreak depends on many factors, some of which are relatively abstract. These include the issue over which the war is fought, the strategies by which it is to be conducted and the stereotype of the enemy. Of course war, as currently practised, cannot be fought without attacking people. Certainly the protocols recognise a distinction between initiation and conduct and have been developed to establish principles that are applicable once the conflict is in progress.

14 Throughout the paper the word 'disinhibits' will refer to some circumstance that operates to remove behavioural restraints that would otherwise be in effect.

15 Evidence of the profound influence of culture as a force against either pre-humanisation or dehumanisation is provided by John Shy, University of Michigan History Department, in comments about some native American tribes (for example, Military Studies Group, University of Michigan, 4 December 1992). Within social psychology there is some formal research on norms and the relationship between norms and behaviour although the behaviour is far removed from that of war. Cialdini presents a valuable background and empirical test of this relationship: R. B. Cialdini, 'A Focus Theory of Normative Conduct; Recycling the Concept of Norms to Reduce Littering in Public Places', *Journal of Personality and Social Psychology*, 58 (1994) 1015–26. The two concepts of norms that he discusses, descriptive and injunctive, do not quite conform to the definitions here. Descriptive norms refer to actual behaviour rather than beliefs, that is they refer to an objective reality. Injunctive 'refers to rules or beliefs as to what constitutes morally approved and disapproved conduct' (p. 1015). The concept of norm in the present chapter refers to the typical (descriptive) view of the moral belief (oughtness) governing conduct during war or other inter-group violence. Confusions in the terminology may be aided by ignoring this paragraph.

16 *New York Times*, 25 January 1995; *McClean's* (Canada), 28 March 1994, 30 January 1995.

17 Turner and Surace provide a specific test of the hypothesis: R. H. Turner and S. H. Surace, 'Zoot-suiters and Mexicans: Symbols in Crowd Behavior', *The American Journal of Sociology*, 62 (1956) 14–20.

18 L. Berkowitz, *Aggression: A Social Psychological Analysis* (New York: McGraw Hill, 1962); L. Berkowitz, 'Social Motivation', in G. Lindzey and E. Aronson (eds), *The Handbook of Social Psychology*,

2nd ed., Volume 3, (Reading, Mass.: Addison-Wesley, 1969); L. Berkowitz, *Aggression: Its Causes, Consequences and Control* (New York: McGraw-Hill, 1993).

19   An early study is that of La Piere: R. T. La Piere, 'Attitudes vs. Actions', *Social Forces*, 13 (1934) 230–7.

20   A few references that identify the history of these efforts are: T. W. Adorno, E. Frenkel-Brunswik, D. J. Levinson and R. N. Sanford, *The Authoritarian Personality* (New York: Harper and Row, 1950); M. Rokeach, *The Open and Closed Mind* (New York: Basic Books, 1960); Stanley Milgram, *Obedience to Authority* (New York: Harper and Row, 1974); H. C. Kelman and L. H. Lawrence, 'Assignment of Responsibility in the Case of Lt. Calley: Preliminary Report on a National Survey', *Journal of Social Issues*, 28 (1972) 177–212; H. C. Kelman, 'Violence without Moral Restraint: Reflections on the Dehumanisation of Victims and Victimisers', *The Journal of Social Issues*, 29 (1972) 25–62; H. C. Kelman and V. L. Hamilton, 'Availability for Violence: A Study of U.S. Public Reactions to the Trial of Lt. Calley', in J. D. Ben-Dak (ed.), *The Future of Collective Violence: Societal and International Perspectives* (Lund, Sweden: Studentlitteratur, 1974); H. C. Kelman and V. L. Hamilton, *Crimes of Obedience* (New Haven, Conn.: Yale University Press, 1989).

21   S. M. Cohen, *Arms and Judgment–Law, Morality and the Conduct of War in the Twentieth Century* (Boulder, Colo.: Western Press, 1989); F. Kalshoven, *Constraints on the Waging of War. International Committee of the Red Cross* (Dordracht, The Netherlands: Martinus Nijhoff, 1987); A. Roberts and R. Guelff (eds), *Documents on the Laws of War* (Oxford: Clarendon Press, 1989); D. Schindler and J. Toman, *The Laws of Armed Conflicts – A Collection of Conventions, Resolutions and Other Documents* (Geneva and Leiden: A. W. Sijthoff, Henry Dunant Institute, 1973).

22   The samples, location, dates, sizes and topics that are the basis for the results are as follows: sample 1, Wayne State University (WSU), January 1992, n = 354, general principles; sample 2, WSU, September, 1992, n = 423, general principles, three versions; sample 3, WSU, January, 1993, n = 286, events; sample 4, WSU, September, 1993, n = 330, events; sample 5, University of Michigan (UM), December, 1992, n = 321, principles (three versions) and events; sample 6, American University, December, 1993, n = 237, events; sample 7, UM Naval Reserve Officer Training Corps (ROTC, training for service as officers in the regular US armed forces), December, 1993, n = 65, principles (three versions) and events; sample 8, University of Canterbury (New

Zealand), May, 1994, n = 60, principles (three versions) and events. I am indebted to Mark Lumley at Wayne State University, Tom Collier and Michael Riordan at the University of Michigan, Joyce Francis at American University and Pat Regan at the University of Canterbury for their assistance in data collection. The generous cooperation of my colleagues has allowed a great deal of research to be conducted without any special research grants (although I do keep an open mind on the matter of funding).

23   The levels are not required to be the same just as in mathematics the same aptitude is relevant among items that differ in difficulty. Nevertheless a person with more than average competence is expected to score high relative to the group both when the items are easy as well as when they are difficult. Whether or not items (variables) have similar profiles is generally obtained from the correlation between them across subjects. If the correlation is high the two variables (items) are considered similar. A high correlation results when there is an ability to predict, reasonably well, a person's rank position on one item from knowledge about the rank position on another. Once a set of items are shown to be similar, a more reliable measure of an individual's position on that (assumed) underlying factor can be obtained by adding the scores on the separate items together. Again, this method of analysis and application of findings is more or less identical to that employed for establishing and measuring arithmetic ability. Once data analyses have identified a set of problems that are highly correlated with each other, a more reliable score for an individual's ability is obtained when results from a number of problems are combined.

24   A more technical presentation of the results is in S. G. Levy, 'Attitudes Toward the Conduct of War', *Conflict and Peace: The Journal of Peace Psychology*, 2 (1995) 179–97.

25   These victim–attacker attributes are consistent with those cited in other contexts, for example Donagan's discussion of atrocities during the English civil wars: Donagan, 'Atrocity, War Crime, and Treason in the English Civil War'.

26   R. Clark, *The Fire this Time: U.S. War Crimes in the Gulf* (New York: Thunders Mouth, 1992).

27   This is an instance in which, at the present time, the data are primarily historical interviews with participants. However it again must be emphasised that the participants have many motives for providing self-serving explanations whereas the respondents in these studies appear to have no comparably compelling inducement to do so. Therefore it is reasonable, particularly in view of the regularity of the findings, to

conclude that the psychological bases that have been identified should become the primary hypotheses about these factors for both partici- pants and observers. Most interviews with participants provide self- identified motives that have been included here in the separate descriptions of victims and attackers, for example, obeying orders (Eichmann, My Lai participants), out of control or doing what others were doing (My Lai), serving a worthy cause (participants in the Mil- gram research). For the latter see Milgram *Obedience to Authority*. Refer also to Kelman and Hamilton, 'Availability for Violence' and W. Shirer, *The Rise and Fall of the Third Reich: A History of Nazi Germany* (New York: Simon and Schuster, 1960). It is likely that the same bases, but in attenuated intensity, apply to bystanders. Although the explana- tion supported by this research is only a fraction of the complete expla- nation, it may represent an important portion.

28   The results of some preliminary analyses that address this question will be presented at the Peace Science Society (International) North American meetings which are to be held at Ohio State University in October, 1995.

29   L. Riefenstahl (director), *Triumph of the Will* (Germany, 1935); H. Schirk (director), *The Wansee Conference* (Germany, 1984); B. Trent (director), *Panama Deception* (North Carolina: Empowerment Project, 1992); and J. Knoop, *Report from Iraq* (Washington, DC: Institute for Policy Studies, 1991).

30   Minard demonstrated the striking effect of social context on attitudes toward blacks in West Virginia coal mines. In his study, attitudes toward the same target (blacks) changed depending upon the social environment – on the job compared to the social community outside of the mines. R. D. Minard, 'Race Relationships in the Pocahontas Coal Field', *Journal of Social Issues*, 8 (1952) 29–52. A similar expla- nation is applicable to the study with filmed documentaries, but rather than the actual social context it is the perceived relationship of the questions being asked of the respondent to the documentary material that had previously been seen. For a recent study of the effect of film on attitudes see L. Butler, C. Koopman, and P. Zimbardo, 'The Psychological Impact of Viewing the Film JFK: Emotions, Beliefs, and Political Behavioral Intentions', *Political Psychology*, 16 (1995) 237–57.

31   Attempts to minimise the deaths of Iraqis in the Gulf hostilities fail both on the grounds of internal consistency as well as information from other sources. See for example J. G. Heidenrich, 'The Gulf War: How Many Iraqis Died?', *Foreign Policy, 90* (1993) 108–25. Some questions

about Heidenrich's analysis are in Letters, *Foreign Policy*, 91 (1993) 182–192; reports of specific incidents are in Clark, *The Fire this Time*. An illustrative criticism is that Heidenrich employed an invariant 3:1 wounded to killed ratio. However Jordan reported a 1:8 ratio in the Six Day War with Israel (a death relationship that is 24 times that of Heidenrich's) and in the Battle of Iwo Jima in World War Two only 1000 of 22 000 Japanese defenders survived, a 1:21 ratio (63 times that employed by Heidenrich).

32   C. A. Kiesler, B. Collins and N. Miller, *Attitude Change* (New York: Wiley, 1969), pp. 191–237.

33   The importance of superordinate goals on reducing hostility between groups was an important outcome reported by Sherif in the Robber's Cave studies. M. Sherif, 'Experiments in Group Conflict', *Scientific American*, 195(5) (1956) 54–8.

34   R. Stagner, 'Fascist Attitudes: An Exploratory Study', *Journal of Social Psychology*, 7 (1936) 309–19.

35   Adorno, *et al.*, *The Authoritarian Personality*; Rokeach, *The Open and Closed Mind*. Authoritarianism was argued by Rokeach to represent a reliance on leadership of the left. He therefore argued for a broader concept that would incorporate a mental rigidity that would apply to the political left as well as the right, that is to say, 'dogmatism'.

36   Milgram, *Obedience to Authority*.

37   Kelman and Hamilton, *Crimes of Obedience*.

38   S. G. Levy, 'An Examination of the Relationship between Systemic Punishment and Systemic Frustration', *Bulletin of the Psychonomic Society*, 13 (1979) 330–2.

39   A. H. Barton, *Communities in Disaster* (Garden City, NY: Anchor, 1970); O. R. Holsti, 'The 1914 Case', *American Political Science Review*, 59 (1965) 365–78; Rokeach, *The Open and Closed Mind*.

40   E. Harburg, 'Socio-ecological Stress, Suppressed Hostility, Skin Color, and Black White Male Blood Pressure: Detroit', *Psychosomatic Medicine*, 35 (1973) 276–96. See also Levy, 'An Examination of the Relationship between Systemic Punishment and Systemic Frustration', for a discussion of the difference between systemic punishment and systemic frustration and research illustrating the difference.

41   A series of studies have related anxiety to authoritarianism or dogmatism, for example D. J. Hanson and A. M. Bush, 'Anxiety and Dogmatism', *Psychological Reports*, 29 (1971) 366; Rokeach, *The Open and Closed Mind*; S. M. Sales, 'Economic Threat as a Determinant of Conversion Rates in Authoritarian and Nonauthoritarian Churches', *Journal of Personality and Social Psychology*, 23 (1972) 420–8 and S.

M. Sales, 'Threat as a Factor in Authoritarianism: An Analysis of Archival Data', *Journal of Personality and Social Psychology*, 28 (1973) 44–57.

42 Freud's theoretical discussion and the analysis and discussion by Shils and Janowitz based on interviews with German soldiers in World War Two who had surrendered are relevant. S. Freud, *Group Psychology and the Analysis of the Ego* (New York: Bantam, 1960; originally published, 1921); E. A. Shils and M. Janowit, 'Cohesion and Disintegration in the Wehrmacht in World War II', *Public Opinion Quarterly*, 12 (1948) 280–315.

43 Support for this position is in M. Rejai (with K. Phillips), *Leaders of Revolution* (Beverly Hills: Sage, 1979).

44 Shirer, *The Rise and Fall of the Third Reich*.

45 B. Bettleheim, 'Individual and Mass Behavior in Extreme Situations', *Journal of Abnormal and Social Psychology*, 38 (1943) 417–52.

46 *New York Times*, (5 March 1978, 31 August 1975, 16 May 1975, 4 May 1975, 19 May 1975).

47 R. Brown, *Social Psychology* (New York: The Free Press, 1965).

48 Freud, *Group Psychology and the Analysis of the Ego*.

Bibliography

Adorno, T. W., Frenkel-Brunswik, E., Levinson, D. J. and Sanford R. N., *The Authoritarian Personality* (New York: Harper and Row, 1950).

Agarwal, A. and Narain, S., *Global Warming in an Unequal World – a Case of Environmental Colonialism* (New Delhi: Centre for Science and Environment, 1990).

Alvarez, W. and Asaro, F., 'The Extinction of the Dinosaurs', in J. Bourriau (ed.), *Understanding Catastrophe* (Cambridge: Cambridge University Press, 1992).

Ambrose, S. E., *Rise to Globalism*, 7th ed. (London: Penguin, 1993).

Archer, M. S., *Culture and Agency: The Place of Culture in Social Theory* (Cambridge: Cambridge University Press, 1988).

Archibugi, D., 'From the United Nations to Cosmopolitan Democracy', in D. Archibugi and D. Held (eds), *Cosmopolitan Democracy*.

Archibugi, D. and Held, D. (eds), *Cosmopolitan Democracy* (Cambridge: Polity Press, 1995).

Aron, R., *Peace and War* (London: Weidenfield and Nicholson, 1966).

Ashley, R., 'The Poverty of Neo-Realism', *International Organisation* 38 (1988) 225–61.

Bahn, P. and Flenley, J., *Easter Island, Earth Island* (London: Thames and Hudson, 1992).

Bailey, M. G. L. 'Do Irish Bog Oaks date the Shang Dynasty?', *Current Archeology* 117 (1989), 310–13.

Bailey, M. G. L., 'Dendrochronology and Past Environments', in A. M. Pollard (ed.), *New Developments in Archeological Science* (Oxford: British Academy, 1992).

Bailey, M. G. L., 'Dendrochronology Raises Questions about the Nature of the AD 536 Dust-Veil Event', *Holocene* 4 (1994) 212–7.

Bailey, M. G. L. and Munro, M. A., 'Irish Tree-Rings, Santorini and Volcano Dust Veils', *Nature* 332 (1988), 344–6.

Banuri, T. *et al.*, *Equity and Social Considerations*, Intergovernmental Panel on Climate Change, Working Group III Report, Chapter 3, Draft 7.1, 1995.

Barraclough, G. (ed.), *The Times Atlas of World History* (London: Times Books, 1994).

Barry, B., 'The Ethics of Resource Depletion', in B. Barry, *Democracy, Power and Justice* (Oxford: Oxford University Press, 1989).

Barry, B., 'Justice as Reciprocity', in B. Barry, *Democracy, Power and Justice*.

Barry, B., *Theories of Justice: A Treatise on Social Justice*, Volume 1, (Hemel Hempstead: Harvester Wheatsheaf, 1989).

Barton, A. H., *Communities in Disaster* (Garden City, New York: Anchor, 1970).

Beetham, D., *The Legitimation of Power* (London: Macmillan, 1991).

Beitz, C., *Political Theory and International Relations* (Princeton, NJ: Princeton University Press, 1979).

Beitz, C., 'Cosmopolitan Ideals and National Sentiment', *Journal of Philosophy*, 80 (1983) 591–600.

Beitz, C., 'The Reagan Doctrine in Nicaragua', in S. Luper-Foy (ed.), *Problems of International Justice* (Boulder, Colo.: Westview Press, 1988).

Benhabib, S., *Situating the Self: Gender, Community and Postmodernism in Contemporary Ethics* (Cambridge: Polity, 1992).

Berger, P. L. and Luckmann, T., *The Social Construction of Reality: A Treatise in the Sociology of Knowledge* (Harmondsworth: Penguin, 1991).

Bergesen, H. O., 'A Legitimate Social Order in a "Greenhouse" World: Some Basic Requirements', *International Challenges*, 11 (1991) 21–30.

Berkowitz, L., *Aggression: A Social Psychological Analysis* (New York: McGraw Hill, 1962).

Berkowitz, L., 'Social Motivation', in G. Lindzey and E. Aronson (eds), *The Handbook of Social Psychology*, 2nd ed., Volume 3, (Reading, Mass.: Addison-Wesley, 1969).

Berkowitz, L., *Aggression: Its Causes, Consequences and Control* (New York: McGraw-Hill, 1993).

Bettleheim, B., 'Individual and Mass Behavior in Extreme Situations', *Journal of Abnormal and Social Psychology*, 38 (1943) 417–452.

Booth, K. and Smith, S. (eds), *International Relations Theory Today* (Cambridge: Polity Press, 1995).

Boutros-Ghali, B., 'Empowering the United Nations', *Foreign Affairs*, 71 (Winter 1992–3) 89–102.

Bowker, M. and Brown, R. (eds), *From Cold War to Collapse: Theory and World Politics in the 1980s* (Cambridge: Cambridge University Press, 1992).

Brammer, R., 'Up and Down Wall Street: Oil Change', *Barron's*, 6 March 1995 3–4.

Brandt Commission, *Common Crisis North-South: Cooperation for World Recovery* (London: Pan, 1983).

Brenton, T., *The Greening of Machiavelli* (London: Earthscan/RIIA, 1994).

Brown, C., *International Relations Theory: New Normative Approaches* (Hemel Hempstead: Harvester Wheatsheaf, 1992).

Brown, C., '"Really Existing Liberalism" and International Order', *Millennium*, 21 (1992) 313–28.

Brown, R., *Social Psychology* (New York: The Free Press, 1965).

Brown, R. and Herrnstein, R. J., *Psychology* (Boston: Little, Brown, 1975).

Brown, S., *New Forces, Old Forces, and the Future of World Politics* (Boston, Mass.: Little, Brown, 1988).

Brown, S., *New Forces, Old Forces and the Future of World Politics: Post-Cold War Edition* (New York: Harper Collins, 1995).

Bull, H., *The Anarchical Society: A Study of Order in World Politics* (London: Macmillan, 1977).

Bull, H., (ed.), *Intervention in World Politics* (Oxford: Clarendon Press, 1984).

Burnheim, J., *Is Democracy Possible?* (Cambridge: Polity Press, 1985).

Burnheim, J., 'Democracy, Nation States and the World System', in D. Held and C. Pollitt (eds), *New Forms of Democracy* (London: Sage, 1986).

Butler, L., Koopman, C. and Zimbardo, P., 'The Psychological Impact of Viewing the Film JFK: Emotions, Beliefs, and Political Behavioral Intentions', *Political Psychology*, 16 (1995) 237–257.

Butterfield, H. and Wight, M. (eds), *Diplomatic Investigations: Essays in the Theory of International Politics* (London: Allen and Unwin, 1966).

Buzan, B., *People, States and Fear: An Agenda for International Security Studies in the Post-Cold War Era*, 2nd ed. (Hemel Hempstead: Harvester Wheatsheaf, 1991).

Buzan, B., 'From International System to International Society: Structural Realism and Regime Theory Meet the English School', *International Organization* 47 (1993) 327–52.

Buzan, B. and Jones, R. J. B. (eds), *Change and the Study of International Relations: The Evaded Dimension* (London and New York: Pinter and St Martin's Press, 1981).

Buzan, B., Jones, C. and Little, R., *The Logic of Anarchy: From Neorealism to Structural Realism* (New York: Columbia University Press, 1993).

260 *Bibliography*

Buzan, B. and Little, R., 'The Idea of the International System: Theory Meets History', *International Journal of Political Science*, forthcoming.

Buzan, B. and Little, R., *An Introduction to the International System: Theory Meets History* (Oxford: Oxford University Press, forthcoming).

Camilleri J. A. and Falk J., *The End of Sovereignty?* (Aldershot: Edward Elgar, 1992).

Carr, E. H., *The Twenty Years' Crisis, 1919–1939: An Introduction to the Study of International Relations* 2nd ed. (London: Papermac, 1981).

Castles, F. G., *Politics and Social Insight* (London: Routledge, 1971).

Castles, S. and Miller, M. J., *The Age of Migration: International Population Movements in the Modern World* (London: Macmillan, 1993).

Christenson, G., '*Jus Cogens*: Guarding Interests Fundamental to International Society', *Virginia Journal of International Law* 28 (1988) 585–648.

Cialdini, R. B., 'A Focus Theory of Normative Conduct; Recycling the Concept of Norms to Reduce Littering in Public Places', *Journal of Personality and Social Psychology*, 58 (1994) 1015–1026.

Clark, R., *The Fire this Time: U.S. War Crimes in the Gulf* (New York: Thunders Mouth, 1992).

Claude, I. L. Jnr, *Power and International Relations* (New York: Random House, 1962).

Cohen, G. A., 'Self-Ownership, World-Ownership and Equality', in F. S. Lucash (ed.), *Justice and Equality Here and Now* (Ithaca, NY: Cornell University Press, 1986).

Cohen, S. M., *Arms and Judgment-Law, Morality and the Conduct of War in the Twentieth Century* (Boulder, Colo.: Western Press, 1989).

Collingwood, R. G., *The Idea of History* (London: Oxford University Press, 1946).

Connolly, W. E. (ed.), *Legitimacy and the State* (Oxford: Basil Blackwell, 1984).

Connolly, W. E., *The Terms of Political Discourse*, 3rd ed. (Oxford: Blackwell, 1993).

Conquest, R., *The Harvest of Sorrow: Soviet Collectivization and the Terror-Famine* (London: Hutchinson, 1986).

Corbridge, S., 'Colonialism, Post-Colonialism and the Political Geography of the Third World', in J. Taylor (ed.), *Political Geography of the Twentieth Century*.

Cox, R. W., 'Gramsci, Hegemony and International Relations: An Essay in Method', *Millennium* 12 (1983) 162–75.

Cox, R. W., *Production, Power and World Order: Social Forces in the Making of History* (New York: Columbia University Press, 1987).

Cox, R. W., 'Rethinking the End of the Cold War', *Review of International Studies*, 20 (1994) 187–99.

Dark, K. R., *Civitas to Kingdom* (London: Pinter, 1994).

Dark, K. R., *The Waves of Time* (forthcoming).

Deudney, D., 'The Mirage of Eco-War', in I. H. Rowlands and M. Greene (eds), *Global Environmental Change and International Relations*.

Deudney, D., 'The Case Against Linking Environmental Degradation and National Security', *Millennium*, 19 (1990) 461–76.

Dobson, A., *Green Political Thought* (London: Unwin Hyman, 1990).

Donagan, B., 'Atrocity, War Crime, and Treason in the English Civil War', *The American Historical Review*, 99 (1994) 1137–1166.

Donelan, M. (ed.), *The Reason of States: A Study in International Political Theory* (London: Allen and Unwin, 1978).

Doyle, M., 'Liberalism and International Relations', in R. Beiner and W.J. Booth (eds.), *Kant and Political Philosophy* (New Haven, Conn.: Yale University Press, 1993).

Dunn, J., 'Introduction: Crisis of the Nation State?', in J. Dunn (ed.), *The Contemporary Crisis of the Nation State?*

Dunn, J. (ed.), *The Contemporary Crisis of the Nation State?* (*Political Studies*, 42 (1994), Special issue).

Dyer, H., 'Environmental Ethics and International Relations', *Paradigms: Kent Journal of International Relations*, 8 (1994) 59–72.

Earle, T. (ed.), *Chiefdoms: Power, Economy and Ideology* (Cambridge: Cambridge University Press, 1991).

Eckersley, R., *Environmentalism and Political Theory: Toward an Eco-centric Approach* (London: UCL Press, 1992).

Einstein, A., 'The Laws of Science and the Laws of Ethics', in H. Feigl and M. Brodbeck (eds), *Readings in the Philosophy of Science* (New York: Appleton-Century Crofts, 1953).

Evans, J. R. and Ward, L. R. (eds), *The Social and Political Philosophy of Jacques Maritain* (London: Geoffrey Bles, 1956).

Falk, R., 'The World Order between Inter-State Law and the Law of Humanity: The Role of Civil Society Institutions', in D. Archibugi and D. Held, *Cosmopolitan Democracy*.

Feifer, G., *Tennozan* (New York: Ticknor and Fields, 1992).

Forde, S., 'Classical Realism' in T. Nardin and D. Mapel (eds), *Traditions of International Ethics* (Cambridge: Cambridge University Press, 1992).

Foucault, M., 'The Subject and Power', in H. L. Dreyfus and P. Rabinow (eds.), *Michel Foucault: Beyond Structuralism and Hermeneutics* (Hemel Hempstead: Harvester, 1982).

Forbes, I. and Hoffman, M. (eds), *Political Theory, International Relations, and the Ethics of Intervention* (London: Macmillan, 1993).

Franck, T. M., *The Power of Legitimacy Among Nations* (New York: Oxford University Press, 1990).

Franck, T. M., 'The Emerging Right to Democratic Governance', *American Journal of International Law* 86 (1992) 46–91.

Franck, T. M. and Rodley, N., 'After Bangladesh: The Law of Humanitarian Intervention by Force', *American Journal of International Law*, 67 (1973) 275–305.

Frank, A. G., 'A Theoretical Introduction to 5000 Years of World Systems History', *Review* 13 (1990) 155–248.

Frank, A. G. and Gills, B. K. (eds), *The World System. Five Hundred Years or Five Thousand?* (London: Routledge, 1993).

Frankel, J., *National Interest* (London: Macmillan, 1970).

Freud, S., *Group Psychology and the Analysis of the Ego* (New York: Bantam, 1960; originally published, 1921).

Friedan, J. A. and Lake, D. A., *International Political Economy*, 2nd ed. (London: Unwin Hyman, 1991).

Friedman, J., *Cultural Identity and Global Process* (London: Sage, 1994).

Fukuyama, F., *The End of History and the Last Man* (London: Hamish Hamilton, 1992).

Gaddis, J. L., *Strategies of Containment: A Critical Appraisal of Postwar American National Security Policy* (Oxford: Oxford University Press, 1982).

Gauthier, D., *The Logic of Leviathan* (Oxford: Oxford University Press, 1969).

Gellner, E., *Nations and Nationalism* (Oxford: Blackwell, 1983).

Gershman, C., 'The United Nations and the New World Order', *Journal of Democracy*, 4 (1993) 5–16.

Gewirth, A., 'Ethical Universalism and Particularism', *Journal of Philosophy*, 85 (1988) 283–302.

Gibbons, M. (ed.), *Interpreting Politics* (Oxford: Blackwell, 1987).

Giddens, A., *The Constitution of Society: Outline of the Theory of Structuration* (Cambridge: Polity Press, 1984).

Gill, S. and Law, D., *The Global Political Economy: Perspectives, Problems and Policies* (Brighton: Wheatsheaf, 1988).

Gills, B. K. and Frank, A. G., 'World Systems Cycles, Crises and Hegemonial Shifts, 1700 B.C. to 1700 A.D.', *Review* 15 (1992) 621–87.

Gilpin, R., *War and Change in World Politics* (Cambridge and New York: Cambridge University Press, 1983).

Gilpin, R., *The Political Economy of International Relations* (Princeton, NJ: Princeton University Press, 1987).

Gleick, P. H., 'Water and Conflict: Fresh Water Resources and International Security', *International Security*, 18 (1993) 79–112.

Global Environmental Change, 'Greenhouse equity', Special Issue of *Global Environmental Change*, 2 (June 1992).

Goldstein, J., *Long Cycles: Prosperity and War in the Modern Age* (New Haven, Conn. and London: Yale University Press 1988).

Goodin, R., 'What Is So Special about Our Fellow Countrymen?', *Ethics*, 98 (1988) 663–686.

Gow, J., *Legitimacy and the Military: The Yugoslav Crisis* (London: Pinter, 1992).

Graham, G., 'The Justice of Intervention', *Review of International Studies*, 13 (1987) 133–146.

Gray, J., *Liberalism* (Milton Keynes: Open University Press, 1986).

Gray, J., *Beyond the New Right: Markets, Government and the Common Environment* (London: Routledge, 1993).

Grubb, M., 'The Greenhouse Effect: Negotiating Targets', *International Affairs*, 66 (1990) 67–89.

Grubb, M. J., *Energy Policies and the Greenhouse Effect: Volume One* (London: Dartmouth/RIIA, 1990).

Grubb, M. J., Sebenius, J. K., Magalhaes, A. and Subak, S. 'Sharing the Burden', in I. Mintzer (ed.) *Confronting Climate Change: Risks, Implications and Responses* (Cambridge: Cambridge University Press, 1992).

Grubb, M. J., Koch, M., Munson, A., Sullivan, F. and Thomson, K., *The Earth Summit Agreements: A Guide and Assessment* (London: Earthscan/RIIA, 1993).

Habermas, J., *Legitimation Crisis* (London: Heinemann Educational, 1976).

Habermas, J., *Moral Consciousness and Communicative Action* (Cambridge: Polity Press, 1990).

Haglund, D. G. and Hawes, M. K. (eds), *World Politics: Power, Interdependence and Dependence* (Toronto: Harcourt Brace Jovanovich, 1990).

Hall, J. A., *Powers and Liberties* (Harmondsworth: Penguin, 1985).

Halliday, F., *Rethinking International Relations* (London: Macmillan, 1994).

Hamilton, V. L., 'Who is Responsible? Toward a Social Psychology of Responsibility Attribution', *Social Psychology*, 41 (1978) 316–328.

Hamilton, V. L., 'Chains of Command: Responsibility Attribution in Hierarchies', *Journal of Applied Social Psychology*, 16 (1986) 118–138.

Hamilton, V. L., 'Conceptions of Authority and Obedience: Moscow, 1990', American Psychological Association Centennial Convention, Washington, D.C., 17 August, 1992.

Hanson, D. J. and Bush, A. M., 'Anxiety and Dogmatism', *Psychological Reports*, 29 (1971) 366.

Harburg, E., 'Socio-ecological Stress, Suppressed Hostility, Skin Color, and Black White Male Blood Pressure: Detroit', *Psychosomatic Medicine*, 35 (1973) 276–296.

Hardin, R., *Collective Action* (Baltimore, Md.: Johns Hopkins University Press, 1982).

Hastings, M. and Jenkins, S., *The Battle for the Falklands* (London: Michael Joseph, 1983).

Hayes, P. and Smith, K. (eds), *The Global Greenhouse Regime: Who Pays?* (London: Earthscan 1993).

Heater, D., *Citizenship: The Civic Ideal in World History, Politics and Education* (London and New York: Longman, 1990).

Heffner, R. D., *A Documentary History of the United States* (New York: Mentor Books, 1965).

Hegel, G. W. F., *Elements of the Philosophy of Right* (Cambridge: Cambridge University Press, 1991).

Heidenrich, J. G., 'The Gulf War: How Many Iraqis Died?', *Foreign Policy*, 90 (1993) 108–125.

Held, D., 'Sovereignty, National Politics and the Global System', in D. Held, *Political Theory and the Modern State* (Cambridge: Polity Press, 1989).

Held, D., 'From City States to a Cosmopolitan Order?', in D. Held (ed.), *Prospects for Democracy* (Cambridge: Polity Press, 1993).

Held, D., *Democracy and the New International Order* (London: Institute for Public Policy Research, 1993).

Held, D., *Foundations of Democracy: The Principle of Autonomy and the Global Order* (Cambridge: Polity Press, forthcoming, 1995).

Hindess, B., 'Imaginary Presuppositions of Democracy', *Economy and Society*, 20 (1991) 173–95.

Hinsley, F. H., *Power and the Pursuit of Peace: Theory and Practice in the History of Relations Between States* (Cambridge: Cambridge University Press, 1963).

Hirst, P., *Associative Democracy* (Cambridge: Polity Press, 1994).

Hobbes, T., *Leviathan*, ed. C. B. Macpherson (Harmondsworth: Penguin, 1968).

Holden, B., *Understanding Liberal Democracy*, 2nd ed. (Hemel Hempstead: Harvester Wheatsheaf, 1993).

Hollis, M. and Smith, S., *Explaining and Understanding International Relations* (Oxford: Clarendon Press, 1990).

Hollis, M. and Smith, S., 'Two Stories About Structure and Agency', *Review of International Studies* 20 (1994) 241–52.

Holsti, O. R., 'The 1914 Case', *American Political Science Review*, 59 (1965) 365–378.

Holsti, O. R., Siverso, R. M. and George, A. L. (eds), *Change in the International System* (Boulder, Colo.: Westview Press and Bowker Publishing, 1980).

Homer-Dixon, T., 'Environmental Scarcity and Intergroup Conflict', in M. T. Klare and D. C. Thomas (eds), *World Security: Challenges to a New Century.*

Hooker, B., 'Rule-Consequentialism, Incoherence, Fairness', *Proceedings of the Aristotelian Society*, 95 (1994) 19–35.

Houghton, J. T., *Global Warming. The Complete Briefing* (Oxford: Lyon Publishing, 1994).

Hunt, I., 'The Permanent Crisis of a Divided Mankind: "Contemporary Crises of the Nation State" in Historical Perspective', in J. Dunn (ed.), *The Contemporary Crisis of the Nation State?*

Hurrell, A., 'A Crisis of Ecological Viability? Global Environmental Change and the Nation State', in J. Dunn (ed.), *Contemporary Crisis of the Nation State?*

Hurrell, A., 'International Political Theory and the Global Environment', in K. Booth and S. Smith, *International Relations Theory Today.*

Hurrell, A. and Kingsbury, B. (eds), *The International Politics of the Environment* (Oxford: Clarendon Press, 1992).

IISS, *Survival*, London, Brasseys.

IISS, *Strategic Survey 1991–92*, London, Brasseys, 1992.

IISS, *Strategic Survey 1992–92*, London, Brasseys, 1993.

IISS, *Strategic Survey 1994–95*, London, Oxford University Press, 1995.

Imber, M. F., *Environment, Security and UN Reform* (London: Macmillan, 1994).

Isaak, R. A., *International Political Economy: Managing World Change* (Englewood Cliffs, NJ: Prentice-Hall, 1990).

Johnston, R. J., 'The Rise and Decline of the Corporate-Welfare State: A Comparative Analysis in a Global Context', in J. Taylor (ed.), *Political Geography of the Twentieth Century.*

Jones, M. A., *The Limits of Liberty: American History 1607–1992* (Oxford: Oxford University Press, 1995).

Jones, R. E., 'The English School of International Relations: A Case for Closure', *British Journal of International Studies* 7 (1981) 1–13.

Jones, R. J. B., *Globalisation and Interdependence in the International Political Economy* (London: Pinter, 1995).

Jones, R. J. B., 'The English School and the Political Construction of International Society', in Roberson, B. A. (ed.), *The English School Revisited* (London: Pinter, forthcoming).

Jordan, A. and O'Riordan, T., *The Precautionary Principle in UK Environmental Policy and Law*, CSERGE Working Paper GEC 94–11 (Norwich: University of East Anglia, 1994).

Kalshoven, F., *Constraints on the Waging of War. International Committee of the Red Cross* (Dordracht, The Netherlands: Martinus Nijhoff, 1987).

Kant, I., *Fundamental Principles of the Metaphysics of Ethics*, trans. T. K. Abbott (London: Longman, 1962).

Kant, I., *Political Writings*, H. Reiss (ed.), (Cambridge: Cambridge University Press, 1991).

Kedourie, E., *Nationalism* revised ed. (London: Century Hutchinson, 1985).

Keegan, J., *A History of Warfare* (London: Hutchison, 1993).

Kegley, C. W., Jnr, 'How Did the Cold War Die? Principles for an Autopsy', *Mershon International Studies Review*, 38, Supplement 1 (March 1994) 11–14.

Kelman, H. C., 'Violence without Moral Restraint: Reflections on the Dehumanization of Victims and Victimizers', *The Journal of Social Issues*, *29* (1973) 25–62.

Kelman, H. C. and Hamilton, V. L., 'Availability for Violence: A Study of U.S. Public Reactions to the Trial of Lt. Calley', in J. D. Ben-Dak (ed.), *The Future of Collective Violence: Societal and International Perspectives* (Lund, Sweden: Studentlitteratur, 1974).

Kelman, H. C. and Hamilton, V. L., *Crimes of Obedience* (New Haven, Conn.: Yale University Press, 1989).

Kelman, H. C. and Lawrence, L. H., 'Assignment of Responsibility in the Case of Lt. Calley: Preliminary Report on a National Survey', *Journal of Social Issues*, 28 (1972) 177–212.

Kelso, A. W., *American Democratic Theory: Pluralism and its Critics* (Westport, Conn.: Greenwood Press, 1978).

Kennan, G., *American Diplomacy 1900–1950* (Chicago: University of Chicago Press, 1950).

Kennedy, P., *The Rise and Fall of the Great Powers* (London: Fontana, 1989).

Keohane, R. O. (ed.), *Neo-Realism and its Critics* (New York: Columbia University Press, 1986).

Keohane, R. O., 'International Institutions: Two Approaches', *International Organisation*, 38 (1988) 379–96.

Kidron, M. and Segal, R., *The New State of the World Atlas*, 4th ed. (London: Simon and Schuster, 1991).

Kiesler, C. A., Collins, B. and Miller, N., *Attitude Change* (New York: Wiley, 1969).

Kimber, R., 'On Democracy', *Scandinavian Political Studies*, 12 (1989) 199–219.

Klare, M. T. and Thomas, D. C. (eds), *World Security: Challenges for a New Century*, 2nd ed. (New York: St Martin's Press, 1994).

Knoop, J., *Report from Iraq* (Washington, D.C.: Institute for Policy Studies, 1991).

Knorr, K. and Trager, F. N. (eds), *Economic Issues and National Security* (Lawrence: Regents, 1977).

Koskenniemi, M., 'National Self-Determination Today: Problems of Legal Theory and Practice', *International and Comparative Law Quarterly* 43 (1994) 241–269.

Krasner, S. D., 'Structural Causes and Regime Consequences: Regimes as Intervening Variables', in S. D. Krasner (ed.), *International Regimes*.

Krasner, S. D. (ed.), *International Regimes*, (Ithaca, NY: Cornell University Press, 1983).

Krasner, S. D., *After Hegemony: Cooperation and Discord in the World Political Economy* (Princeton, NJ: Princeton University Press, 1984).

Kratochwil, F., 'The Embarrassment of Changes: Neo-Realism as the Science of *Realpolitik* Without Politics', *Review of International Studies* 19 (1993) 63–80.

Krause, F., Koomey, J. and Bach, B., *Energy Policy in the Greenhouse: From Warming Fate to Warming Limit* (El Cerrito: International Project for Sustainable Energy Paths, 1990).

La Piere, R. T. 'Attitudes vs. Actions', *Social Forces*, 13 (1934) 230–237.

Lean, G. and Hinrichsen D. (eds), *Atlas of the Environment* (Oxford: Helicon Publishing, 1992).

Lessnoff, M., *Social Contract* (London: Macmillan, 1986).

Levy, J., 'Long Cycles, Hegemonic Transitions, and the Long Peace', in C. W. Kegley (ed.), *The Long Postwar Peace* (New York: Harper Collins, 1991).

Levy, S. G., 'The Psychology of Political Activity', *Annals of Political and Social Science*, 391 (1970) 83–96.

Levy, S. G., 'An Examination of the Relationship between Systemic Punishment and Systemic Frustration', *Bulletin of the Psychonomic Society*, 13 (1979) 330–332.

Levy, S. G., 'Attitudes Toward the Conduct of War', *Conflict and Peace: The Journal of Peace Psychology*, 2 (1995) 179–197.

Linklater, A., *Beyond Realism and Marxism: Critical Theory and International Relations* (London: Macmillan, 1990).

Linklater, A., *Men and Citizens in the Theory of International Relations*, 2nd ed. (London: Macmillan, 1990).

Linklater, A., 'What is a Good International Citizen?' in P. Keal (ed.), *Ethics and Foreign Policy* (St Leonards, NSW: Allen and Unwin, 1992).

Lipschutz, R. 'Reconstructing World Politics: The Emergence of Global Civil Society', *Millennium*, 21 (1992) 389–420.

List, M. and Rittberger, V., 'Regime Theory and International Environmental Management', in H. Hurrell and B. Kingsbury, *The International Politics of the Environment*.

Little, R., 'International Relations and Large-Scale Historical Change', in A. J. R. Groom and M. Light (eds), *Contemporary International Relations: A Guide to Theory* (London: Pinter, 1994).

Loescher, G., *Refugee Movements and International Security*, Adelphi Paper No 268, Institute of Strategic Studies (1991).

Lowi, M., 'Bridging the Divide: Transboundary Disputes and the Case of West Bank Water', *International Security*, 18 (1993) 113–38.

Luard, E., *History of the United Nations*, Volume 1, *The Years of Western Domination* (London: Macmillan, 1982).

McMahan, J., 'The Ethics of International Intervention', in K. Kipnis and D. Meyers (eds.), *Political Realism and International Morality* (Boulder, Colo.: Westview Press, 1987).

McNeil, W. H., *Plagues and Peoples* (Harmondsworth: Penguin, 1979).

McRae, H., *The World in 2020* (London: Harper Collins, 1994).

Malnes, R., *The Environment and Duties to Future Generations. An Elaboration of 'Sustainable Development'* (Oslo: Fridtjof Nansen Institute, 1990).

Manning, C. A. W., *The Nature of International Society* (London: G. Bell and Sons, 1962).

Maritain, J., *Moral Philosophy* (London: Geoffrey Bles, 1964).

Matthews, T., 'The Environment and International Security', in M. T. Klare and D. C. Thomas (eds), *World Security: Challenges for a New Century*.

May, J. D., 'Defining Democracy: A Bid for Coherence and Consensus', *Political Studies*, 26 (1978) 1–14.

Mayall, J., *The Community of States: A Study in International Political Theory* (London: Allen and Unwin, 1982).

Mayall, J., *Nationalism and International Society* (Cambridge: Cambridge University Press, 1990).

Mazrui, A. A., *Towards a Pax Africana* (London: Weidenfeld and Nicolson, 1967).

Meron, T., 'War Crimes in Yugoslavia and the Development of International Law', *American Journal of International Law* 88 (1994) 78–87.

Milgram, S., *Obedience to Authority* (New York: Harper and Row, 1974).
Mill, J. S., 'A Few Words on Non-Intervention' in his *Collected Works,* Vol. 21, *Essays on Equality, Law, and Education,* ed. J. M. Robson (London: Routledge, 1984).
Milligan, D. and Watts Miller, W., (eds.), *Liberalism, Citizenship and Autonomy* (Aldershot: Avebury, 1992).
Minard, R. D., 'Race Relationships in the Pocahontas Coal Field', *Journal of Social Issues,* 8 (1952) 29–52.
Modelski, G., 'The Long Cycle of Global Politics and the Nation-State', *Comparative Studies in Society and History,* 20 (1978), 214–35.
Modelski, G. (ed.), *Exploring Long Cycles* (Boulder, Colo.: Lynne Rienner, 1987).
Morgenthau, H. J., *Politics among Nations,* 5th ed. (New York: Alfred Knopf, 1973).
Morgenthau, H. J., *In Defence of the National Interest: A Critical Examination of American Foreign Policy* (Washington, D.C.: University Press of America, 1982).
Mouffe, C. (ed.), *Dimensions of Radical Democracy: Pluralism, Citizenship, Community,* (London: Verso, 1992).
Mueller, J., *Quiet Cataclysm: Reflections on the Recent Transformation of World Politics* (New York: Harper Collins, 1995).
Mulgan, G. J., 'Democracy Beyond Sovereignty', in G. J. Mulgan, *Politics in an Antipolitical Age* (Cambridge: Polity Press, 1994).
Myers, N. 'Environment and Security', *Foreign Policy,* 74 (1989) 23–41.
Nardin, T. *Law, Morality and the Relations of States* (Princeton, NJ: Princeton University Press, 1983).
Nitze, W., *The Greenhouse Effect: Formulating a Convention* (London: RIIA, 1990).
Nozick, R., *Anarchy, State, and Utopia* (Oxford: Blackwell, 1974).
O'Brien, J, and Palmer, M., *The State of Religion Atlas* (London: Simon and Schuster, 1993).
O'Brien, R., *Global Financial Integration: The End of Geography* (London: RIIA, 1992).
Olson, W. C. (ed.), *The Theory and Practice of International Politics,* 8th ed. (Engelwood Cliffs, NJ: Prentice Hall, 1991).
O'Neill, O., *Faces of Hunger* (London: Allen and Unwin 1986).
O'Neill, O., 'Transnational Justice', in D. Held (ed.), *Political Theory Today* (Oxford: Polity Press 1991).
Organski, A. F. K., *World Politics,* 2nd ed. (New York: Alfred Knopf, 1968).
O'Sullivan, N., *Fascism* (London: Dent, 1983).

Pallemaerts, M., 'From Stockholm to Rio: Back to the Future?', in P. Sands (ed.), *Greening International Law* (London: Earthscan, 1993).

Paterson, M., 'Global Warming: The Great Equaliser?', *Journal für Entwicklungspolitik*, 8 (1992) 217–228.

Paterson, M., *Explaining the Climate Convention: International Relations Theory and Global Warming*, unpublished Ph.D. Thesis, Essex University, 1994.

Pearce, D., 'The Global Commons', in D. Pearce (ed.), *Blueprint 2: Greening the World Economy* (London: Earthscan, 1991).

Pirages, D., 'Demographic Change and Ecological Insecurity', in M. T. Klare and D. C. Thomas (eds), *World Security: Challenges for a New Century*.

Plant, R., 'The Justifications for Intervention: Needs before Contexts', in I. Forbes and M. Hoffman (eds), *Political Theory, International Relations, and the Ethics of Intervention* .

Platt, C., *Medieval England: A Social History and Archeology from the Conquest to 1600 AD* (London: Routledge, 1978).

Plekhanov, G. V., *The Role of the Individual in History* (New York: International Publishers, 1940).

Polanyi, K., *Origins of Our Time: The Great Transformation* (London: Gollancz, 1945).

Popper, K., *The Poverty of Historicism*, 2nd ed. (London: Routledge, 1961).

Rainey, G. E., *Patterns of American Foreign Policy* (Boston: Allyn and Bacon, 1975).

Rawls, J., *A Theory of Justice* (Oxford: Oxford University Press, 1972).

Redclift, M., 'Throwing Stones in the Greenhouse', *Global Environmental Change*, 2 (1993) 90–92.

Rees, D., *Korea: The Limited War* (London: Macmillan, 1964).

Régamy, P., *Non-violence and the Christian Conscience* (London: Darton Longman and Todd, 1966).

Rejai, M. (with K. Phillips), *Leaders of Revolution* (Beverly Hills: Sage, 1979).

The Report of the Commission on Global Governance, *Our Global Neighbourhood* (Oxford: Oxford University Press, 1995).

Ricci, D. M., *Community Power and Democratic Theory* (New York: Random House, 1971).

Richardson, L. F., *Statistics of Deadly Quarrels* (Chicago: Quadrangle Books, 1960).

Rittberger, V. and Mayer, P, (eds), *Regime Theory and International Relations* (Oxford: Clarendon Press, 1993).

Roberts, A. and Guelff, R. (eds), *Documents on the Laws of War* (Oxford: Clarendon Press, 1989).

Rokeach, M., *The Open and Closed Mind* (New York: Basic Books, 1960).

Rosenau, J. N. 'Citizenship in a Changing Global Order', in J. N. Rosenau and E-O. Czempiel, *Governance Without Government*.

Rosenau, J. N. and Czempiel, E-O. (eds), *Governance Without Government: Order and Change in World Politics* (Cambridge: Cambridge University Press, 1992).

Rousseau, J-J., *Emile* (Paris: Garnier Frères, 1964).

Rousseau, J-J., *The Social Contract,* ed. M. Cranston (Harmondsworth: Penguin, 1968).

Rowlands, I. H. and Green, M. (eds), *Global Environmental Change and International Relations* (London: Macmillan, 1992).

Rummel, R., 'Power, Genocide and Mass Murder', *Journal of Peace Research,* 31 (1994) 1–10.

Sales, S. M., 'Economic Threat as a Determinant of Conversion Rates in Authoritarian and Nonauthoritarian Churches', *Journal of Personality and Social Psychology*, 23 (1972) 420–428.

Sales, S. M, 'Threat as a Factor in Authoritarianism: An Analysis of Archival Data', *Journal of Personality and Social Psychology*, 28 (1973) 44–57.

Saward, M., 'Green Democracy?', in A. Dobson and P. Lucardie (eds), *The Politics of Nature* (London and New York: Routledge, 1993).

Schindler, D. and Toman, J., *The Laws of Armed Conflicts – A Collection of Conventions, Resolutions and Other Documents* (Geneva and Leiden: A. W. Sijthoff, Henry Dunant Institute, 1973).

Schneider, S., *Global Warming* (San Francisco: Sierra Club, 1989).

Schore, D. J. and Fletcher, A., *Chronology of Eclipses and Comets AD 1–1000* (Woodbridge: Boydell, 1984).

Scruton, R., *A Dictionary of Political Thought* (London: Pan Books, 1983).

Sebenius, J. K., 'Designing Negotiations Towards a New Regime: The Case Of Global Warming', *International Security*, 15 (1991).

Shaw, M., *Global Society and International Relations* (Cambridge: Polity Press, 1994).

Sherif, M., 'Experiments in Group Conflict', *Scientific American*, 195 (1956) 54–58.

Shiffler, W., *The Legal Community of Mankind* (New York: Columbia University Press, 1954).

Shils, E. A. and Janowitz, M., 'Cohesion and Disintegration in the Wehrmacht in World War II', *Public Opinion Quarterly*, 12 (1948) 280–315.

Shirer, W., *The Rise and Fall of the Third Reich: A History of Nazi Germany* (New York: Simon and Schuster, 1960).

Sholte, J. A., *International Relations of Social Change* (Buckingham: Open University Press, 1993).

Shue, H., *Basic Rights* (Princeton, NJ: Princeton University Press, 1979).

Shue, H., 'The Unavoidability of Justice', in A. Hurrell and B. Kingsbury (eds), *The International Politics of the Environment* .

Shue, H., 'Subsistence Emissions and Luxury Emissions', *Law and Policy*, 15 (1993) 39–59.

Shue, H., 'Environmental Change and the Varieties of Justice: An Agenda for Normative and Political Analysis', paper for conference on 'Global Environmental Change and Social Justice', Cornell University, Ithaca, NY, September 1993.

Shue, H, 'After You: May Action by the Rich be Contingent on Action by the Poor?', *Indiana Journal of Global Legal Studies*, 1 (1994) 343–366.

Singer, J. D. and Small, M., *The Wages of War* (New York: Wiley, 1972).

Singer, P., 'Famine, Affluence and Morality', *Philosophy and Public Affairs*, 1 (1972).

Singer, S. F., 'Earth Summit Will Shackle the Planet, Not Save It', *The Wall Street Journal*, 19 February 1992.

Singer, P., *Practical Ethics,* 2nd ed. (Cambridge: Cambridge University Press, 1993).

Skillen, T., 'Active Citizenship as Political Obligation', *Radical Philosophy*, 58 (1991) 10–13.

Slater, J. and Nardin, T., 'Non-Intervention and Human Rights', *Journal of Politics*, 48 (1986) 86–95.

Smith, A., *National Identity* (Harmondsworth: Penguin, 1991).

Smith, M., 'Ethics and Intervention', *Ethics and International Affairs*, 3 (1989) 1–26.

Spitz, E., 'Defining Democracy: A Nonecumenical Reply to May', *Political Studies*, 27 (1979) 127–8.

Springer, A. L., 'United States Environmental Policy and International Law: Stockholm Principle 21 Revisited', in J. E. Carroll (ed.), *International Environmental Diplomacy* (Cambridge: Cambridge University Press, 1988).

Stagner, R., 'Fascist Attitudes: An Exploratory Study', *Journal of Social Psychology*, 7 (1936) 309–319.

Strange, S., *'Cave! Hic Dragones:* A Critique of Regime Analysis', in S. D. Krasner (ed.), *International Regimes*.

Stubbs, R. and Underhill, G. R. D. (eds), *Political Economy and the Changing Global Order* (London: Macmillan, 1994).

Susskind, L. and Ozawa, C., 'Environmental Diplomacy: Strategies for Negotiating More Effective International Agreements', Harvard Disputes Program, MIT, Cambridge Mass., 1990.

Tainter, J. A., *The Collapse of Complex Societies* (Cambridge: Cambridge University Press, 1988).

Taylor, P. J., *Political Geography: World-economy, Nation-state and Locality* (London: Longman, 1989).

Taylor, P. J. (ed.), *Political Geography of the Twentieth Century. A Global Analysis* (London: Belhaven Press, 1993).

Thiele, L. P., 'Making Democracy Safe for the World: Social Movements and Global Politics', *Alternatives* 18 (1993) 273–305.

Thomas, C., *The Environment and International Relations* (London: RIIA, 1992).

Thomas, C., 'The Pragmatic Case Against Intervention', in I. Forbes and M. Hoffman (eds), *Political Theory, International Relations and the Ethics of Intervention* .

Thomas, C. (ed.), *Rio, Unravelling the Consequences* (London: Cass, 1994).

Thompson, J., *Justice and World Order: A Philosophical Inquiry* (London: Routledge, 1992).

Tickner, J. A., 'Re-visioning Security', in K. Booth and S. Smith (eds), *International Relations Theory Today*.

Turner, B., (ed.), *Citizenship and Social Theory*, (London: Sage, 1993).

Turner, R. H. and Surace, S. H., 'Zoot-suiters and Mexicans: Symbols in Crowd Behavior', *The American Journal of Sociology*, 62 (1956) 14–20.

United Nations, *Framework Convention on Climate Change* (New York: United Nations, 1992).

Urquart, B., 'For a UN Volunteer Military Force', *New York Review of Books*, 10 June 1993.

Vincent, R. J., *Nonintervention and International Order* (Princeton, NJ: Princeton University Press, 1974).

Waever, O., Buzan, B., Kelstrup, M. and Lemaitre, P., *Identity, Migration and the New Security Agenda in Europe* (London: Pinter, 1993).

Walker, R. J. B. and Mendlovitz, S. H., 'Interrogating State Sovereignty', in R. J. B. Walker and S. H. Mendlovitz (eds), *Contending Sovereignties* (Boulder, Colo. and London: Lynne Rienner, 1990).

Wallerstein, I., *The Modern World System: Capitalist Agriculture and the Origins of the European World-Economy in the Sixteenth Century* (New York: Academic Press, 1974).

Walter, A., *World Power and World Money: The Role of Hegemony and International Monetary Order* (Hemel Hempstead: Harvester Wheatsheaf, 1991).

Waltz, K., *Man, the State and War: A Theoretical Analysis* (New York: Columbia University Press, 1954).

Waltz, K., *Theory of International Politics* (Reading, Mass.: Addison-Wesley, 1979).

Walzer, M., *Just and Unjust Wars* (Hammondsworth: Penguin, 1978).

Ware, A., 'Liberal Democracy: One Form or Many?', in D. Held (ed.), *Prospects for Democracy* (*Political Studies*, 40 (1992), special issue).

Watson, A., *The Evolution of International Society: A Comparative Historical Analysis* (London: Routledge, 1992).

Weigel, G., *Tranquillitas Ordinis* (Oxford: Oxford University Press, 1987).

Weiss, E. B., 'Climate Change, Intergenerational Equity and International Law: An Introductory Note', *Climatic Change*, 15 (1989) 327–335.

Weiss, T. G., 'UN Responses in the Former Yugoslavia: Moral and Operational Choices', *Ethics and International Affairs*, 8 (1994) 1–22.

Wendt, A., 'The Agent-Structure Problem in International Relations Theory', *International Organisation*, 41 (1987) 335–70.

Wendt, A., 'Bridging the Theory/Meta-theory Gap in International Relations', *Review of International Studies*, 17 (1991) 383–92.

Wendt, A., 'Levels of Analysis vs. Agents and Structures: Part III', *Review of International Studies*, 18 (1992) 181–216.

Westing, H. (ed.), *Global Resources and International Conflict* (Oxford: Oxford University Press, 1988).

Whelan, F. G., 'Prologue: Democratic Theory and the Boundary Problem', in J. R. Pennock and J. W. Chapman (eds), *Liberal Democracy* (Nomos XXV) (New York: New York University Press, 1983).

Wight, M., *Systems of States* (Leicster: Leicester University Press, 1977).

Wight, M., 'The Theory of International Society' in M. Wight, G. Wight and B. Porter, *International Theory: The Three Traditions*.

Wight, M., Wight, G. and Porter, B. (eds), *International Theory: The Three Traditions* (Leicester: Leicester University Press/RIIA 1991).

Wilkinson, D., 'Civilizations, Cores, World Economics and Oikumnes', in A. G. Frank and B. K. Gills (eds), *The World System. Five Hundred Years or Five Thousand?*

Williams, H., 'International Relations and the Reconstruction of Political Theory', *Politics* 14 (1994) 135–142.

Wolfers, A., *Discord and Collaboration* (London: Johns Hopkins, 1971).

World Commission on Environmental and Development, *Our Common Future* (The Bruntland Report), (Oxford: Oxford University Press, 1987.

World Resources Institute, *World Resources 1990–91* (Washington D.C.: World Resources Institute, 1991).

Young, H. P., *Sharing the Burden of Global Warming* (College Park: University of Maryland, 1991).

Young, O. R., 'Regime Dynamics: The Rise and Fall of International Regimes', in S. D. Krasner (ed.), *International Regimes*.

Young, O. R., 'The Politics of International Regime Formation: Managing Natural Resources and the Environment', *International Organization*, 43 (1989) 349–375.

Young, O. R., 'The Effectiveness of International Institutions: Hard Cases and Critical Variables', in J. N. Rosenau and E-O. Czempiel, *Governance Without Government: Order and Change in World Politics*.

Zacher, M. W., 'The Decaying Pillars of the Westphalian Temple: Implications for International Order and Governance', in J. N. Rosenau and E-O. Czempiel (eds), *Government Without Government: Order and Change in World Politics*.

Index

Gramsci, A. 35
Gray, J. 49, 65, 98, 108
Great Britain 34, 88, 211, 214; *see also* European states
Green, T. H. 50
green politics 136ff
  NGOs 149–50
Greene, M. 154, 178
Grenada 236
Grieve, R. 174
Groom, A. J. R. 19
Grubb, M. 155, 167, 178, 185, 194, 197
Guelff, R. 252
gulags 231
Gulf Stream 170
Gulf War 71, 76–84, 205, 210, 214, 222, 228, 236, 242

Haas, P. M. 160
Habermas, J. 63, 114, 121, 124, 133
Habsburg Empire 157
Hagland, D. 67
Haiti 84, 86, 89, 155
Hall, J. A. 8, 17
Halliday, F. 3, 7, 19, 67
Hamilton, V. L. 245, 252, 254
Hannum, H. 66
Harburg, E. 255
Hardin, R. 163
Harris, A. L. 18
Hawes, M. K. 67
Hayes, P. 197
Heater, D. 156
Heffner, R. D. 92
hegemonic powers, in states-system 34
Hegel, G.W.F. 114, 118, 134, 208, 221
  ethical life 129
Heidenrich, J. G. 254
Held, D. 148, 154, 159, 161, 162
Herrstein, R. J. 250
Hinrichsen, D. 179
Hinsley, F. H. 65

Hiroshima–Nagasaki 236
Hirst, P. 142, 155, 159
history, and global change 14–6
  comparative approaches 14
  and cycles 15
  and disease 176
  and ecological changes 67–81
  particularist approaches 15
  short-term 15
Hitler, A. 246
Hobbes, T. 45–6, 50, 64, 97, 108
Hoffman, M. 108
Holden, B. 32, 113, 135–63, 155
Hollis, M. 37, 38
Holocaust 243; *see also* Nazis
Holsti, O. R. 8, 17
Holy Roman Empire 42
'holy war' 221
Homer-Dixon, T. 167, 178
Hooker, B. 106, 109
Horst, J. 157
Houghton, J. T. 154
humanitarian intervention 5, 94–110, 219, 222
  consequentialism 100–103
  definition 95
  failure of 104–6
  as imperialism 102–3
  and national interest 97–100
  realist objections 95ff
  selectivity in 104–5
Hurrell, A. 149, 152, 154, 161, 162, 167, 178
Hussein, Saddam 76, 80–82, 90, 214, 243
Hutchings, K. 32, 113–34, 147
hydrological changes 169ff

ice caps 170
Imber, M. 167, 168
imperialism 102–3, 121
individual freedom 26–8, 49, 54
institutions, and international relations 10